CQ GUIDE TO

CURRENT AMERICAN
GOVERNMENT

Spring 1999

CQ GUIDE TO

CURRENT AMERICAN GOVERNMENT

Spring 1999

Congressional Quarterly Inc.
Washington, D.C.

Congressional Quarterly Inc.

Congressional Quarterly Inc., an editorial research service and publishing company, serves clients in the fields of news, education, business, and government. It combines the specific coverage of Congress, government, and politics contained in the *CQ Weekly* with the more general subject range of an affiliated service, the *CQ Researcher*.

Congressional Quarterly also publishes a variety of books, including college political science textbooks and public affairs paperbacks on developing issues and events under the CQ Press imprint. CQ Books researches, writes, and publishes information directories and reference books on the federal government, national elections, and politics, including the *Guide to the Presidency*, the *Guide to Congress*, the *Guide to the U.S. Supreme Court*, the *Guide to U.S. Elections*, and *Politics in America*. *CQ's Encyclopedia of American Government* is a three-volume reference work providing essential information about the U.S. government. The *CQ Almanac*, a compendium of legislation for one session of Congress, is published each year. *Congress and the Nation*, a record of government for a presidential term, is published every four years.

CQ publishes the *Congressional Monitor*, a daily report on current and future activities of congressional committees, and several newsletters. CQ is also a leader on the Internet, offering legislative tracking services. Full text of government documents, legislative summaries, committees coverage, vote analyses, and congressional schedules, along with CQ's comprehensive, impartial news, analyses, and information on government and politics are available on the Web: www.cq.com.

Copyright © 1999 by Congressional Quarterly Inc.
1414 22nd Street, N.W., Washington, D.C. 20037

CQ Books on the Web: http://books.cq.com
CQ Books Customer Service: (800) 638-1710; (202) 822-1475

Printed in the United States of America

ISSN: 0196-612X
ISBN: 1-56802-108-9

Contents

Contents

Introduction

Congressional Quarterly's *Guide to Current American Government* is divided into four sections—foundations of American government, political participation, government institutions, and politics and public policy—that correspond with the framework of standard introductory American government textbooks. Articles have been selected from the *Congressional Quarterly Weekly* to complement existing texts with up-to-date examinations of current issues and controversies.

Foundations of American Government. Fundamental aspects of the U.S. Constitution and the federal government are the focus of this section. The featured article charts the progress of a proposed constitutional amendment and gauges its prospects for passage. The Crime Victims Amendment was approved by the Senate Judiciary Committee in July 1998 but must overcome several legislative obstacles if it is to be ratified.

Political Participation. This section reviews current issues in electoral politics. Several stories cover the historic 1998 midterm elections. CQ editors also explore the impact of the Internet on election campaigns, the status of women in Congress, and the implications for democracy of an increasingly disengaged electorate. The actions and influence of special interest groups are illustrated in four additional articles.

Government Institutions. Aspects of Congress, the presidency, the judiciary, and the bureaucracy are discussed in turn. CQ editors take a detailed look at how the impeachment inquiry shaped the agenda of the 105th Congress. To what extent the powers of the presidency were affected by the Starr Report and its aftermath is the focus of a series of articles. The section concludes with investigations of Congress's troubled relationship with the judiciary and the political hazards of taking the 2000 census.

Politics and Public Policy. This section provides in-depth coverage of major social policy issues, including proposed changes in managed health care, privacy concerns on the Internet, the diminishing political popularity of free trade, the battle over the budget surplus, Social Security reform, and student loan rate cuts.

By reprinting articles largely as they appeared originally in the *CQ Weekly*, the *Guide*'s editors provide a handy source of information about contemporary political issues. The date of original publication is noted with each article to give readers a time frame for the events that are described. Although new developments may have occurred subsequently, updates of the articles are provided only when they are essential to an understanding of the basic operations of American government. Page number references to related and background articles in the *CQ Weekly* and the *CQ Almanac* are provided to facilitate additional research on topical events. Both are available at many school and public libraries.

Foundations of American Government

The process for amending the U.S. Constitution is laid out in Article V. The article specifies a two-fold procedure: proposal and ratification. An amendment may be proposed by two-thirds of both houses of Congress or by a constitutional convention called by petition of two-thirds of the states. To be ratified, an amendment must be approved by three-fourths of state legislatures or by constitutional conventions held in three-fourths of the states.

All constitutional amendments so far have been ratified by state legislatures except the Twenty-first, which repealed Prohibition. Advocates of the proposed amendment believed that it stood a better chance of passage in state conventions than in state legislatures, where supporters of Prohibition, or "Drys," seemed to outnumber opponents.

The latest proposed amendment may not reach the ratification stage. As the following article points out, barriers in Congress to passage of the Crime Victims Amendment, approved June 7, 1998, by the Senate Judiciary Committee, are formidable: shallow support in the general Senate, strong objections from conservatives, who feel that the amendment is unnecessary, and fear among some senators that it would lead to years of messy litigation.

Supporters of the amendment assert that it is necessary to protect victims from a judicial system that has forgotten them. Victims' rights are nowhere mentioned in the Constitution, and including them in an amendment would guarantee that victims would not be lost in the legal process.

Arguments on both sides of the issue are compelling, but at this writing the opponents of passage appear to have the upper hand. The amendment procedure outlined in the Constitution ensures that the road to ratification is long and hard. In this case, that road may be all but unpassable.

Crime Victims Amendment Has Steadfast Support, But Little Chance of Floor Time

It took 62 drafts, and the better part of the 105th Congress, but the Senate Judiciary Committee on July 7 finally approved a proposed constitutional amendment designed to bolster the rights of violent crime victims.

The vote on S J Res 44 was 11-6, slightly less than two-thirds of those voting. It would need such a margin in both chambers before it could be sent to the states for ratification.

The measure may be the pending constitutional amendment with the best chance of being approved by Congress in the foreseeable future. It is endorsed by the Clinton administration and has considerable bipartisan support in the Senate.

But it still faces numerous obstacles. Prosecutors are afraid it could complicate the process of putting criminals behind bars. Constitutional purists argue an amendment is unnecessary. And some conservatives argue it would generate years of litigation.

And its support could prove shallow. For instance, Jeff Sessions, R-Ala., said he would vote to send it out of committee but remained uncommitted to it thereafter. Chairman Orrin G. Hatch, R-Utah, acknowledged that getting floor time for its consideration this year would be a struggle.

But its sponsors remain steadfast. They have gone through numerous versions in an attempt to pick up support and prevent defections, and they intend to continue pressing their case. They argue that a constitutional amendment is the only way of addressing a judicial system that has all but forgotten victims.

CQ Weekly July 11, 1998

"What we are trying to do is give victims some status in law," said Dianne Feinstein, D-Calif., who sponsored the measure along with Jon Kyl, R-Ariz.

Among other things, the measure would give violent crime victims the right to be informed of and attend any public proceedings, including court hearings. If they attended, they would have a right to speak or submit a statement. They would have a right to reasonable notice when their assailants are released or escape. They would have a right to express their views in hearings relating to parole or any other type of early release. And they would have a right to restitution.

The thinking that underpins the amendment is that victims are often lost in a legal process that focuses on the balance between prosecutor and prosecuted.

Defendants are granted a series of rights in the Constitution and in case law, starting with their right to be informed of their rights when they are arrested. Some of their most significant rights include a right to speedy trial, to choose not to testify against themselves, to a trial by jury and to be deprived of life or liberty only through "due process of law."

Victims, in contrast, are afforded no rights. In fact, the due process clause has been interpreted to mean their exclusion from trials and sentencing hearings on the grounds that they could influence the jury.

Critics of the measure see it as a violation of federalist principles, in that it would override state constitutions and statutes. They also argue it could greatly complicate the work of prosecutors.

Just creating a working definition of a victim could take years of legislating and litigation, they argue. In some cases there is a clear distinction between an innocent victim and a heinous criminal, but sometimes the victim in one crime is a defendant in another. Conceivably, these victim-defendants could use their newfound rights as leverage in their own cases.

In an extreme case, one could imagine convicted felons demanding release from jail each time there is a hearing in a case for which they are categorized as the victim.

"If there is any one law we can always count on," said Fred Thompson, R-Tenn., an opponent of the measure, "it is the law of unintended consequences."

Thompson's Objections

Thompson raised a number of other objections. He said a victim's right to participate in hearings could make it harder for prosecutors to strike deals with potential informants. He also argued that in some cases there could be hundreds of people defined as victims. Their participation could conflict with a defendant's right to a speedy trial.

Proponents of the measure said they have already addressed these and other concerns through the changes they have made. The measure approved is considerably weaker than earlier drafts. It addresses violent crimes only. It has a number of exceptions, and some of its requirements apply only to the extent they are "reasonable."

Furthermore, the measure gives Congress the power to grant specific exceptions if it can demonstrate a compelling interest in doing so. ◆

Political Participation

The articles in this section examine major components of American politics: elections, campaigns, voters, and interest groups.

The first four articles focus on the midterm congressional elections of 1998. CQ editors have selected stories that address not only the outcomes of the elections but also the implications of those outcomes for the president's agenda, for the organization and operation of the Senate and the House, and for state government.

Democrats fared better than expected in House elections, gaining five seats. It was the first time since 1934 that the party controlling the White House gained seats in an off-year election. Republicans, stung by election results that left them with the slimmest House majority since 1955 (223 to 211), elected a new Speaker, Robert L. Livingston, R-La., and called for a reexamination of the party's agenda.

As this book went to press, House Republicans pressed for additional leadership changes. Although Majority Leader Dick Armey retained his post, withstanding challenges from Steve Largent and Jennifer Dunn, and Tom DeLay was unopposed for another term as majority whip, other Republican leaders were swept aside by the party's desire for change. GOP Conference chairman John A. Boehner lost his post to rising star J. C. Watts, and Thomas M. Davis III unseated John Linder for chairmanship of the National Republican Congressional Committee. Moreover, three new committee chairmen were chosen: C. W. Bill Young (Appropriations), Larry Combest (Agriculture), and David Dreier (Rules).

Whereas House elections prompted changes in Republican Party leadership, the results in the Senate were far less ground shaking. All but three of the thirty-four senators running for reelection were returned to office, and the Republican majority (55 to 45) stayed the same. With House Republicans divided and lacking clear direction, Senate majority leader Trent Lott, R-Miss., sought to fill the leadership vacuum by devising a postelection strategy that would unify his party and reclaim lost political ground.

Following the election coverage are additional stories—about campaigns, voters, and interest groups—that contribute to our understanding of American political participation. They demonstrate that participation has been both helped and hindered by recent developments on the political scene. An article on how the Internet has changed the way election campaigns are conducted suggests that technology has improved communication between candidates and voters, while stories on women in Congress and the increasingly disengaged electorate offer reasons for declining voter turnout, a sign that better communication does not necessarily lead to increased participation.

Articles on influential interest groups, including the Disney Company, technology firms, the oil industry, and even state legislatures show a different side of political participation. Well financed, highly organized, and politically sophisticated, the most effective groups wield enormous clout on Capitol Hill. For them, political participation is less about communication than about money—and the well-executed media campaign.

Leaders seem disinclined to bridge differences despite the growing ranks of centrists

Voters' Plea for Moderation Unlikely To Be Heeded

With both Republicans and Democrats claiming an election mandate of sorts for their own partisan programs, it already seems that leaders of the 106th Congress are preparing to ignore the plea for compromise that came from voters in the Nov. 3 balloting.

The conflict between strict conservatism and a more moderate approach is certain to be at the heart of the debate among House Republicans over who should replace Speaker Newt Gingrich, R-Ga., and other leaders in the new session, and whether to continue to pursue the highly partisan impeachment proceedings against President Clinton. [Robert L. Livingston, R-La., became Speaker on Nov. 18. — Ed.]

And while Democrats in Congress seemed to benefit more from the voters' hunger for more moderate politicians, African-Americans, Hispanics and labor unions are sure to demand special rewards from policy-makers for their assistance in saving the party that controls the White House from suffering the usual midterm election rout.

Middle-of-the-road compromises are available to the leaders of the newly elected 106th Congress as they prepare to come to Washington for organizational meetings in mid-November. They could, for example, bridge their differences over how to spend the budget surplus by both cutting taxes and fixing Social Security. But the prospects for such a solution seemed remote amid the recriminations that characterized the days immediately after the election.

Ultimately, the election brought little turnover in either the House or Senate. The incoming House, containing 223 Republicans, 211 Democrats and one independent, gives the GOP the slimmest majority there since 1955. In the Senate, the breakdown stands pat at 55 Republicans, 45 Democrats.

As usual, incumbents will dominate the new Congress. All but seven of the 401 House members seeking re-election are being returned to office. Just three of the 34 senators up this year were defeated — Alfonse M. D'Amato, R-N.Y., Lauch Faircloth, R-N.C., and Carol Moseley-Braun, D-Ill.

Despite these status quo results, Gingrich initially touted the election as the "first time in 70 years that Republicans kept control of the House for a third term." Democrats gloated that it was the first time since 1934 that the party controlling the White House gained seats in an off-year election — and the first time since James Monroe in 1822 that the president's party picked up House seats in his sixth year in office.

But the only ideological group that could undeniably claim victory was the one made up of centrist-minded lawmakers.

The House "Blue Dogs" — a group of moderate to conservative Democrats — added six new faces to their caucus,

giving it a strong voting bloc of 30 members. That bloc will wield significant power next year in a chamber with only a narrow six-seat difference between Republicans and Democrats.

"The radical center has been strengthened," said Rep. Charles W. Stenholm, D-Texas, a Blue Dog leader. Stenholm said his group would reach out to moderate Republicans in hopes of creating an even larger bloc that neither party leadership will be able to ignore.

Likewise, in the Senate, some members looked at what the voters had said and called for a move away from extremism.

"The new Republican Party, if it is to be successful in future elections, must be a party of inclusion," said Sen. John McCain, R-Ariz. "We must open our doors and our arms and welcome those who share our values and our conservative philosophy into the GOP."

McCain pointed out that he was able to attract 55 percent of the Hispanic vote in Arizona, and 65 percent of women voters — both traditionally part of the Democratic base.

A Strengthened Center

Across the country, moderates proved victorious on the congressional and state levels. The Bush brothers — George W. and Jeb — won governorships in Texas and Florida with the help of Hispanic and black voters. In California, Gray Davis, once considered too conservative and boring to win, became the first Democrat in 16 years to be elected governor. And in North Carolina, John Edwards, a tough-on-crime Democrat who favors the death penalty and local control of education, pulled enough conservative votes to defeat Faircloth.

Even liberal New York Rep. Charles E. Schumer, who led an aggressive, bitter campaign to unseat D'Amato, called for moderation and conciliation in his Nov. 3 victory speech.

"Campaigns more often than not must focus on the things that divide us," he said. "But government and public service must focus more on the causes that unite us."

But there were few, if any, signs that these pleas for moderation would be heeded enough to break the polarization that has gripped Congress for much of the past two decades. In the House, in fact, conservatives argued that the Republican Party would have done better on Election Day if GOP leaders had been less willing to compromise with Clinton on spending issues at the end of the 105th Congress.

Blue Dogs

Moderate Democrats picked up four House seats on Election Day that had been held by Republicans.
• Ken Lucas, a Democrat who opposes abortion rights and

Future voter Channelle Miller, 7 months old, looks on as her father, Calvin, holds her up with one arm and votes with the other at a polling booth Nov. 3 in south central Los Angeles.

favors school prayer, captured the seat in Kentucky's 4th District that had been held for 12 years by GOP Rep. Jim Bunning, who ran successfully for the Senate.

• Ronnie Shows, a Democrat who opposes abortion rights and gun control, picked up Mississippi's 4th District seat held by retiring GOP Rep. Mike Parker.

• Mike Thompson, a moderate Democrat, took the 1st District seat of retiring Republican Rep. Frank Riggs in California.

• Moderate Democrat Dennis Moore defeated 3rd District Republican Rep. Vince Snowbarger in Kansas.

All four candidates received financial backing from the Blue Dogs during their campaigns. Another two Blue Dog candidates — Baron Hill and David Phelps — won seats left open by retiring Democratic incumbents Lee H. Hamilton in Indiana's 9th District and Glenn Poshard in Illinois' 19th District.

Stenholm said early in the election cycle that Democratic leaders realized they could no longer rely on a liberal, one-size-fits-all approach in recruiting candidates.

Party leaders recognized that they needed to recruit moderate candidates if they were to have a chance of winning marginal districts. He said conservative Democrats will also be the key to gaining a House majority in 2000.

"If there is a change in control, it will come from our blue puppies," he said, adding that moderates will have a large say over the Democratic agenda in the coming years.

"It's impossible, with a narrow margin in the House, for the Democratic leadership to ignore our agenda," Stenholm said. "Our 30 Blue Dogs, if you went to a liberal agenda, would lose reelection."

Issues

Other conservative Democrats expressed the hope that Republicans would learn a lesson from the elections and turn their focus more toward meat-and-potatoes issues such as education and jobs, rather than ideological issues such as abortion and gun control.

"We will see Republicans who are less ideological, who represent insecure seats and feel a strong need to coalesce with Democrats," said David Heller, president of Main Street Communications, a Democratic media firm that worked with Blue Dog candidates Lu-

cas and Phelps this year.

"The most important conclusion of the election is, voters are concerned about things that affect their lives on a day-to-day basis," he said.

Republican consultant Frank Luntz agreed: "It's quality-of-life issues that matter, making people's lives easier and simpler. The party that focuses on those concepts will win."

Many analysts say Republicans made a mistake this year by shifting their focus away from such basic issues. In the final days before the elections, national Republicans ran a series of ads in key districts questioning Clinton's character and trying to link all Democrats to the presidential sex scandal.

Republicans think "you fire up the core constituency of the party, and you bring them out because they're not so much interested in stop signs and local projects as making a big splash in national politics," said political scientist Jonathan Krasno of the Brennan Center for Justice at New York University. He described that strategy as a mistake.

"They still use sort of ideological appeals as one of their main recruiting tools," Krasno said, but "Americans are overwhelmingly moderate and pragmatic."

Krasno said a good example of down-home issues defeating broad ideology was in South Carolina, where Democrats held on to their Senate seat in the face of a tough Republican challenge.

Democratic Sen. Ernest F. Hollings emphasized his seniority and his ability to bring federal money back to the state for pet projects. His challenger, GOP Rep. Bob Inglis, campaigned for smaller government, even at the expense of South Carolina interests.

South Carolina also showed how the Clinton scandal failed to play into Republican hands. The state GOP vowed to link every Democrat to the White House and place Clinton's face on every piece of political literature.

But in the end, Democrats held on to every one of their congressional seats and even defeated the Republican governor.

Because the Clinton scandal did not give Republicans the political edge they were hoping for, their enthusiasm for Clinton's impeachment is likely to be diminished in the new Congress. But Clinton's harshest opponents on the House Judiciary Committee, such

Re-Energized 'New Deal' Coalition Boosts Democrats for 2000

The coalition of interest groups that propelled many Democrats to success on Nov. 3 could bring about an end to the Republican House majority as early as 2000.

"If the Democrats win the presidency in 2000, I would bet that they'll take the House," said David W. Rohde of Michigan State University, co-editor of a series of books on congressional elections.

The party controlling the White House almost always loses seats in midterm elections, but Democrats defied history and conventional wisdom in putting back together much of their old New Deal coalition.

Outreach efforts by the party and its allies to encourage blacks, Hispanics, union members, gays, women and Jews to get out and vote succeeded in the low-turnout mid-term environment. The party even restored some of its luster in the eyes of white men in certain races by nominating conservative or centrist candidates.

Democrats picked up five seats in the House and put a halt to their string of overall losses in Senate and gubernatorial contests.

Republicans were left arguing whether appeals to their own conservative base had been too weak, or had been so strong as to drive away potential voters. (*Story, p. 8*)

GOP base turnout had been taken almost as a given in prognostications leading up to the elections, as conservatives were expected to cast votes in anger over President Clinton's behavior.

Instead, many conservatives had grown dispirited as they saw Clinton appearing to survive yet another scandal. They also were angry at congressional Republicans for the less-than-frugal end-of-session budget deal. (*1998 CQ Weekly, p. 2986*)

Polling for the Christian Coalition found that on Nov. 3 nearly a quarter of the conservative Christians who voted for Republicans in

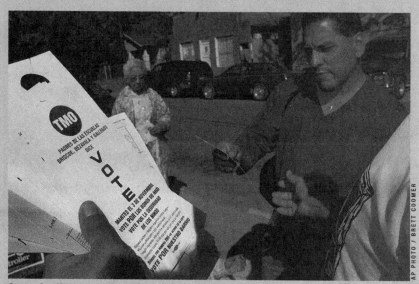

Campaign literature printed in Spanish is handed out near a polling place in Houston to help Spanish-speaking voters on Nov. 3.

1994 switched their support to Democrats this year.

"Conservatives in Washington are not going to glide to victory by taking our voters for granted," said Randy Tate, executive director of the Christian Coalition.

Many independent observers, though, saw the best hope for the GOP in following the model of the Bush brothers, Jeb and George W., who racked up impressive wins in the Florida and Texas gubernatorial races, respectively, by openly appealing to black and Hispanic voters. (*Governors, p. 16*)

But if Republicans were left mending fences, Democrats were celebrating the return of core groups to the fold.

Black voters were not only angry about GOP impeachment efforts but pleased with their own standing in the economy as well.

"The black community did not want a repeat of 1994," when low black turnout helped the GOP take control of the House, said David A. Bositis, senior political analyst at the Joint Center for Political Studies in Washington. "Clinton gets the credit

[for the good economy], and they don't want to see him impeached."

The black share of the vote did not increase nationally from 1994, but it did grow in battleground states of the South. Blacks were an essential factor in electing statewide Democratic candidates in Maryland, the Carolinas, Alabama and Georgia, where the black vote increased from 19 percent of the state's total vote in 1994 to 29 percent in 1998, according to exit polls.

EMILY's List, which raises money for Democratic women candidates, spent $3 million in a coordinated campaign with the Democratic Party in 20 states to encourage women to vote. The gender gap may have grown widest in California's governor's race, where the Republican share of the female vote dropped from a bare majority in 1994 to just 35 percent.

The union household share of the national vote rose from 14 percent in 1994 to 22 percent in 1998. In contrast to 1996, when labor spent more than $30 million on issue ads, this time unions invested heavily in turnout efforts.

DEPARTING THE HILL

Defeated for Re-election HOUSE (7)

Jon D. Fox, R-Pa. (13)   Michael Pappas, R-N.J. (12)   Rick White, R-Wash. (1)
Jay W. Johnson, D-Wis. (8)   Bill Redmond, R-N.M. (3)
Jay C. Kim, R-Calif. (41) **   Vince Snowbarger, R-Kan. (3)

Retiring from the HOUSE (23)

Jon Christensen, R-Neb. (2) *   Joseph P. Kennedy II, D-Mass. (8)   Dan Schaefer, R-Colo. (6)
Harris W. Fawell, R-Ill. (13)   Scott L. Klug, R-Wis. (2)   David E. Skaggs, D-Colo. (2)
Vic Fazio, D-Calif. (3)   Thomas J. Manton, D-N.Y. (7)   Bob Smith, R-Ore. (2)
Elizabeth Furse, D-Ore. (1)   Joseph M. McDade, R-Pa. (10)   Gerald B.H. Solomon, R-N.Y. (22)
Henry B. Gonzalez, D-Texas (20)   Paul McHale, D-Pa. (15)   Louis Stokes, D-Ohio (11)
Lee H. Hamilton, D-Ind. (9)   Mike Parker, R-Miss. (4)   Esteban E. Torres, D-Calif. (34)
Jane Harman, D-Calif. (36) **   Bill Paxon, R-N.Y. (27)   Sidney R. Yates, D-Ill. (9)
W.G. "Bill" Hefner, D-N.C. (8)   Frank Riggs, R-Calif. (1) ***

Defeated for Re-election SENATE (3)

Carol Moseley-Braun, D-Ill.   Alfonse M. D'Amato, R-N.Y.   Lauch Faircloth, R-N.C.

Retiring from the SENATE (4)

Dale Bumpers, D-Ark.   Daniel R. Coats, R-Ind.   Wendell H. Ford, D-Ky.   John Glenn, D-Ohio

Ran for SENATE (8)

Rep. Scotty Baesler, D-Ky. (6), **lost**   Rep. Bob Inglis, R-S.C. (4), **lost**
Rep. Jim Bunning, R-Ky. (4), **won**   Rep. Mark W. Neumann, R-Wis. (1), **lost**
Rep. Michael D. Crapo, R-Idaho (2), **won**   Rep. Charles E. Schumer, D-N.Y. (9), **won**
Rep. John Ensign, R-Nev. (1), **lost**   Rep. Linda Smith, R-Wash. (3), **lost**

Ran for GOVERNOR (3)

Sen. Dirk Kempthorne, R-Idaho, **won**
Barbara B. Kennelly, D-Conn. (1), **lost**
Rep. Glenn Poshard, D-Ill. (19), **lost**

* Lost in Nebraska's May 12 GOP gubernatorial primary.
** Lost in California's June 2 primary.   *** Withdrew from California Senate race.

as Bob Barr, R-Ga., are by no means ready to give up just when they think their goal of ousting Clinton is within grasp.

Congressional expert William Connelly, a political science professor at Washington and Lee University in Virginia, said congressional Republicans should learn from their governors, who won 23 of the 36 governorships in play on Election Day. There was a net loss of one governorship for Republicans, but they still control 31 of the 50 states.

"Congressional Republicans would do well to look at their governors," Connelly said. "The governors are addressing issues close to home, not fighting symbolic issues. Congressional Republicans seemed more inclined to push the politics of symbolism."

Two big losses for Republican governors came in the deep South, where Govs. Fob James Jr. of Alabama and David Beasley of South Carolina counted on religious conservatives as their bedrock of support.

Steven Schier, chairman of the political science department at Carleton College in Minnesota, said the Democratic election gains were due not to voters' overwhelming support for the Democratic agenda, but rather to voters' desire to embrace any agenda.

"This was about as insignificant an election with regard to issues as I can remember," he said.

Schier described the Democratic legislative agenda as "happy talk," but said it proved more attractive to voters than the Republicans' emphasis on Clinton's affair with former White House intern Monica Lewinsky.

"A positive message on the issues, however tepid it may be, is better than no issues," Schier said. "The Republicans were trying to emphasize the negativity of Clinton. And two negatives don't translate into an attraction."

Campaign 2000

Voices of moderation in both parties also may be drowned out by preparation for the 2000 election, which is expected to be even more contentious as a result of this year's outcome.

"This election makes 2000 look like Armageddon," said Gary Jacobson, a political science professor at the University of California, San Diego. "There is an excellent chance that whoever wins the White House will win both houses of Congress."

Because of the political maneuvering that will take place over the next two years, some observers predict that little legislating will take place on Capitol Hill — despite the narrow majority and opportunities for bipartisan compromise.

"Legislatively, little will happen," said Democratic consultant Mark Mellman. "Democrats and Republicans will be playing hard to win the White House and the congressional majority. It will be a very polarized place." ◆

Leadership posts are up for grabs as disaffected Republicans force Gingrich out

Shakeup in the House

Rep. Robert Livingston, chairman of the Appropriations Committee, announced his candidacy for the speakership outside the Capitol on Nov. 6.

House Republicans knew their post-election conversations would be consumed with whether certain transgressions merited removal from office.

What surprised them was the subject of those talks. Instead of discussing whether to impeach President Clinton for lying about an affair, they forced Speaker Newt Gingrich, R-Ga., to step down from his leadership post after the party lost a net five House seats in the Nov. 3 election. Other leaders were expected to face serious challenges as well.

Gingrich's Nov. 6 decision to resign came just hours after he drew a challenge from a candidate with the stature and connections to beat him — Ap-

CQ Weekly Nov. 7, 1998

propriations Committee Chairman Robert L. Livingston, R-La. More candidacies were expected to follow.

In the four years since it took the House in a conservative revolution, the GOP's agenda seemed to run out of steam. Until now, Gingrich has survived criticism from rank-and-file members who felt that he tended to become disengaged and was unable to form broad coalitions needed to run the House.

In choosing his successor Nov. 18, Republicans must address the splits within their ranks, primarily the fissure that divides conservatives and moderates — a division that reflects a broader struggle within the national party. [Republicans selected Livingston as Gingrich's successor. — Ed.]

No matter who wins the other lead-

ership posts, it is clear House GOP members wanted a shift in strategy, perhaps to something more pragmatic, but certainly to an agenda they can better articulate to voters.

Gingrich's decision not to seek another term put practically every leadership post up for grabs. It followed days of recriminations among GOP members over who was to blame for the election results, which handed House Republicans the thinnest margin a majority has held in 46 years.

The election "has shown us unequivocally that the American people want more than politicians with good speeches," Livingston said. "They want politicians with ideas — and ideas that work." Too often the party's message "has gotten lost in the haze of high rhetoric and miscast priorities; lost in a management style where process is subordinated to polls and self-initiated crises."

In contrast to Gingrich, whom he repeatedly referred to as a friend, Livingston said he would be more of a "stay at home type" of Speaker, dealing with "day-to-day governing" of the House.

He would also be more pragmatic than Gingrich and less of a visionary. As Speaker, he would likely concentrate more on the nuts and bolts of advancing a legislative agenda than Gingrich, a discipline that would be invaluable in working with such a thin Republican margin.

Other posts were at stake besides the speakership. Steve Largent of Oklahoma announced Nov. 6 that he would challenge Majority Leader Dick Armey of Texas, while George P. Radanovich of California, Rick A. Lazio of New York and Peter Hoekstra of Michigan were possible opponents for House Republican Conference Chairman John A. Boehner of Ohio.

"It's abundantly clear that on Nov. 3 the Republican Party hit an iceberg," Largent said. "And I think the question that's before our conference today is whether we retain the crew of the Titanic or look for some new leadership."

"To paraphrase Raymond Chandler, congressional Republicans are feeling the edge of the carving knife and studying each other's necks," said John J. Pitney Jr., an associate professor of government at Claremont McKenna College in California.

This is only the second time since the Civil War that the party not in control of the White House lost seats in a midterm election, and many Republicans were seriously considering a shakeup as a result. The party is left with 223 seats, compared with 211 Democrats and one Independent.

"All of my political instincts say we've lost two in a row, we need a leadership change," said Mark Souder, R-Ind.

No matter who is in charge, managing the assemblage will be even more of a chore. The election sliced the Republicans' scant, hard-to-manage 11-vote majority into an even thinner six-vote edge.

"If you thought the 105th Congress was chaotic, the 106th is going to be even more so," said William F. Connelly Jr., a professor of politics at Washing-

106th Congress		105th Congress	
Republicans	223	Republicans	228
Democrats	211	Democrats	206
Independent	1	Independent	1

REPUBLICANS	
Net loss	-5
Freshmen	17
Incumbents re-elected	206
Incumbents defeated	6

DEMOCRATS	
Net gain	+5
Freshmen	23
Incumbents re-elected	188
Incumbents defeated	1

ton and Lee University in Virginia.

Republicans could be held hostage on any particular vote not just by a faction, but by a small gathering of disgruntled members. Any huddle of a half-dozen Republicans could be a cabal. Absences brought about by the flu or the weather could tip the balance of power on any given day.

"If a plane is late from California, they could lose a vote," said a Democratic leadership aide, with evident glee.

Majority Whip Tom DeLay, R-Texas, has had the difficult job of assembling a majority for every vote. Because of his success in that tough assignment, DeLay seems the most secure of GOP leaders. "There aren't many members saying, 'I want to be the person responsible for getting to 218,' " Souder said.

The Republicans' loss of House seats and the disarray that followed also throws further doubt on their ability to assemble a majority to impeach Clinton. It becomes more likely that lawmakers will ultimately seek an alternative punishment, such as censure. (1998 CQ Weekly, p. 2986)

Indeed, many Republicans blame the party's obsession with Clinton and his possible impeachment for their electoral setback. Other criticisms, depending on one's ideology, included the leadership's inability to develop and communicate a broad message, its unwillingness to stick to a conservative agenda and the lack of legislative accomplishments.

Hardly anyone seemed to focus, as Gingrich urged, on the fact that Re-

publicans won their third consecutive House election for the first time since the Great Depression.

For the current crop of House Republicans, the Great Depression now refers to their mood — fears that their hard-earned majority status is slipping away.

A Growing Discontent

GOP lawmakers had commented privately throughout the year that their leaders were less cohesive and effective than they had been in the early days of Republican control of the House in 1995.

Then, of course, the party had its "Contract With America" to unite behind. Dissension in the ranks grew after the partial government shutdowns in the winter of 1995-96, and the so-called disaster relief debacle last year, when the party linked unrelated matters to emergency flood relief, delaying the aid. Misgivings about Gingrich crystallized with the aborted coup against him in July 1997, plotted with the consent of some party leaders. (1997 Almanac, p. 1-11)

Gingrich survived the overthrow attempt and strengthened his hand this year. But the ill will blossomed again when lawmakers stitched together an unwieldy omnibus fiscal 1999 appropriations bill (PL 105-277) and when GOP leaders made a failed, last-ditch attempt to improve their electoral standing with television commercials that focused on Clinton's affair with former White House intern Monica Lewinsky. (Omnibus appropriations, 1998 CQ Weekly, p. 2885)

"The last couple of months have been a giant screw up," said E. Clay Shaw Jr., R-Fla.

Even party stalwart Henry J. Hyde, R-Ill., chairman of the Judiciary Committee, commented, "Leadership takes credit when things go right. They ought to take blame when things go wrong."

Ralph Hellman, a former DeLay aide who now lobbies for the National Federation of Independent Business, said, "I think everyone is trying to blame each other when the reality is dealing with an 11-seat majority is just a bear. A six-seat majority is going to be even tougher."

Gingrich, never at a loss for words, sounded stumped when talking to reporters Nov. 4. "I frankly don't understand all the things that happened yesterday," he admitted, "and I'm not sure anyone else in the country does either."

Gingrich acknowledged that Republicans had underestimated how quickly people tired of the Lewinsky scandal, though he said the media was preoccupied with it. But he also said that the GOP should have been more aggressive in telling voters "what we're trying to do is find a way to reform government, cut taxes, save Social Security, win the war on drugs, reform education and strengthen national defense."

With barely two weeks between Election Day and the meeting for members to choose their leadership team, there is little time to gin up a campaign and develop coalitions. That they are scattered across the country and dependent on reaching one another by telephone makes it even more difficult.

And it is difficult for outsiders to assess how a leadership campaign is faring because, more so than on most issues, it is a member-to-member process with little input from staff and less desire than usual to tell all to the press.

Nagging Doubts

Gingrich built a strong following within the party for having led Republicans to control of the House after 40 years in the minority.

But there have been persistent, nagging doubts about his ability to lead Republicans in the majority. He may ultimately be seen as a transitional figure, someone whose divisiveness alienated many mainstream voters and who was unable to build a large and stable coalition. (*1998 CQ Weekly, p. 2085*)

"Before you can govern Congress as a majority in the House, you have to learn to govern yourself, that is, your own factions," Connelly said. "It's not clear he's successfully made the transition from opposition to governing. The House Republican Party overall is having trouble making that transition."

Added one Republican strategist: "We've got a leadership problem. We've got a followership problem too."

Conservatives were especially bitter about the outcome. "I felt like '94 was a referendum on the President's failed leadership," Largent told the Tulsa World. "I think '98 was a referendum on the Republicans' failed leadership."

Shortly after the election, Gingrich began taking the offensive to save his job, reaching out to members by phone.

New House Panel Chairmen

The most powerful committee job in the House likely will be up for grabs this month with Appropriations Chairman Robert L. Livingston, R-La., running for House Speaker.

Livingston said Nov. 6 he would challenge Speaker Newt Gingrich, R-Ga., who reportedly decided within hours not to run for re-election.

Competition for the Appropriations post could be intense. Gingrich picked Livingston over three more-senior members in 1994, and two of them remain — C.W. Bill Young of Florida and Ralph Regula of Ohio. (*1998 CQ Weekly, p. 2978*)

Further down the Appropriations roster, the retirement of Joseph M. McDade, R-Pa., opens the way for Joe Knollenberg, R-Mich., to become chairman of the Energy and Water Subcommittee. But if the decision is based on overall committee seniority, the chairmanship would go most likely to Ron Packard of California, a close Livingston ally and now chairman of the Military Construction Subcommittee. In all, Republicans will have three open seats to fill; Democrats will have six.

Other key committee changes:

• **Rules.** David Dreier, R-Calif., will take the helm of the committee that sets floor procedure, succeeding Gerald B.H. Solomon, R-N.Y., who is retiring. Dreier is a little more polished than the more emotional Solomon, but the overall agenda is set by the House leadership.

• **Agriculture.** Larry Combest, R-Texas, will take over as chairman from Bob Smith, R-Ore., who is retiring. Combest has served on the Agriculture Committee his entire House career and has good relations with Agriculture Secretary Dan Glickman.

• **International Relations.** The new ranking Democrat, Sam Gejdenson of Connecticut, could hardly be more different from his predecessor, Lee H. Hamilton of Indiana, who is retiring.

Gejdenson is an emotional fire-

cracker more prone to partisan shouting matches or effusive speeches than the low-key, measured Hamilton. But Gejdenson may be able to work with Chairman Benjamin A. Gilman, R-N.Y. Gejdenson wants to make deals. Gejdenson and Gilman also are among the strongest supporters of Israel in the House.

The committee loses Vince Snowbarger, R-Kan., a major opponent of paying debts to the United Nations. His defeat and the shrinking GOP majority may make it easier to get U.N. funds through the House without abortion restrictions.

• **Ways and Means.** Both the chairman and ranking Democrat are leaving the Social Security Subcommittee, which could play a significant role next year as Congress debates legislation to overhaul the federal retirement system.

Subcommittee Chairman Jim Bunning, R-Ky., was elected to the Senate. His successor is likely to be moderate Amo Houghton, R-N.Y., former Corning Glass Works chief executive officer.

Ranking Democrat Barbara B. Kennelly of Connecticut failed in her gubernatorial bid. She may be replaced by either Benjamin L. Cardin of Maryland or Sander M. Levin of Michigan.

• **Commerce.** Joe L. Barton, R-Texas, is expected to take over as chairman of the Energy and Power Subcommittee, replacing retiring Dan Schaefer, R-Colo.

Possible candidates to replace Barton as chairman of the Oversight Subcommittee: Dennis Hastert, R-Ill., and Fred Upton, R-Mich.

• **Education and the Workforce.** Michael N. Castle, R-Del., a moderate, is in line to replace the retiring Frank Riggs, R-Calif., as chairman of the Early Childhood, Youth and Families Subcommittee, which will have a key role in rewriting the Elementary and Secondary Education Act next year. Some education groups are courting Rep. Howard P. "Buck" McKeon, R-Calif.

"He's very open and receptive and he's listening to members' concerns and trying to learn what can be done better," a leadership aide said Nov. 5.

Christina Martin, Gingrich's press secretary, issued a statement Nov. 6 expressing the Speaker's resolve to run for another term.

Hours later, Gingrich held a conference call with confidants saying that he had a change of heart.

"The Republican conference needs to be unified, and it is time for me to move forward where I believe I still have a signficiant role to play for our country and our party," Gingrich said in a statement released late in the day. "I urge my colleagues to pick leaders who can both reconcile and discipline, who can work together and communicate effectively."

Livingston's Loyalty

Livingston had previously been upfront both about his interest in serving as Speaker and his loyalty to Gingrich. After the election, he seemed more serious about the former than the latter.

He said earlier in the year that he wanted the job. He quickly followed through, rounding up commitments from more than 100 members who said they would support him if Gingrich stepped down during the next two years.

This early spadework could turn out to be enormously valuable for Livingston, who posed his challenge to Gingrich with two weeks' notice and most members ensconced in their districts.

He also comes across reasonably well on television — a talent many rank-and-file members are desperate to see in the leadership team — has an ability to raise money, has shown his leadership abilities as chairman of Appropriations and has allies in different factions. (*1998 CQ Weekly, p. 979*)

Challenging Gingrich involved upending the man who handpicked him as Appropriations chairman four years ago and enabled him to bypass three more senior members.

And yet Livingston, in a phone conversation with Gingrich on Nov. 4, broached the subject of Gingrich stepping down.

Livingston could face criticism from some who have seen his red-hot temper. Hard-core conservatives believe he is too quick to compromise with De-

mocrats. Moderates might find him less receptive than Gingrich, who has of late been particularly open to the ideas of more centrist members.

Livingston, according to several people who have spoken to him, was said to be reluctant to form a leadership slate. However, he might need to build a coalition that includes conservatives in order to coerce enough votes from the party's right wing.

Ways and Means Committee Chairman Bill Archer of Texas said Nov. 6 that he was considering running for Speaker. Aides to James M. Talent of Missouri said he was mulling a bid as well.

With Gingrich out as Speaker, much of the rest of his team may have to struggle to stay in place. Armey, Boehner and Conference Vice Chairman Jennifer Dunn of Washington all said they planned to seek re-election to their posts.

Armey has long been seen as the most vulnerable GOP leader. Bill Paxon, R-N.Y., was gearing up to challenge him earlier this year, with DeLay's blessing, before Paxon abruptly announced his retirement. (*1998 CQ Weekly Report, p. 472*)

The name most frequently mentioned as a potential opponent against Armey was Largent, a rock-ribbed conservative from the feisty Class of '94. J.C. Watts of Oklahoma and Hoekstra were also being mentioned for an undetermined leadership slot.

Many Republican lawmakers were calling for making the post of chairman of the National Republican Congressional Committee an elected position instead of one appointed by the Speaker. That would likely mean a replacement for John Linder, R-Ga., who has been widely criticized in the wake of the election. Jim McCrery of Louisiana and Thomas M. Davis III, R-Va., are possible candidates.

And if Livingston ascends into leadership, that would leave an important vacancy at Appropriations. C.W. Bill Young, R-Fla., would be next in line, though there would almost certainly be some jostling for it.

Developing an Agenda

The election amplified the views of Republicans who complained about the lack of an identifiable agenda. "I think that there are a few people spending a disproportionate share of their time trying to kill the messenger

when what we should be doing is refining the message," said Sherwood Boehlert, R-N.Y.

The agenda could be a more centrist one. "They need to have an agenda that is sufficiently appealing to their conservative base to galvanize them and yet at the same time they have to be able to broaden their appeal to moderate voters," said Ronald M. Peters Jr., who heads the Carl Albert Congressional Research and Studies Center at the University of Oklahoma.

"Clearly we have to find a more positive, inclusive message and stay on it . . . and talk about issues in a way that the general public understands and relates to," said Lazio, a moderate.

Many conservatives, naturally, were leery of that approach. "We need to give our conservative base some red meat," said Richard H. Baker, R-La. "At least they would see somebody fighting for what they believe in." That could mean an all-out struggle for a large tax cut or education vouchers usable for private schools.

But some conservatives were receptive to a wider appeal. Republicans have to "formulate an agenda out there that will appeal to moderates and conservatives, said Robert L. Ehrlich Jr., R-Md. "And it's not just cutting capital gains."

Moderates and conservatives even spoke to one another about forming a coalition to unseat one or more incumbent leaders, particularly Boehner and Linder.

"Republicans, as always, are fractious," said Pitney, "and they define the problem differently. It will take an enormous amount of skill and discipline to bring them together."

Democrats, meanwhile, said they were eager to step into the breach. They will have two relatively low-key races for leadership positions of their own during the week of Nov. 16, to replace caucus Chairman Vic Fazio of California and Vice Chairman Barbara B. Kennelly of Connecticut, both of whom are retiring.

They are eager to talk about the issues that they believe brought them to the brink of retaking the House. "People don't want deadlock," said Minority Leader Richard A. Gephardt, D-Mo., adding that Democrats will still push for a managed care patients' bill of rights, more money for teachers and classrooms, and saving the surplus for Social Security. ◆

Senate GOP chief must rally party as it confronts issues that play to Democratic strengths

Lott's Leadership Burden Grows

Charles E. Schumer shows relief at defeating New York's Alfonse M. D'Amato.

In Illinois, Republican Peter Fitzgerald beat incumbent Carol Moseley-Braun on Nov. 3.

John Edwards delighted Democrats with his North Carolina victory over Lauch Faircloth.

In the aftermath of the meltdown of the House Republican leadership, Senate Majority Leader Trent Lott, R-Miss., is suddenly confronting a crucially important mission: Come up with a winning game plan, and quickly.

With Speaker Newt Gingrich out and the GOP leadership in the House up for grabs, it is up to Lott and his leadership team to develop an agenda that can rally dispirited and divided congressional Republicans.

That will not be easy. Many of the marquee battles of the 106th Congress — from overhauling Social Security to curbing abuses by health maintenance organizations — will be fought on the Democrats' turf.

Buoyed by the election results, Democrats have charged out of the blocks with an aggressive legislative program. Several components, such as imposing rules on managed health care, are leftover proposals that were blocked by the GOP in the 105th Congress. "They're ready, we just have to push the 'print' button," said a Democratic strategist.

By contrast, most of Lott's troops are in a blue funk, more interested in affixing blame for the disappointing electoral showing than in crafting new legislative plans. And Lott — the fast-talking Southerner who is much more adept at tactics than strategy — is facing his toughest challenge since he

replaced former Kansas Sen. Bob Dole as majority leader two years ago.

The stakes are enormous. Democrats will be trying to pull off a political triple-play in 2000, retaining control of the White House while retaking the Senate and House. "It's the ultimate political year," said Marshall Wittmann, director of congressional relations for the House at the conservative Heritage Foundation.

The battle for control of the Senate is likely to be particularly hard fought. Republicans must defend 19 seats, but Democrats will have only 14 seats in play. In a sign of the Democrats' growing confidence, Missouri Gov. Mel Carnahan recently announced he would challenge Republican Sen. John

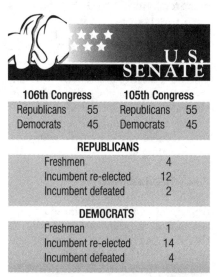

U.S. SENATE

106th Congress		105th Congress	
Republicans	55	Republicans	55
Democrats	45	Democrats	45

REPUBLICANS	
Freshmen	4
Incumbent re-elected	12
Incumbent defeated	2

DEMOCRATS	
Freshman	1
Incumbent re-elected	14
Incumbent defeated	4

Ashcroft, a leading conservative and a possible presidential candidate.

So far, Lott's only solution has been to pitch for a major tax cut, which has undeniable appeal for the GOP's restive conservative base but stands little chance of becoming law. Significantly, Lott came under fire when a Republican-backed tax cut died in the Senate in the fall without coming to a vote. But a full-scale discussion of the agenda will probably wait until Republicans meet in early December to reorganize for the next Congress.

Senate Republicans fared far better at the polls than their House counterparts. The GOP retained its 55-45 seat edge. But just a few months ago, it dreamt of 60 seats, enough to overcome a partisan filibuster.

Instead, it preserved the numerical status quo, which prompted some Republicans to recall old adages about the thrills of playing to a tie or kissing your sister. "I've already heard from several unhappy senators," said John McCain, R-Ariz., after easily winning his third term. "We just lost a golden opportunity."

It is uncertain whether the rumbles of discontent will cost any senior Republicans their leadership positions. In recent years, Senate Republicans have had less of a taste for internecine warfare than their House colleagues, for whom palace intrigue has become practically second nature.

The turmoil in the House has taken

Moynihan To Retire in 2000

Democratic Sen. Daniel Patrick Moynihan of New York jumped to the head of the next parade of congressional retirees, announcing on a TV talk show Nov. 6 that he will not seek a fifth term in 2000.

His decision became public just three days after New York's other senator, Republican Alfonse M. D'Amato, was unseated by Democratic Rep. Charles E. Schumer. (*Senate, p. 12*)

State party officials and other sources named a long list of potential candidates even before Moynihan's announcement was official.

State Comptroller H. Carl McCall, who had refused Nov. 5 to rule out a primary run against Moynihan, appeared certain to go, and may be joined in the Democratic field by Rep. Nita M. Lowey; Housing and Urban Development Secretary Andrew M. Cuomo; New York City Public Advocate Mark Green; and environmental lawyer Robert F.

Moynihan said on Nov. 6 that he would not seek re-election in 2000.

Kennedy Jr., whose father held the seat from 1965 to 1968.

Among the Republicans certain to take a look at running were New York City Mayor Rudolph W. Giuliani and Rep. Rick A. Lazio. Speculation was also rampant that D'Amato might try to mount a comeback.

Moynihan, 71, who is the ranking Democrat on the Finance Committee, was the panel's chairman when it took up Clinton's proposal to overhaul health insurance policy.

He earned the enmity of the White House by declaring in January 1994, "We don't have a health care crisis in this country. We do have a welfare crisis."

When the Republican-controlled 105th Congress produced a welfare overhaul (PL 104-193) that ended guarantees of federal support to the poor, Moynihan unsuccessfully lobbied Clinton not to sign it. (*1996 Almanac, p. 6-3*)

Moynihan's mother ran a saloon in New York City's Hell's Kitchen, and he remains part Irish bartender, part Harvard professor. After rising to prominence in the academic community, he became a Cabinet or sub-Cabinet official in four successive administrations.

He was the architect of President Richard M. Nixon's failed "guaranteed income" plan and a 1988 welfare overhaul. He also caused himself great trouble when he counseled "benign neglect" toward minorities.

---

some heat off Lott for now. Still, many GOP activists and rank-and-file senators were noticeably underwhelmed by his performance in this fall's budget showdown with President Clinton.

Chuck Hagel, R-Neb., a fierce critic of Lott's, has signaled he may challenge Mitch McConnell of Kentucky for the chairmanship of the National Republican Senatorial Committee, which does fundraising and candidate recruitment.

The New Battleground

Lott and other GOP leaders face some familiar problems as they begin planning for the 106th Congress. Minority Leader Tom Daschle, D-S.D., is a master at using the Senate's rules to stymie GOP initiatives. In light of the Democrats' election successes and the fading hopes for Clinton's impeachment, Daschle should be even bolder next year.

Lott also knows that to achieve any meaningful legislative victories, Republicans must compromise with Clinton and Democrats. But striking such deals, whether on the 1997 balanced-budget package or this fall's massive omnibus spending bill (PL 105-277), drives the

GOP's conservative base to distraction.

Those tensions — between conflict and compromise, among parties and within the GOP's ranks — will be present as Congress struggles with a number of major issues next year:

• **Social Security.** Clinton has repeatedly outmaneuvered Republicans on Social Security, so Lott and other GOP leaders are understandably wary of rushing forward with a plan to ensure the solvency of the nation's retirement system.

Republicans generally favor permitting Americans to invest a portion of their payroll taxes in equity markets. But Clinton and Vice President Al Gore will come under intense pressure from unions and other core Democratic supporters to fight privatization plans.

The battle lines could form early — the House Ways and Means Committee has scheduled a hearing on Social Security's future on Nov. 19, and the White House will hold a conference on that subject next month.

• **Taxes.** Social Security is closely tied to the question of tax cuts, which is the GOP's top priority. Clinton's mantra of "save Social Security first" effectively

prevented Republicans from enacting a tax cut in 1998.

Until the Social Security issue is somehow taken off the table, any sizable tax cuts probably will not pass. "I don't see that Republicans have enough votes to do tax cuts," said veteran lobbyist John Motley, senior vice president for government and public affairs at the Food Marketing Institute.

• **Education.** The elections proved that politicians ignore this issue at their political peril. Next year, Congress will tackle education policy when it considers reauthorizing the Elementary and Secondary Education Act (PL 103-382), which originally was part of President Lyndon B. Johnson's Great Society program.

Republicans will press for school vouchers and tax-deferred educational savings accounts. Democrats will renew their push to fund 100,000 new teachers and school construction. Given the political stakes, the debate likely will be bitter and divisive.

• **Budget.** The GOP's message on budget and appropriations sounds as if it was written by the rock band The Who

Some Senate Panels May Shift Focus As New Chairmen Come to Power

Democrats may have been eager to defeat New York Republican Sen. Alfonse M. D'Amato, but at least they could cut deals with him as chairman of the Banking Committee.

That may not be true of D'Amato's successor, Phil Gramm, R-Texas, onetime economics professor and rock-ribbed free-market thinker who often seems to have little tolerance for the views of others.

Banking panel Democrats fear the often bipartisan committee will become yet another ideological battleground.

"I think the Democrats on that committee often thought there was a deal at the end of the rainbow" with D'Amato, said Jake Lewis, a banking specialist for Ralph Nader's Center for the Study of Responsive Law. "I think there will be no illusion with Gramm. Therefore, I think, look for the Democrats on the Senate Banking Committee to act more like Democrats from the start."

D'Amato's defeat is one of the few major changes in the Senate committee landscape for the 106th Congress. Among others:

Armed Services

Republican John W. Warner of Virginia takes over the chairmanship from 95-year-old Strom Thurmond, R-S.C., who is staying in the Senate.

Gramm is a free-market thinker who seems to have little tolerance for other points of view, leading some to fear the Banking panel will become an ideological battleground.

Courtly in style and less partisan than Thurmond, Warner has a clear agenda for changing defense policy that includes larger budgets, fewer deployments of U.S. ground troops in murky ethnic conflicts such as Bosnia and a greater reliance on Navy fleets and ship-borne Marine Corps units.

Republican social conservatives have largely gotten over their anger with Warner for refusing to endorse Oliver L. North in the 1994 Virginia Senate race, but he may still have to prove his conservative credentials.

Elsewhere on the committee,

James M. Inhofe, R-Okla., is expected to replace retiring Daniel R. Coats of Indiana as chairman of the AirLand Forces Subcommittee. A staunch conservative, Inhofe has been an aggressive Clinton administration critic in chairing the Readiness Subcommittee, which may now fall to Pat Roberts, R-Kan.

With the departure of conservative Sen. Dirk Kempthorne, R-Idaho, the chairmanship of the Personnel Subcommittee could go to Olympia J. Snowe, R-Maine, a moderate who could use the panel to focus more attention on military health care and issues involving women.

Rules

Mitch McConnell, R-Ky., is expected to take over as chairman, replacing Warner. Daniel K. Inouye of Hawaii is expected to assume the top Democratic spot, replacing the retiring Wendell H. Ford of Kentucky.

Senate Rules plays a more subsidiary role than its House counterpart, but that would change in the increasingly unlikely event that the House votes to impeach President Clinton — Rules would be called on to review and possibly propose revisions in Senate rules and procedures governing a trial. The committee has not conducted such a review since the Senate prepared to try President

— "We won't get fooled again."

In 1996, and again this year, Clinton used the threat of a government shutdown to force Republicans into humiliating concessions on spending bills. To neutralize that threat, GOP leaders are already vowing to finish the fiscal 2000 budget and appropriations bills on time.

But the failure of Republicans to produce a budget last year owed less to procrastination than the party's deep internal divisions over using the budget surplus to finance tax cuts. Those differences persist. In addition, the policy-related "riders" that conservatives

attach to spending bills will continue to provoke partisan conflict.

Perhaps more important, the $500 billion omnibus bill made a mockery of the budget caps of the 1997 deal. That extra spending could force appropriators to make painful cuts next year, unless there is a bipartisan deal to lift the caps.

All of these issues and numerous others —including trade, foreign policy, campaign finance and Democratic proposals to raise the minimum wage — will be debated in an atmosphere that will be unusually politicized for a non-election year.

The 2000 presidential campaign will

begin in earnest next fall, which means that major bipartisan deals will have to be accomplished before then. The Senate is loaded with potential presidential contenders — from John Kerry of Massachusetts and Bob Kerrey of Nebraska, among Democrats, to Ashcroft and McCain on the GOP side.

Motley is worried that the business community's legislative priorities might suffer in the overheated political atmosphere. He expects that many Republicans will feel pressure to support an increase in the minimum wage. "I'm not confident a floor fight over the minimum wage could be won," he said.

Andrew Johnson in 1868.

McConnell may also convene hearings on the efficiency of the "motor voter" law (PL 103-31) making it easier to register to vote when applying for a driver's license. McConnell, the leading critic of the legislation championed by Ford, says the law opened the door to voter fraud.

Commerce, Science and Transportation

Ford's retirement will lead to the naming of West Virginian John D. Rockefeller IV as ranking Democrat on the Aviation Subcommittee. Ford had close ties to airlines, given Kentucky's big hub airports, while Rockefeller is likely to be an advocate for small towns increasingly abandoned by scheduled airlines. Rockefeller could have a busy year: Commerce Chairman John McCain, R-Ariz., insisted on authorizing the Federal Aviation Administration for only six months in the omnibus spending bill (PL 105-277) to ensure he could reopen debate early in 1999 on his proposal to add landing slots at crowded airports.

Energy and Natural Resources

Jeff Bingaman, D-N.M., will become the ranking Democrat with the retirement of Dale Bumpers, D-Ark.

As a Westerner, Bingaman is likely to be much closer to Chairman Frank H. Murkowski, R-Alaska, on issues involving public lands, forests and energy. Bumpers frequently sided with environmentalists on timber issues and mining reform.

Murkowski has pledged that his committee will adopt by June a bill dealing with issues surrounding the deregulation of electric rates by states, something he refused to do in 1998 when he had to deal with Bumpers. Murkowski and Bingaman agree on the need to clarify state and federal regulatory responsibilities.

Environment and Public Works

Kempthorne's departure to become governor of Idaho leaves open the chairmanship of the Drinking Water, Fisheries and Wildlife Subcommittee. Warner's step up on Armed Services may leave open the top seat on the Transportation and Infrastructure Subcommittee. Potential successors, such as Robert C. Smith, R-N.H., and Craig Thomas, R-Wyo., were assessing several committee options.

Governmental Affairs

Joseph I. Lieberman of Connecticut is expected to take over the top Democratic slot opened by the retirement of Sen. John Glenn, D-Ohio.

Carl Levin of Michigan was next in line but opted instead to stay on as ranking Democrat on the Armed Services Committee. Lieberman, a moderate Democrat who often teams with less ideological members on both sides of the aisle, is likely to work closely with committee Chairman Fred Thompson, R-Tenn.

Banking, Housing and Urban Affairs

One of the big losers in D'Amato's departure could be mass transit

systems in the Northeast. As Banking chairman, he controlled the transit authorization and snared a big increase for mass transit in the six-year transportation bill. Gramm is likely to be more inclined to spread mass transit money around, especially to fast-growing cities in the West.

A prime area of partisan confrontation next year will be issues such as the 1977 Community Reinvestment Act (PL 95-128), which requires federal regulators, when weighing a bank's application for a merger or new branch, to also consider whether the institution has lent to all segments of its community.

At the end of the 105th Congress, Gramm and his frequent Banking panel ally, Richard C. Shelby, R-Ala., blocked movement of a measure (HR 10) to rewrite the nation's financial services laws because they opposed a provision to apply community reinvestment requirements to financial conglomerates and to increase penalties for non-compliance.

Because of Gramm's strong feelings, the measure's supporters and other observers question whether he will be able to move an overhaul bill, which remains a top priority for much of the financial services industry. (*Financial services, 1998 CQ Weekly, pp. 2733, 2659*)

Gramm issued a statement on Nov. 4 attempting to assuage their fears. He called HR 10 "an obvious priority" for the committee next year.

The New Line-Up

What is striking about the new Senate is how similar it looks to the old Senate. Only three incumbents were defeated — Republicans Alfonse M. D'Amato, N.Y., and Lauch Faircloth, N.C., and Illinois Democrat Carol Moseley-Braun.

But the surprising success of a number of endangered Democrats, such as Barbara Boxer in California, means that the Senate will not undergo a major partisan or ideological transformation, as occurred in 1996 and 1994.

There will be subtle changes. With Moseley-Braun's defeat, the Senate has no African-American members.

Senate Minority Whip Wendell H. Ford, D-Ky., is retiring. His spot will be filled by Nevada Democrat Harry Reid, who still must survive an official recount for his razor-thin victory over GOP Rep. John Ensign to be official. Overall, there will be eight newcomers — four Republicans and four Democrats. Among the freshmen are Jim Bunning, R-Ky, a McConnell ally and Hall of Fame baseball pitcher, and Evan Bayh, Ind., a rising Democratic star. The election of Democrat Blanche Lincoln of Arkansas, a former House member, keeps the number of women in the chamber at nine.

Lobbyists on other issues say that, as

far as their priorities were concerned, the elections changed little.

Neither side appeared to pick up any ground in the battle over banning the procedure some critics refer to as "partial birth" abortions.

Wisconsin Democrat Russell D. Feingold's victory over Rep. Mark W. Neumann encouraged campaign finance advocates, because Feingold — who cosponsored, with McCain, the leading campaign finance bill (S 25) — had limited his own political spending. But it did not appear as if the McCain-Feingold bill picked up any supporters as a result of the elections. ◆

Gubernatorial victors, including two Bushes, will help position party for redistricting

For GOP, a Few Points of Light

Republicans, looking for a silver lining in the Nov. 3 elections, may find one at the state level, where they managed to hold on to the lion's share of the nation's governorships.

Republican governors will not only have a big say in redesigning the congressional map after the 2000 census, but they will be in position to help deliver key states to the next GOP presidential candidate.

But the GOP lost the biggest prize — California — and suffered other defeats that kept the outlook at the state level less than completely rosy.

"Governors cannot completely dominate this process, but they can play a role," said Norman Ornstein of the American Enterprise Institute, a Washington, D.C., think tank.

State elections in 1998 held many surprises — none bigger than the success in Minnesota of Reform Party candidate Jesse "The Body" Ventura, a former professional wrestler.

Democrats consoled themselves with an unexpectedly lopsided victory in California, where they took the keys to the governor's mansion for the first time in 16 years.

Democrats may also be running in more favorable congressional districts throughout the South in the first decade of the next millennium, as their party's candidates unseated Republican governors in South Carolina and Alabama and retained an open seat in Georgia (the only state not to elect a Republican governor in this century).

Although it continues to favor Republicans, the South is clearly not a one-party region, favoring the GOP, as it had been for Democrats in the decades leading up to the civil rights era of the 1960s.

But Republicans also received good news in the region, winning their first gubernatorial election in Arkansas since 1980 and watching the Bush brothers, George W. and Jeb, coast to victories in Texas and Florida.

Sons of former President George

Former President George Bush and his wife, Barbara, congratulate their youngest son, Jeb, on his election as governor of Florida at a victory party Nov. 3 in Miami.

Bush, they will be the first brothers to simultaneously preside over two states since Nelson and Winthrop Rockefeller held sway over New York and Arkansas in the late 1960s. And with control of two of the biggest prizes in electoral votes, the Bush brothers will hold a decidedly prominent place on the political landscape.

Gov. George W. Bush, the presumed front-runner for the GOP presidential nomination in 2000, has helped his party grow in Texas by appealing to blacks and Hispanics.

"I showed Texans ... that one can adhere to the conservative philosophy and implement policies that are compassionate," Bush said Nov. 4.

The lessons of his re-election success were not lost on his brother Jeb, who narrowly lost the 1994 gubernatorial contest in Florida after saying he would probably do "not much" for African-Americans if elected.

This time around, Jeb Bush's message was far more inclusive, and both

brothers spoke about the importance of "compassionate conservatism" in their acceptance speeches.

Republicans, who have won control of a majority of statehouses during this decade, received further evidence that the political model of their party's gubernatorial wing may hold broader appeal than their more confrontational congressional squad.

Socially moderate Republican governors were re-elected, sometimes by large margins in the Northeast, traditionally a Democratic stronghold.

Tom Ridge of Pennsylvania, George E. Pataki of New York and John G. Rowland of Connecticut all vanquished their Democratic opponents by margins of at least 20 percent. Argeo Paul Cellucci of Massachusetts and Lincoln C. Almond of Rhode Island prevailed in races by lesser margins.

"It's clear that social moderation and fiscal conservatism is the successful model for Republicans," said University of California, San Diego political

Activists attend an election night rally against a Washington state ballot initiative banning affirmative action practices in government and college admissions. The measure passed.

state's presidential vote in 1992. Although he slipped to 12 percent there in 1996, the state also gave 7 percent of its Senate vote that year to Reform candidate Dean Barkley.

The Golden Prize

Lt. Gov. Gray Davis' strong, 20 point victory margin over GOP state Attorney General Dan Lungren in California gave Democrats the most important win of the entire election cycle.

California is expected to gain as many as five seats after the 2000 census because of burgeoning population growth. With Democrats also controlling the California legislature, the party has high hopes of drawing congressional lines to maximize its strength. (Democrats now hold 28 of California's 52 House seats.)

But Republicans also scored a crucial gain in Florida with Jeb Bush's easy win over Democratic Lt. Gov. Buddy MacKay. Bush's victory makes Florida the first Southern state since Reconstruction to give the GOP control of both the legislature and governorship.

Florida is poised to gain seats after the census, as is Texas, where George W. Bush's landslide win helped Republicans down the ballot. The election of Rick Perry as the first Republican lieutenant governor in state history means that Bush can explore a presidential run without worrying about his party losing control back home in Austin.

The race in Georgia between Democratic state Rep. Roy Barnes and millionaire Republican businessman Guy Millner had been considered a toss-up. But Millner, the GOP nominee for governor in 1994 and Senate in 1996, fell short once again.

Democrats control the legislature in Georgia, another state expected to gain House seats after 2000.

"There were a number of people that thought that was a prime area for a Republican gain, [but it] didn't really happen," said William Pound of the National Conference of State Legislatures. "The legislature will be a battleground in 2000."

Democrats also exceeded expectations in South Carolina and Alabama by running pro-gambling, pro-education campaigns.

Democratic Lt. Gov. Don Siegelman of Alabama unseated his boss, GOP Gov. Fob James Jr., by calling for a state lottery to fund education.

In South Carolina, former state De-

scientist Gary Jacobson. "That's the clearest message of this election."

Redistricting Impact

Jacobson, an expert on House elections, was skeptical about the effect gubernatorial outcomes would have on post-census redistricting, pointing out that the courts have not been shy in recent years about throwing out maps that are too blatantly partisan.

Nevertheless, governors will hold considerable sway over the process. And with the GOP majority in the House down to a six-seat margin, the new maps will significantly influence control of Congress after 2002.

Democrats are better positioned to shape the new district lines in their favor in some key states, but even taking into account the loss of California, eight of the 10 most populous states will be governed by Republicans.

Republicans held closely contested open seats in Ohio and Illinois, and GOP candidates will succeed retiring Democrats in Colorado, Nebraska and Nevada, in addition to Florida.

Aside from California, Republicans were also unable to hold on to the gubernatorial slots that opened in Minnesota and Iowa.

The result was a net loss of one governorship for the GOP, taking the party down to 31.

Democrats, who controlled 31 governorships when Bill Clinton took office as president in 1993, remain well

behind at 17.

Ventura and independent Gov. Angus King of Maine, who enjoyed a 40-percentage point re-election romp, will mind the store in the remaining two states.

Both of their states have nonpartisan leanings. King is the second independent governor to serve in Maine since the 1970s.

And Minnesota had previously demonstrated its responsiveness to the fiscally conservative, socially liberal Reform Party message.

Ross Perot took 24 percent of the

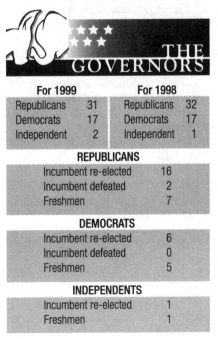

THE GOVERNORS

For 1999		For 1998	
Republicans	31	Republicans	32
Democrats	17	Democrats	17
Independent	2	Independent	1

REPUBLICANS

Incumbent re-elected	16
Incumbent defeated	2
Freshmen	7

DEMOCRATS

Incumbent re-elected	6
Incumbent defeated	0
Freshmen	5

INDEPENDENTS

Incumbent re-elected	1
Freshmen	1

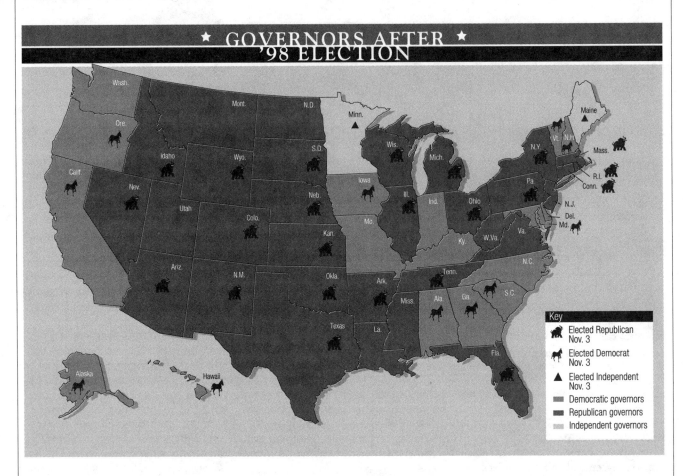

★ GOVERNORS AFTER ★
'98 ELECTION

Key
🐘 Elected Republican Nov. 3
🐴 Elected Democrat Nov. 3
▲ Elected Independent Nov. 3
▨ Democratic governors
▨ Republican governors
▨ Independent governors

mocratic Rep. Jim Hodges surprised Republican Gov. David Beasley in large degree because of heavy financial backing of his campaign from video poker interests.

But the stunning Minnesota victory of Ventura ruined Democratic hopes of picking up this Republican-held seat. Democrats ran third in both Minnesota and Maine.

Ventura was undaunted by his new and unexpected challenge.

"I've jumped out of an airplane 34 times," he said. "I've dove 212 feet under water. I've done a lot of things that defied death. And this isn't defying death. It's just common sense and hard work."

State Legislatures

Republicans, however, lost ground nationwide in state legislative elections, breaking the historical axiom that the president's party loses state legislative seats in midterm elections.

Democrats gained about 45 legislative seats nationwide and made a net gain of three legislative chambers, leaving them in control of 53 legislative chambers to the Republicans' 45, according to the state legislative group.

Oklahoma Gov. Frank Keating, who

will soon assume control of the Republican Governors' Association with current Chairman Beasley's defeat, conceded it was not good news for the GOP.

"I would say that we took some buckshot, but we're still in the air," said Keating, who won a second term by a solid 17 percentage point margin.

Republicans gained only a handful of state legislative seats in the South, which is something of a victory for Democrats. The GOP-leaning South remains competitive for the once-dominant Democratic Party.

"The erosion was stopped in this election," said Pound. "Whether that's temporary or permanent [remains] a good question."

Despite a surge for Democrats in state legislatures, Pound said, there is no overriding trend, with gains occurring in scattered states for parochial reasons. "There's no pattern to it," he said. "It's all over the country."

Redistricting is particularly crucial in states that are losing congressional seats, and many of those states are in the Northeast, where Democratic strength is centered.

One feature of the election that Republicans are sanguine about is the return of GOP incumbents in states that

are traditionally Democratic.

In Massachusetts, GOP Acting Gov. Cellucci, who assumed office after President Clinton unsuccessfully nominated Gov. William F. Weld as ambassador to Mexico in 1997, survived a strong challenge from Democratic state Attorney General Scott Harshbarger.

In Rhode Island, Republican Almond beat back a challenge from Myrth York, improving his margin in a rematch. Almond beat York by 4 percentage points in 1994, but brought his margin up to 9 this time.

And in New Mexico, Republican Gov. Gary E. Johnson held back a strong challenge from Martin Chavez, the mayor of Albuquerque.

But there were missed GOP opportunities as well. In Maryland and Hawaii, Republicans thought they had an unusual chance to unseat incumbents in traditionally Democratic territory. They fell short in both instances, so Parris N. Glendening of Maryland and Benjamin J. Cayetano of Hawaii will each serve four more years.

Republicans were most successful in states where they ran on centrist, kitchen-table themes — a tactic that might cause some strategic rethinking by national Republican leaders.

★ GOVERNORS AND ★
GOVERNORS-ELECT

Listed below are the governors and governors-elect and the year for the next gubernatorial race. The names of the governors elected or re-elected Nov. 3 are in bold. The Republicans captured four seats held by Democrats; the

Democrats returned the favor. But Republicans lost one seat to Minnesota's Reform Party. Two states, New Hampshire and Vermont, hold gubernatorial elections every two years.

Alabama – **Donald Siegelman, D** (2002)
Alaska – **Tony Knowles, D** (2002)
Arizona – **Jane Dee Hull, R** (2002)
Arkansas – **Mike Huckabee, R** (2002)
California – **Gray Davis, D** (2002)
Colorado – **Bill Owens, R** (2002)
Connecticut – **John G. Rowland, R** (2002)
Delaware – Thomas R. Carper, D (2000)
Florida – **Jeb Bush, R** (2002)
Georgia – **Roy Barnes, D** (2002)
Hawaii – **Benjamin J. Cayetano, D** (2002)
Idaho – **Dirk Kempthorne, R** (2002)
Illinois – **George Ryan, R** (2002)
Indiana – Frank L. O'Bannon, D (2000)
Iowa – **Tom Vilsack, D** (2002)
Kansas – **Bill Graves, R** (2002)
Kentucky – Paul E. Patton, D (1999)
Louisiana – Mike Foster, R (1999)
Maine – **Angus King, I** (2002)
Maryland – **Parris N. Glendening, D** (2002)
Massachusetts – **Argeo Paul Cellucci, R** (2002)
Michigan – **John Engler, R** (2002)
Minnesota – **Jesse Ventura, Reform** (2002)
Mississippi – Kirk Fordice, R (1999)
Missouri – Mel Carnahan, D (2000)

Montana – Marc Racicot, R (2000)
Nebraska – **Mike Johanns, R** (2002)
Nevada – **Kenny Guinn, R** (2002)
New Hampshire – **Jeanne Shaheen, D** (2000)
New Jersey – Christine Todd Whitman, R (2001)
New Mexico – **Gary E. Johnson, R** (2002)
New York – **George E. Pataki, R** (2002)
North Carolina – James B. Hunt Jr., D (2000)
North Dakota – Edward T. Schafer, R (2000)
Ohio – **Bob Taft, R** (2002)
Oklahoma – **Frank Keating, R** (2002)
Oregon – **John Kitzhaber, D** (2002)
Pennsylvania – **Tom Ridge, R** (2002)
Rhode Island – **Lincoln C. Almond, R** (2002)
South Carolina – **Jim Hodges, D** (2002)
South Dakota – **William J. Janklow, R** (2002)
Tennessee – **Don Sundquist, R** (2002)
Texas – **George W. Bush, R** (2002)
Utah – Michael O. Leavitt, R (2000)
Vermont – **Howard Dean, D** (2000)
Virginia – James S. Gilmore III, R (2001)
Washington – Gary Locke, D (2000)
West Virginia – Cecil H. Underwood, R (2000)
Wisconsin – **Tommy G. Thompson, R** (2002)
Wyoming – **Jim Geringer, R** (2002)

"We see the customers," said Pennsylvania Gov. Ridge, a GOP moderate who won re-election by 27 points. "And they're not as interested in the ideology or the partisanship of what we're doing. They want to see results."

Voter Initiatives

Along with electing lawmakers, voters in states across the country cast their ballots on a number of proposals that Congress failed to enact on the federal level.

In Arizona and Massachusetts, voters approved campaign finance overhaul initiatives that provide public funding for candidates and lower the limits on political contributions. Congress this year failed to pass a broad overhaul of the campaign finance system. (*Campaign finance, 1998 CQ Weekly, p. 2402*)

Another area where Congress debated but did not enact legislation this year was a possible tax increase on tobacco products. But on Election Day, California voters appeared to have approved an initiative backed by the unlikely coali-

tion of Hollywood celebrities Rob Reiner and Charlton Heston, president of the National Rifle Association, and former GOP Rep. Michael Huffington to raise the cigarette tax by 50 cents a pack in the state. The estimated $500 million to $700 million that would be raised per year would go to early childhood education and anti-smoking programs. (*Tobacco, 1998 CQ Weekly, p. 1669*)

The biggest winner among the more than 230 initiatives and referendums on state ballots this year was approval of marijuana for medical use.

In all, in five states where the issue was on the ballot — Alaska, Arizona, Nevada, Oregon and Washington — voters passed initiatives to allow doctors to prescribe marijuana for patients with serious or terminal illnesses.

M. Dane Waters, president of the Initiative and Referendum Institute, a nonpartisan Washington, D.C., group that tracks state issues, predicted the clean sweep would guarantee that more states will vote on medical marijuana initiatives in 1999 and 2000.

"The people spoke on Election

Day and made it clear they were hungry for true reform," said Waters. "The voters addressed the tough issues that elected officials have been unwilling to deal with, as well as voted down those reforms they weren't quite ready for."

Although the District of Columbia had the marijuana issue on the ballot, Congress slipped a provision into the omnibus spending law (PL 105–277) prohibiting the votes from being counted. In Colorado, a court challenge invalidated the initiative. (*Spending, 1998 CQ Weekly, p. 2885*)

Another measure approved by the voters was a Washington state initiative banning affirmative action programs in state and local governments. Meanwhile, in Alaska and Hawaii, voters overwhelmingly voted to ban homosexual marriages. The two amendments to the states' constitutions follow a law passed by Congress and signed by Clinton in 1996 (PL 104-199) that bars federal recognition of same-sex marriages. (*1996 Almanac, p. 5-26*) ◆

More and more campaigns find a solid Internet presence important

Home Page as Hustings: Candidates Work the Web

Political strategists can debate how the Monica Lewinsky investigati on will play out in the fall elections, but many already agree on one definite political impact: The scandal introduced thousands of potential voters to the world of cyberspace.

News of the affair between the former White House intern and President Clinton first broke on the Internet, and scandal-followers repeatedly returned to the World Wide Web for regular updates.

"Monica was probably the biggest" issue that prompted people to log on to the Web, said Andrew L. Sernovitz, president and CEO of the Association for Interactive Media, a Washington lobbying group for Internet companies.

There were plenty of Internet users before the name Lewinsky ever hit the press, but the controversy is a prime example of how more Americans are turning to the Internet for information.

And as the number of Web surfers continues to grow, more politicians are using it as an inexpensive campaign tool that can reach millions of voters with a simple stroke of a key.

The potential of political Web sites is nearly unlimited. They not only give voters in-depth information about the candidates and their positions, but they can draw voters and volunteers into campaigns.

"In 1996, we saw the first interest of major statewide campaigns in having a Web site, but it was mostly brochure-ware," said Jonah Seiger, co-founder of mindshare Internet Campaigns, a Washington-based media strategy group. "In 1998, we're starting to see candidates realize the true power of the Internet, seeing them integrate it into the whole campaign strategy."

Survey Findings

A survey by Congressional Quarterly, under the auspices of Campaigns & Elections magazine, shows the growing reliance of political campaigns on the Internet. The survey asked 270 campaigns for federal, state and local office across the country about their attitudes toward the Internet.

The majority of campaigns surveyed — 63 percent — have Web sites, while another 21 percent plan to have one running at some point in the future.

And 56 percent of the campaigns polled said they thought the Internet was "a very important" communications tool that "is already changing political campaigns."

Cyberspace Explosion

An April Commerce Department study showed the number of Internet users worldwide has exploded from 3 million in 1994 to 100 million in 1998 — most of them in the United States. An August survey by Nielsen Media Research showed a 35 percent increase in U.S. users since last year, to 70.5 million — about one-third of the adult population.

A poll conducted in November 1997 by Arlington, Va.-based The Luntz Research Cos. showed that Web users are more politically aware than their "unconnected" counterparts. While only 49 percent of "unconnected" Americans surveyed could name Newt Gingrich, R-Ga., as House Speaker, 79 percent of those who were

Quick Contents

Candidates for political office this year have discovered a new tool for getting their message out — the Internet. And a new survey found that 63 percent of 270 campaigns for federal, state and local office have Web sites to communicate with the voters. Experts say that number will grow in the next century.

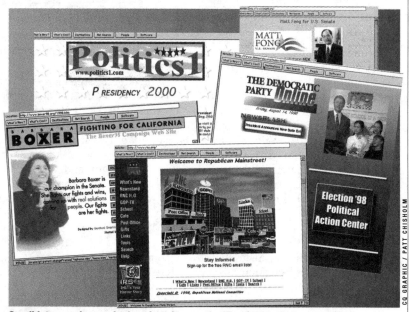

Candidates are increasingly using sites on the World Wide Web, some with splashy graphics, to enlist volunteers and win over "connected" voters.

CQ GRAPHIC / PATT CHISHOLM

"connected" knew who he was.

Although most Web users who visit a campaign site are likely to already be interested in the candidate, Internet experts agree that the sites are a prime way to solidify voter support.

"A Web site has the ability to close [the deal] for people. Television spots might get them interested, but the Web site will influence undecided voters, and that's who you want," said Sernovitz.

Candidates on the Net

The impact of the Internet on the political arena is becoming apparent. Several prominent statewide candidates have made the Internet a campaign tool this year as they head into the fall elections.

Democratic incumbent Barbara Boxer bought banner ads on the Web sites of three local newspapers during the California Senate primary elections in June. Banner ad space can be purchased on most Internet publications at about one-fifth of the cost of television ads.

When browsers of these cyberspace newspapers clicked onto Boxer's banner ads — which flashed her name, picture and slogan on the computer screen — they were automatically transported to Boxer's Internet campaign site. There, they could read about her policy positions, order campaign paraphernalia, or sign up as volunteers.

Rob Patton, technical director of Boxer's campaign, said Boxer was the only political candidate he knew of in California — and one of only a handful across the country — who bought banner ads for their campaigns. The Boxer camp is now discussing purchasing more cyberspace ads for the general campaign.

Boxer faces a tough race in November against GOP nominee Matt Fong. Fong has his own Internet campaign site with news articles about the race, biographical information, and a volunteer sign-up available.

Jeb Bush, the Republican candidate for Florida governor, has attracted national attention to his Web site with its daily news updates about the race and on-line sales of "Jeb ware" — hats, T-shirts and buttons.

The site features "Photos From The Road." Bush campaign aides carry digital cameras at every campaign stop, then put the photo disks into a laptop and post pictures on the Web site.

In November, Bush will face Democratic Lt. Gov. Buddy MacKay, who also has a Web site featuring press releas-

No Tolerance for 'Spam'

Even the name sounds distasteful. "Spamming," the cyberspace term for sending out mass junk e-mail, is considered the biggest mistake a political campaign can make when using the Internet. For all the help the Web can do campaigns, spamming is political suicide.

"Candidates who use spam will do so at their own peril," said Jonah Seiger, co-founder of the Washington, D.C.-based mindshare Internet Campaigns, a media strategy group. "It's free speech, but it's bad strategy."

The negative impact of spamming was demonstrated in July during the governor's race in Georgia. Just days before the primary election, Democratic candidate Steve Langford apologized to voters after his campaign sent out 500 unsolicited e-mails.

"While we believe strongly in the freedom of speech, we also believe that it is inappropriate to send unwanted information to people who must pay for the capacity to receive it," Langford's campaign manager Lee Raudonis said in a statement.

Raudonis said he was "horrified" at some of the angry messages his office received in response to the e-mail.

The situation was complicated even further when the campaign — on the advice of the WorldTouch Network company, which helped facilitate the mailing — fabricated a return address, so the campaign's e-mail box would not be inundated with messages bouncing back to their origin. As a result, Web users had no way of responding directly to the e-mail.

Despite the apology, Langford's Internet service provider threatened to terminate his service for forging a return address, calling it a "flagrant violation" of anti-spam policy.

"I recognize that what we did was inappropriate, and I am very sorry for any problems this may have caused," Raudonis said, adding that if Langford were elected governor, he would consider legislation to prevent such problems in the future.

In the July 21 primary, Langford came in fourth in the six-way race.

Other Problems

Rep. Jane Harman, who ran unsuccessfully for the Democratic nomination for California governor in June, narrowly escaped a similar controversy.

Harman had contracted with a media consulting group to have her name included in a Democratic slate e-mail to be sent, unsolicited, to 1 million California voters.

But even before the mailing was sent out, the complaints started to roll in.

"When we announced we were going to do that, we got a lot of flak from anti-spam groups who engaged us in a heated discussion," said Robert Barnes, president of Informed Voter Network, a California media consulting group that works with Democratic candidates.

After hearing the flood of complaints, Barnes' company scaled back its plans. The company instead launched an "opt-in" Internet ad campaign that flashed a political announcement onto computer screens when Web users signed on to their Internet accounts. If the users wanted more information, they could click one button; if they didn't, they clicked another.

"Our goal is to help elect our clients, not harm them," Barnes said.

Spamming has become so controversial that the Senate in May passed legislation (S 1618) aimed at curbing its use, and a House subcommittee this month passed a similar bill (HR 3888). (*1998 CQ Weekly*, pp. 1314, 2189)

And Internet experts warn that political candidates who send spam risk alienating voters. "Spam has become associated with unscrupulous marketing. It's not good for your image," Seiger said.

Seiger added that most people list spammers at the top of their annoyance list — above direct mailers and telemarketers.

"They're at the intolerable level," he said.

es and campaign schedules.

"One of the advantages of the Internet is it's more interactive. It's a complement to radio and TV. There's not a lot you can fit into a 30-second radio spot," said Mike Connell, president of New Media Communications, which developed Bush's campaign Web site.

Connell also designed the Web sites of the Iowa Republican Party, the Ohio Republican Party and the GOP gubernatorial candidate in Ohio, Bob Taft. Visitors to Taft's site can see videos of his television ads, hear weekly taped messages from him, request free bumper stickers and sign up to volunteer.

In Georgia, Democratic gubernatorial candidate Roy Barnes has a unique feature on his Web site. A "campaign cam" is mounted to a wall of Barnes' campaign office, transmitting live video pictures of campaign aides working during the day.

"It's been fantastic," said Harlan Barnes, the candidate's 25-year-old son and the campaign's technical director. "For our supporters, it makes them feel like they're connected."

National Impact

The Republican and Democratic parties are well aware of the growing political importance of the Internet. Both the Republican National Committee and the Democratic National Committee are planning to upgrade their Internet sites in the weeks leading up to the November elections.

"We want to encourage people to be active in politics, to encourage greater registration. It will be more user friendly, easier to search and a lot more fun to use," said RNC spokesman Mike Collins.

Among the new features on the RNC site will be a national map that Web users can click on to register to vote in their home states. The site has direct links to state boards of elections.

In August, the DNC added a feature to its site that allows voters to link to the Web sites of Democratic candidates and state parties across the country. As with the RNC site, Democratic viewers can register to vote.

Both parties say they also encourage their candidates to set up their own campaign Web sites.

Linda Sinoway, the DNC's interactive media director, estimated that about half of all Democratic candidates for federal and statewide office have their own sites.

Collins said that 32 of the country's state Republican parties have Web sites and that more than 75 percent of GOP candidates running for federal office have created them, too. "Outside of talk radio, there has never been a device that can empower ordinary citizens like the Internet," he said. "It will be the medium of the next decade."

Bridging the Generation Gap

Meanwhile, the Internet is being used to bridge the generation gap, as well.

This summer, the American Association of Retired Persons, which represents 33 million Americans, joined with MCI Telecommunications and Rock the Vote — a group that promotes voting among younger Americans — in launching a new site for voter registration.

The site — NetVote '98 — is broken down into a series of simple buttons that guide the user through an on-line version of a typical voter registration. Two weeks later, the completed application card arrives at the user's home with pre-paid return postage. The user just signs the card and mails it back to his local board of elections.

Although the majority of the country's senior citizens are already registered to vote — 77 percent, according to AARP — the group said it hopes the Web site will bring in a new generation of voters.

"Our members are the parents and grandparents of people who don't vote. We're working to pass it down to the next generation," said Denise Orloff, a spokeswoman for AARP. "Our members vote, but that's not enough."

Polls show that Internet users are generally younger than the overall population, and as the Internet becomes a mainstay in schools across the country, those students will grow into voting-age Web users.

"When those kids get out of high school — if you ignore that segment, you are ignoring a huge block of voters," said Lee Magness, president of Politicalnet.com, a Houston firm that designs political Web sites. "The Internet will play the most critical role in campaigns, if not this election, at least in 2000."

Chris Casey, author of the book "The Hill on the Net: Congress Enters the Information Age," said the Internet can encourage volunteers and other grass-roots supporters, who in turn generate more votes.

"The Internet is non-intrusive.

While the television viewer has to sit through your commercial because they want to watch the rest of Melrose Place, the Web user has to search out your Web site," Casey said.

Campaign Web sites have another advantage: Candidates can monitor voter interests simply by watching how they peruse the Internet. Most sites have the ability to track what sections browsers are visiting the most. If, for example, a campaign site has several different pages describing positions on health care, crime and taxes, the candidate can track which issue is drawing the most visits. Then, the candidate can gear the campaign toward the most popular issue.

"It is like an unknown poll," said Jeff Gallino, managing partner of Boundary Light, a consulting firm that created the Web site of Democratic Senate candidate Dottie Lamm in Colorado.

Lamm's site allows visitors to sign up as volunteers and make donations online. It also offers regular updates on the race. Lamm is challenging Republican Sen. Ben Nighthorse Campbell, who has a site that displays biographical information and press releases.

And Web sites have the advantage of being available 24 hours a day, unlike print or broadcast ads. "It's not like television, where you send an ad out into the ether and hope people aren't in the bathroom when it airs," said mindshare's Seiger.

Special-Interest Groups

Candidates are not the only ones enamored with the potential of the Internet. Special-interest groups are making use of it to promote political candidates. Among them are the League of Conservation Voters, which works on environmental issues, and the Campaign for Working Families, a conservative political action committee headed by Gary Bauer, which list candidates they support on their Web pages. Others, such as the conservative think tank Free Congress Foundation, provide viewers links to state Republican parties, which in turn have links to all the GOP candidates in that state.

Still in its infancy, the Internet is not yet faced with federal regulations that require such policies as equal free time for candidates on television and radio. For now, the only guidelines being applied to the Internet are those that already exist for print or broadcast campaigning.

Political Web Sites

Here is a selection of political Web sites:

www.politicsonline.com A comprehensive site that offers up-to-date articles about how the Internet is affecting this year's elections, and gives wannabe politicians tips on how to use the Internet as a campaign tool. The site includes links and information on almost every political issue that can come up in a political race to help candidates "rebut an opponent's attacks" on the campaign trail. The site is run by Phil Noble & Associates, a consulting firm headquartered in Charleston, S.C.

www.vote-smart.org Project Vote Smart, a nonprofit, nonpartisan organization, aims to help voters make "informed decisions." The group has collected extensive biographical and political infomation on more than 13,000 federal and state candidates and lawmakers. Browsers can click on the names of candidates and lawmakers and find their responses to the group's survey on a variety of policy issues. Browsers can also find information on state ballot initiatives, and historical data on past elections.

www.campaignwebreview.com A twice-monthly on-line publication written by three experts in the field of politics and communications. The nonpartisan publication profiles ballot initiatives and candidate races where the Internet is being used as a campaign tool. It is aimed at educating the public about the growing use of the Internet in politics.

www.penncen.com/psotd The "Political Site of the Day" — maintained by the Web site development company Kessler Freedman Inc. — offers a new link every day to an unusual political Web site. Browsers can link to, among other places, the Michael Jordan for President home page, the 70th Anniversary of the Sacco and Vanzetti Execution site, and the Boycott Nike home page.

www.mindshare.net The home page of the mindshare Internet Campaigns media strategy group advertises the company's services, but browsers can also link to a variety of news stories about the use of the Internet in political campaigns. The site contains numerous surveys and reports about Internet use and trends.

www.womenvote.org A nonpartisan site run by the Women's Leaders Online Fund, a group aimed at educating female voters. It provides personalized voting guides that allow users to compare their stances with the positions of House and Senate members. Browsers can select from more than 20 policy categories, click on what issues are most important to them and then check to see how their lawmakers voted.

www.wired.com An on-line publication that offers daily news stories of particular interest to Internet users. The publication contains a special section with news stories on politics in cyberspace.

www.politics1.com An independent, nonpartisan site that allows browsers to search states for all candidates running for federal and statewide office. The site contains links to many candidates with Web sites, as well as almost every state political party. It also includes a cyberspace store for political memorabilia.

Here are addresses for Web sites mentioned in this story:
www.rnc.org Republican National Committee
www.democrats.org Democratic National Committee
www.boxer98.org Sen. Barbara Boxer, D-Calif.
www.fong98.org California Republican Matt Fong for Senate
www.jeb.org Florida Republican Jeb Bush for Governor
www.mackay98.org Democratic Lt. Gov. Buddy MacKay of Florida
www.barnesgovernor.org Georgia Democrat Roy Barnes for Governor
www.guymillner98.org Georgia Republican Guy Millner for Governor
www.dottielamm98.com Colorado Democrat Dottie Lamm for Senate
www.nighthorse98.com Sen. Ben Nighthorse Campbell, R-Colo.
www.netvote98.mci.com On-line voter registration site sponsored by MCI, American Association of Retired Persons and Rock the Vote.

"We don't have any real regulations concerning the Internet," said Ron Harris, spokesman for the Federal Election Commission. "One day, I'm sure we'll have to. Right now it's mainly on a case-by-case basis."

For all the help the Internet can offer a political candidate, experts warn that it can be a double-edged sword.

Because Internet users are generally more politically sophisticated than non-users, they often have high expectations. If the candidate's Web site does not meet those expectations, voters can be turned off. "There's all those people wanting to give you a chance. When you disappoint them, you lose that vote," said Sernovitz.

As more and more politicians begin to experiment with Web sites, Sernovitz advises them to take it seriously. "A campaign would never consider letting a 17-year-old do the printing for a campaign brochure. But I guarantee you'll see campaigns letting young volunteers do their Web sites," he said.

And while most Internet experts predict that no candidate will win an election this fall solely because of his use of the Internet, many say the right use of the system can make a difference in close elections.

Graeme Browning, author of "Electronic Democracy: Using the Internet to Influence American Politics," said the Internet may not push a candidate to victory this year, but it definitely could in the future.

"Possibly in the year 2000, or maybe more in 2004, we will see someone win an election because of a Web site," Browning said. "I think the Internet will replace TV, or at least it will be 50-50 in importance to political campaigns." ◆

Polls signal a loss of recent years' momentum, and the Clinton scandal may be to blame

For Women Candidates, An Uncertain Season

What a difference six years makes. In 1992, the high-profile sex scandals surrounding the Navy's Tailhook convention and Supreme Court nominee Clarence Thomas energized women activists across the country, helping to elect a record number of female lawmakers to Congress. The number of women in the House nearly doubled to 48, and the number of female senators tripled (albeit to six), prompting pundits to dub 1992 "The Year of the Woman."

But today's sex scandal enveloping President Clinton and former White House intern Monica Lewinsky could have a different impact on women running for Congress.

Three women who celebrated their election to the Senate in 1992 — Barbara Boxer of California, Carol Moseley-Braun of Illinois and Patty Murray of Washington — are now among the year's most vulnerable Democrats. [In spite of their vulnerability, Boxer and Murray were reelected in 1998. Moseley-Braun, however, was defeated. — Ed.] To be sure, all were considered top Republican targets before the president's peccadillos took over the headlines, but the scandal has been used against them, and their polling numbers have begun to decline recently. Women could lose one or more of their Senate seats. (1998 CQ Weekly, pp. 1858, 2640)

The numbers are a little more favorable for women in the House. Only four of the House's 54 women are leaving Congress this year, and five others are favored to win open-seat races — for a net gain of at least one. Several other women candidates are running strong campaigns against incumbents or for open seats. But the numbers signal a loss of momentum since 1992, when 24 new women were swept into the House, or even 1994 and 1996, in each of which 11 new women arrived. During the same time, four women were elected to the Senate and one left, bringing the current total to nine.

Leaders of women's political groups fear the never-ending stream of lurid details about Clinton's affair with Lewinsky will disgust Democratic voters — particularly women — and discourage them from going to the polls in November.

The 1992 landslide gains for women — from 28 to 48 in the House and from two to six in the Senate — were attributed to several factors. The 1992 House bank scandal, which revealed that hundreds of lawmakers had routinely overdrawn their House bank accounts, weakened many members and prompted a dozen to quit, leaving women with good chances of defeating long-term incumbents or winning seats left open by retirements. Redistricting after the 1990 census also opened up new seats. Of the 24 new women elected to the House in 1992, 22 were open-seat victors. (Bank scandal, 1992 Almanac, p. 23; redistricting, p. 25-A)

But it was the nationally televised image of Anita F. Hill being grilled by an all-male Senate Judiciary Committee about her sexual harassment charges against Supreme Court nominee Thomas, as well as charges of sexual abuse of women at the Navy's 1991 Tailhook convention, that brought women's issues to the front of the political debate. Female candidates took advantage of the sexual political divide and ran as outsiders pushing for change. (Thomas confirmation, 1991 Almanac, p. 274; Tailhook, 1992 Almanac, p. 519)

"Anita Hill was beyond a sex scandal," said Debbie Walsh, director of the program for women public officials at Rutgers University's Center for the American Woman and Politics. "Here was this woman coming forward before this all-male institution with not a single woman to hear her story. That's what set people off. It was not just sexual harassment. This year, there isn't that dynamic."

Instead, this year's stories of improper sexual behavior are prompting women to tune out the political debate. Women who in 1992 thought their activism would make a difference in how elected leaders treated women now say they feel discouraged.

Women in Congress

	Nominees	Winners
1986	64 House	23 (12 D, 11 R)
	6 Senate	1 (1 D)
1988	59 House	25 (14 D, 11 R)
	2 Senate	0
1990	69 House	28 (19 D, 9 R)
	8 Senate	1 (1 R)
1992	106 House	47 (35 D, 12 R)
	11 Senate	5 (5 D)
1994	112 House	47 (30 D, 17 R)
	9 Senate	3 (1D, 2R)
1996	120 House	51 (35 D, 16 R)
	9 Senate	2 (1D, 1R)
1998	121 House	58 (41D, 17R)
	10 Senate	8 (5D, 1R)

SOURCE: Center for the American Woman and Politics at Rutgers University

Three Endangered Senators

In 1992, a group of Democratic women broke previous electoral records and made the mostly white, male Senate more diverse than it had ever been.

The women seized upon the nationwide fascination with such issues as the sexual harassment charges against Supreme Court nominee Clarence Thomas, ran as outsiders and promised to shake up the male-dominated government.

But today, three of those women — Sens. Barbara Boxer of California, Carol Moseley-Braun of Illinois and Patty Murray of Washington — are struggling for their political lives.

The vulnerability of Boxer and Moseley-Braun could result in a drop in the number of women in the Senate, from its current high of nine. Murray is also vulnerable, but her opponent is a woman.

Republicans had placed the three women at the top of their target list long before news broke of President Clinton's affair with former White House intern Monica Lewinsky.

Moseley-Braun has been embroiled in controversies surrounding her personal life and campaign fundraising. Boxer has been a GOP target since winning in 1992 with just 48 percent of the vote, and Murray has similarly been vulnerable since winning with 54 percent.

But the Clinton scandal is now being used against the women by their GOP challengers and could be the fatal blow to their re-election bids this fall.

Tables Turned

In October 1991, then-Rep. Boxer was one of seven women House members to march over to the Senate to urge a delay in the vote on Thomas' nomination until the sexual harassment charges could be exam-

ined. *(Thomas confirmation, 1991 Almanac, p. 274)*

After her election in 1992, Boxer again attacked the sexual misconduct of a high-profile man — former Sen. Bob Packwood, R-Ore. (1969-

Moseley-Braun, who faces a tough re-election bid, rallies Aug. 20 with other state Democrats at the Illinois State Fair in Springfield.

95) — and called for his resignation. *(Packwood, 1995 Almanac, p. 1-47)*

But Boxer's outspoken criticism of those men is now coming back to haunt her. Her GOP challenger, state Treasurer Matt Fong, has invoked the Thomas and Packwood cases in his race to defeat Boxer in November. Fong has accused her of remaining conspicuously quiet on the Clinton affair.

"When it comes time [to criticize] Democrats, you have a different standard than for Republicans," Fong charged in an August debate. "Barbara, your silence on this issue is deafening."

On the Senate floor this summer, Boxer criticized Clinton's personal behavior, but she has continued to praise his policies, giving him credit for the booming economy. She also has said she would welcome the president to a fundraiser with her this fall. Her situation is even more awkward because her daughter is married to first lady Hillary Rodham Clinton's brother, Tony Rodham.

A recent poll by the Los Angeles Times showed Boxer trailing Fong by 5 percentage points among likely

voters. The poll has a margin of error of 4 percentage points.

The poll also showed that 30 percent of those surveyed were less likely to vote for Boxer because of her response to Clinton's admitted sexual misconduct.

Polling Deficit

In Illinois, the state Republican Party has called on Moseley-Braun to cancel an October fundraiser with Clinton. The state GOP chair has blasted Moseley-Braun for "trad[ing] campaign dollars for justifiable moral indignation."

But Moseley-Braun, desperate for campaign cash in her race against millionaire state Sen. Peter Fitzgerald, says she has no plans to cancel. Like Boxer, Moseley-Braun has criticized Clinton's personal behavior but has stood with him on his policy agenda.

Fitzgerald's campaign has attacked Moseley-Braun's muted criticism of Clinton, saying she "can't have it both ways."

A recent poll by the Chicago Sun-Times put Moseley-Braun 15 points behind Fitzgerald — her largest polling deficit so far this year.

In Washington state, Murray is also being hurt by the scandal in her re-election bid against Republican Rep. Linda Smith.

During Murray's first run for the Senate in 1992, she made the most of the heightened interest in women's issues and ran on the slogan that she was a "Mom in tennis shoes."

Today, Smith is using that slogan against the incumbent, charging that Murray has stayed mum on the Clinton scandal and "turned her tennis shoes in for a pair of Hush Puppies."

Murray said she was "upset and angry" at Clinton's personal conduct. But she has tried to stay clear of the fray, instead focusing on issues such as health care and education.

Democratic Sens. Murray, Moseley-Braun, Boxer, Dianne Feinstein and Barbara A. Mikulski wave to crowd at 1996 convention.

Walsh said many women are torn because Clinton had been perceived as a "pro-woman" politician. Women who may have supported him on issues such as abortion, health care and education are now disgusted with his personal behavior. Candidates find themselves in the position of trying to decide how far to distance themselves from him.

"Some of these women Democrats will be in an awkward position," said Florida GOP Rep. Tillie Fowler, who was elected in 1992. "On the one hand, they want the Democratic Party support, but if they want to get that values edge, they need to be out there, rightfully, deploring the president. It's a Catch-22."

Said Walsh: "Clarence Thomas was not seen as a friend to certain kinds of women's issues as Bill Clinton is. This is much more complicated."

Patricia Ireland, president of the National Organization for Women (NOW), said some women may be "disillusioned" with Clinton, for whom they had voted in the hope that he would be a strong spokesman for women's rights. "They're somewhat turned off by the feeling there's no hope of making progress or changing the issues," Ireland said. Women, she said, do not like Clinton, nor do they like Independent Counsel Kenneth W. Starr. "They're saying a pox on both their houses." (*1998 CQ Weekly, p. 2647*)

Regardless of how Clinton's prob-

lems play out in November, women have already set a record this year for the most female nominees ever running for the House.

With the primary season now complete, a record 121 women have been nominated for House seats, including 76 Democrats and 46 Republicans.

The previous record was set in 1996, when 120 women were nominated.

Women also came close to tying the record for the number of Senate nominees. Ten women — seven Democrats and three Republicans — have been nominated this year. The record for female Senate nominees is 11, set in 1992. Walsh said more and more women are expected to run for office with each passing election.

Also this year, Washington state's race between Murray and Rep. Linda Smith is only the third woman vs. woman Senate race in history. (In 1960, Sen. Margaret Chase Smith, R-Maine, (1949-73) defeated Democratic challenger Lucia Cormier, and in 1986, Sen. Barbara Mikulski, D-Md., defeated GOP challenger Linda Chavez.)

Voter Turnout

Unlike Clarence Thomas and Tailhook, the Clinton scandal appears to be suppressing the female vote.

"In 1992, seeing the image of Anita Hill, millions of women voted who never voted before," said Rep. Jane

Harman, D-Calif., who was first elected in 1992. "There were clearly positive feelings toward Hill and against an all-male Senate Judiciary Committee, so the goal was clear: to change the face of Congress. In 1998, the feelings toward this president are so ambivalent. So many deplore his conduct, including me, but they applaud the positions he has taken on issues. Now the situation is more ambiguous."

Polls have shown that Democrats are much less likely to vote this fall compared with Republicans or even independents. A bipartisan poll released Sept. 8 by Republican pollster Ed Goeas and Democratic pollster Celinda Lake showed that 70 percent of Republicans are "extremely likely" to vote in November, compared with 63 percent of independents and 61 percent of Democrats. In a year when pundits predict record-low turnouts, even a small deficit in Democratic votes could spell trouble for the party.

This hurts women because both women voters and women congressional candidates tend to be Democrats.

A poll conducted in June by the women's political fundraising group EMILY's List showed that women overall are less likely than men to go to the polls this fall. The poll showed that 80 percent of men who voted in 1996 say they will vote again this year, compared with 75 percent of women — and that was before Clinton admitted Aug. 17 to an improper relationship with Lewinsky.

"The whole scandal-laden atmosphere has turned off women voters," said Stephanie Cohen, communications director for EMILY's List, which has called for Clinton to be censured rather than impeached. "There's so much noise out there, but there's no great debate in Congress on issues. Women are thinking, 'These elections have nothing to do with me; they have no impact on my life.' "

In particular, EMILY's List has found that women least likely to vote this November are those who are older, black, or Hispanic and those who work outside the home. The group has kicked off a $3 million get-out-the-vote campaign aimed at women less likely to vote. Workers will contact voters by mail and phone to encourage them to vote for female candidates who support abortion rights and other issues important to the organization.

Turning the Tables

Leaders from other liberal women's groups, including NOW, held a news conference Sept. 24 to speak out against impeaching Clinton, and to call on women across the country to vote in November. They said it was not too late to use the scandal to energize women.

"If we don't want to see Newt Gingrich ride into the White House on Ken Starr's coattails, then we'd better support the candidates who will make sure that Congress gets back to business," Ireland said. "If we want to see continued progress on the issues that count, then we must vote for the candidates who will champion our cause."

Joining Ireland were leaders of the Feminist Majority Foundation, the National Council of Negro Women and the Women's Institute for Freedom of the Press. Ireland and others said they would work to encourage women to vote. Eleanor Smeal, president of the Feminist Majority, said it was women's groups in 1992 that turned the Thomas and Tailhook scandals into issues that energized women voters, and that those groups can do it again.

Ireland agreed. "I hope it will help women running for Congress," she said. "I believe we can turn it in that direction, but that only happens if we have a

strong movement." Smeal and Ireland said they will try to spread the message that unless women vote this year, the gains they made in 1992 could be lost.

Values

Many women politicians think the scandal may have a silver lining.

Polls have shown that the talk about infidelity and kinky sex have pushed the issue of character and values to the top of voters' priority lists.

In the bipartisan Goeas-Lake poll, "declining moral values" topped the list as the nation's most important problem according to voters — tied

Ireland said women's groups would work to encourage women to vote despite disappointment in Clinton.

with crime and drugs.

And female politicians agree that women are generally perceived — accurately or not — as being more honest and trustworthy than men. "Women are trusted to run their lives better," said Rep. Elizabeth Furse, D-Ore., first elected to the House in 1992. "People don't see women as having affairs. True or not, they see women as more trustworthy. There could be a move this year to elect more women."

Republican Fowler agreed.

"Women could get a boost. On the values part of it, women probably have a slight edge," Fowler said. "Women are looked to as being above all this, more honest, less likely to engage in this kind of conduct." But Democratic women will have to distance themselves from

Clinton to win on the values issue, she said, and that could be difficult.

Good Chances in House

The number of women in the Senate could drop slightly next year because of the vulnerability of Boxer and Moseley-Braun, but the number of women in the House will probably increase slightly. Only four female lawmakers are leaving the House: Barbara B. Kennelly, D-Conn., is running for governor; Smith, R-Wash., is running for the Senate against Murray; Furse of Oregon is retiring, and Harman of California lost her bid for the gubernatorial nomination.

But those female losses are likely to be more than made up for by five new women who are all but certain to win election to open seats:

● In California's District 34, Democratic state assemblywoman Grace Napolitano is expected to easily win the race to succeed retiring Democratic Rep. Esteban E. Torres.

● Two open seats in Illinois are likely to be filled by women. Democratic state Rep. Jan Schakowsky is expected to replace retiring Democratic Rep. Sidney R. Yates in the overwhelmingly Democratic 9th District, and two women are going head-to-head for the 13th District seat of retiring Republican Rep. Harris W. Fawell. Republican State Rep. Judy Biggert is favored over Democratic consultant Susan Hynes.

● Two women are also vying to replace retiring 2nd District Rep. Scott L. Klug, R-Wis. They are state Rep. Tammy Baldwin, a Democrat, and former state Insurance Commissioner Josephine Musser, a Republican.

● In Ohio, county prosecutor Stephanie Tubbs Jones, a Democrat, is expected to replace retiring Democratic Rep. Louis Stokes in the 11th District.

Several other women have good chances of being elected. Many are trying to sort out what impact the Clinton scandal will have on them.

"Women in my district have expressed concerns as mothers, daughters and grandmothers about the whole issue of truthfulness and integrity," said Jean Leising, a Republican candidate who is facing Democrat Baron Hill for the open 9th District seat of retiring Rep. Lee H. Hamilton, D-Ind. "I believe that will motivate them to vote. That's a push for me." ◆

As turnout ebbs, get-out-the-vote efforts are increasingly in the hands of special interests

The Disengaging Voter

Barely more than one-third of eligible citizens are expected to visit their local polling places this Nov. 3, an impoverished turnout rate that can be taken as a sign that huge segments of the electorate feel little connection to the goings-on in Washington.

"We're going to have a situation in 1998 . . . where we'll probably have a lower turnout rate than any time since 1794," said University of Texas political scientist Walter Dean Burnham. "That should tell you something."

Steadily diminishing turnout rates have contributed to the decline of centrism in national politics. With more and more of the populace abstaining, candidates have to tailor their messages to appeal to the more ideologically engaged citizens who do bother to go to the polls, from Christian conservatives to environmental "greens."

"The broadest effect of turnout decline is that it makes our politics a politics only of the interested and the zealous," said Curtis Gans, director of the Committee for the Study of the American Electorate (CSAE).

As the parties partially sacrifice their historic role as grass-roots voter mobilizers in favor of fundraising and candidate consulting, the vacuum they are leaving is being filled to some extent by special interest groups such as labor unions and conservative Christian political organizations.

The AFL-CIO is planning to spend more than three times as much money during the 1998 cycle on "get-out-the-vote" efforts as on issue advertising. (*1998 CQ Weekly, p. 2866*)

And the Christian Coalition is planning to spend $1 million on turnout efforts such as phone calls and direct mail, plus an additional $1 million on 45 million voter guides to be distributed in churches Nov. 1.

"What you get is private organizations like the Christian Coalition or the labor unions actually performing the functions of a political party," said Paul Kleppner, a political scientist at

Northern Illinois University and author of a book on the history of U.S. voter turnout.

"It is the misfortune of the Democrats that unions are declining in numbers and therefore significance, and the Christian Coalition is increasing in numbers and significance," he said.

Republicans are taking a calculated risk this November, counting on their base of conservative supporters to come out and cast a vote against Democrats to vent their anger about President Clinton's affair with former White House intern Monica Lewinsky.

Although Democrats have been cheered by recent polls suggesting that the broad populace is more supportive of Clinton than of congressional Republicans who are pressing forward with impeachment proceedings, they are disheartened that their numbers are not as strong among the smaller universe of people who are actually likely to vote.

"The whole story is going to be turnout," predicted National Republican Congressional Committee (NRCC) Chairman John Linder of Georgia.

Democratic pollster Celinda Lake has identified "waitress moms" — working women under the age of 55 with children at home and no college degree — as a potentially decisive demographic group in this year's elections.

"It gave me a nice safe feeling to know that the fate of America is in the sensible hands of gals who smoke and call customers 'Hon,' " Maureen Dowd of The New York Times quipped in her Oct. 18 column.

EMILY's List, a political action committee (PAC) aimed at electing women candidates, is spending $3 million this fall to get women to vote. (*1998 CQ Weekly, p. 2639*)

During the latter half of the 19th century, turnout rates in counties in Northern states such as Ohio and Indiana regularly topped 90 percent, although less than half the adult population was then eligible.

Politics in the age before television,

the Internet and other modern distractions was much more of a participatory sport, with ward heelers and precinct captains paying regular visits to homes and workplaces. The old party machines converted votes into power — including the ability to provide patronage jobs and other favors.

"If you have local situations where you have robust party organizations, you will have higher turnout than where you don't," Burnham said. "[But] such organizations are rapidly becoming museum pieces and aren't likely to work as well in suburban and exurban areas."

Political rhetoric following the Civil War was often inflammatory as parties vied for the tiny percentage of potential swing voters who were not already strongly allied with one party or the other.

Parties in Decline

Modern politicians have the opposite problem. Instead of fighting over a few voters not already spoken for, today there are a multitude of abstainers who simply cannot be reached, meaning candidates have to be sure to energize their dwindling cores of support.

"There's this sort of disconnection between your average citizen and the political process," said Ruy A. Teixeira, a political analyst at the labor-backed Economic Policy Institute in Washington and author of the book, "The Disappearing American Voter."

"We know that people only vote if they feel a connection between the outcome and their individual vote."

Today, a plurality of voters do not identify themselves as members of either major party. And a majority of citizens did not bother to vote even during the presidential contest of 1996. Turnout among voting age citizens was 49 percent in 1996, the poorest showing in a presidential year since 1924.

"There is sort of a vicious circle involved," said Duke University political scientist John H. Aldrich.

"If you feel detached from the system, you don't vote, and nothing much changes, and it enhances that don't-bother-voting feeling."

Activists are no longer the old doorbell ringers sent down from Chicago City Hall. Instead, they are usually more concerned with promoting a particular issue — health care, for instance, or education — than the overall health of the party slate.

And candidates must fashion a message that rings ideological bells in order to appeal to the minority of citizens still politically engaged and voting.

Their main vehicle for doing so is television, where ads are nearly always intended to change how people will vote, rather than convincing them that they should turn out to vote. If negative TV ads turn off one of your opponent's potential supporters, that translates into one less vote against you, even if that vote is never cast.

Which leads to opportunities for mischief. Primary voting turnout is so low that numerous major-party congressional candidates were nominated this year by just 5 percent of the local voting age population.

"Since it's in all likelihood the ideologues who will comprise the 5 percent, you sort of wipe out the reasonable middle from politics," Kleppner said.

Primary Turnout

According to a CSAE analysis of 1998 primary voting, record low turnout levels were reached in Republican and Democratic primaries in 22 states and the District of Columbia.

If not for a big bump up in California, where turnout in the June primary increased by nearly a third over 1994 levels, overall primary voting would have dropped 20 percent from that year's level nationwide.

Turnout in California was boosted by a controversial ballot initiative, Proposition 226, which would have curtailed political spending by unions; it was defeated in the face of a $24 million campaign led by organized labor.

"Whatever base voting was being pushed on the Democratic side of the aisle really was around 226, as opposed to generic party turnout," said Gale Kaufman, who served as campaign consultant to the union effort.

Issue campaigns may or may not motivate more voters than candidate campaigns, but party organizations in states expecting to see landslide elections in their gubernatorial or Senate contests

Midterm Turnout Rates

Following are turnout rates as a percentage of the voting age population for midterm primaries and elections since 1962.

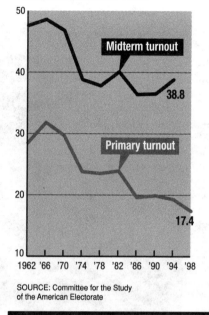

SOURCE: Committee for the Study of the American Electorate

are left with a tough motivational pitch to make.

In Texas, where Republican Gov. George W. Bush is expected to be reelected by a landslide, his state party is planning to spend up to $4 million trying to turn out the vote. But even Royal Masset, political director of the Texas GOP, worries that big-bucks expenditures may not be enough. (*1998 CQ Weekly*, p. 2876)

"The direct mail doesn't get them to turn out," he said. "I'm not sure the telephone does either."

Like many political scientists, Masset believes that people do not vote because of a deep disaffection with politics.

"There's no doubt that interest in government is dropping," Masset said. "People feel disconnected from parties, and think there's no difference between the parties, despite our rhetoric being different."

The two major parties, which often pursue campaign contributions from overlapping pools of donors, now share a hard line on issues such as crime and defense, and both speak in support of fiscal conservatism and business interests.

The differences between the parties are noticeable mostly on issues that

candidates are sometimes wary of bringing up, such as abortion, for fear that strong positions might drive away some voters. And so candidates in recent cycles, rather than loudly declaring their own firmly held beliefs, have taken to declaring their opponents are "extreme" or "out of step."

This is a tactic, for instance, that some Democrats are employing as a way of going back on the offensive in the wake of Clinton's sex scandal.

"Democrats are finding that attacking Republicans for conducting a partisan witch hunt against the president is a good way of energizing their supporters," said Douglas Muzzio, a pollster and professor of public affairs at Baruch College in New York.

Poor Voting Habits

There has been a disproportionate decline in voting rates among the poor and less educated — perhaps giving the lie to the notion that voter apathy is the result of contentment with a healthy economy in peacetime.

Those making less than $15,000 a year, adjusted for inflation, are voting 34 percent less in presidential elections and 48.5 percent less in midterm elections than they did in the mid-1960s, while voting participation has declined among those who did not progress beyond fourth grade by 47.7 percent in presidential elections and 59.8 percent in midterms.

According to Raymond E. Wolfinger, an elections expert at the University of California, Berkeley, the demographic groups most likely not to vote are "the young and the restless" — citizens under 35, and those who have not lived in the same residence for at least two years.

But turnout has declined among all groups except the elderly since 1960, which was the high-water mark for voter turnout since women's suffrage.

During the last 40 years, the country as a whole has grown older and less residentially mobile but more educated — enhancing the overall demographic profile that is supposed to mean greater voting participation.

Meanwhile, registration laws have been liberalized at both the federal level and in many states, yet electoral participation has dropped.

"There is no structural thing that can be done that will in any significant way mitigate the problem," Gans said. ◆

Behind scenes, image-conscious company builds an imposing lobbying presence

Disney in Washington: The Mouse That Roars

On a recent Tuesday afternoon when the Senate halls were humming, Walt Disney Co. chairman Michael D. Eisner dropped in for an unpublicized chat with Senate Majority Leader Trent Lott. What did Eisner want? Plenty, it turned out.

At the top of his list was a request for Congress to help his company's highest priority: HR 2589, a bill to extend the soon-to-expire copyright on Mickey Mouse. [Congress passed the bill, renamed S 505, on October 7.—Ed.]

Before he left the spacious offices of the majority leader at the U.S. Capitol on June 9, Eisner was assured that his company's pet bill would get the help it needed.

"He was very much interested in seeing the copyright bill," Lott said of their brief conversation. "It's being considered. I think we need to do it. I agree with him."

The unheralded conversation between the Senate majority leader and the corporate executive with close Democratic ties demonstrated the bipartisan reach and the behind-the-scenes lobbying tactics of the nation's biggest entertainment company.

At stake are billions of dollars in revenue for the media giant. Critics — including consumer groups, librarians and other entertainment companies — question whether one company should get preferential treatment for sweeping legislation it wants to ensure that the company can continue charging premium prices for videos and other products featuring Mickey Mouse and a menagerie of other popular cartoon characters.

The bill would extend by 20 years the 75-year copyright that covers movies. It would grant Disney exclusive rights to the images for another generation and make it harder for them to be reproduced by other manufacturers when copyrights run out.

Disney's campaign, conducted almost entirely behind the scenes, is typical of what industry insiders say is a company that jealously guards its image as a marketer of family entertainment instead of a savvy business and

CQ Weekly Aug. 8, 1998

political force.

In Hollywood, where partisanship reigns and Democrats have dominated, Disney strictly avoids tilting toward either party.

"Mickey Mouse is not a Republican or a Democrat," said Joe Shapiro, who oversaw Disney's Washington lobbying office in the early 1990s. "If you take a strong position either way, you are looking at offending rough-

ASSOCIATED PRESS

Eisner with Mickey Mouse, Disney's greatest treasure. The company asked Congress to extend the copyright on its cartoon characters, including Mickey Mouse, Dumbo, Donald Duck, and Snow White and the Seven Dwarfs.

ly half of the people. Michael Eisner is very informed about public policy issues. But as a matter of personal style, he's not out front. I believe he doesn't think it's appropriate."

Nevertheless, the Disney empire opened an office and hired lobbyists in Washington in 1990, and it has become an influential force on legislation. Among its activities:

• It is one of the top media conglomerates contributing to political campaigns. Recipients of campaign money include members of key committees such as Sen. Patrick J. Leahy, D-Vt., a family friend of Eisner and ranking Democrat on the Judiciary Committee, and Rep. Howard Coble, R-N.C., chairman of the Judiciary Subcommittee on Arts and Intellectual Property, which oversees copyright issues. It has contributed nearly $800,000 to political campaigns in the 1997-98 cycle. (*Chart, p. 35*)

• It has courted members of the congressional delegations from California and Florida, where its theme parks pump billions of dollars a year into local economies in Orlando, Fla., and Anaheim, Calif.

• It has begun a major reorganization that will combine the lobbying firepower of Disney and its subsidiary ABC Inc., under Preston Padden, who left his job as president of ABC Television Network Inc. to take over the task of upgrading Disney's lobbying operation. Disney spent more than $1.5 million on lobbying last year.

• It took a leading role in Hollywood in promoting closer ties to Republican leaders to help move legislation. On June 29, three weeks after Eisner's meeting with Lott, Disney sent John F. Cooke, executive vice president for corporate affairs, to a meeting hosted by another major Hollywood company, Universal Studios, a subsidiary of The Seagram Co. Ltd., in Studio City, Calif., to discuss legislation with Speaker Newt Gingrich, R-Ga., and Reps. David Dreier and Mary Bono, both from California. (*Story, p. 32*)

In February, the company paid $2,700 to host Gingrich and his wife, Marianne, for three days at Disney Institute, the company's educational facility in Orlando. Gingrich gave a speech and visited Disney's new Animal Kingdom theme park.

Low Profile

But Disney is discrete about its strategy. Eisner, Cooke and other Dis-

ney executives declined to be interviewed for this article about the company's activities on Capitol Hill.

"We regard our lobbying as proprietary to us. We don't wish to talk about it," said spokesman Thomas J. Deegan.

Shapiro, the company's former general counsel, links the company's reticence to a corporate culture built around protecting the company's image as a maker of family entertainment.

"We don't want to be obtrusive in making our point," said Shapiro, who left the company four years ago. "How does it enhance Disney value to shareholders to have the company perceived as a bunch of high-powered lobbyists? We want them to think of the people at Disney as clever filmmakers and theme park operators."

But Padden, 49, who is one of four executive vice presidents and who reports directly to Eisner, signaled that he is about to change some things. In an interview with Congressional Quarterly, he said he would be trying to formulate a new style and a new agenda for the Disney lobbying office.

And he made clear that Disney's policy of not discussing its lobbying operation with the media could change under his leadership.

"We're working out a style for the office and an agenda," he said. "The two companies [ABC and Disney] merged two years ago, but the lobbying offices were kept separate. Now we are looking at combining resources. We think we can help each other achieve our goals."

Disney's Agenda

Corporate mergers and acquisitions have transformed Disney from a specialist in children's entertainment into a media conglomerate with holdings in broadcast and cable television stations, theme parks, and professional hockey and baseball teams.

And with its empire growing, Disney is faced with a burgeoning array of legislative needs from Capitol Hill, forcing it to reorganize and broaden its lobbying base.

But Disney learned its lesson about Washington the hard way.

In 1994, the company suffered a stinging defeat when it belatedly came to Capitol Hill to build congressional support and overcome local opposition to the proposed Disney's America theme park near the Shenandoah Na-

tional Park in Virginia. Eisner intervened personally to host a luncheon on Capitol Hill and a glamorous movie premiere for "The Lion King."

The movie showing backfired when picketers showed up with signs reading, "No Orlando in Virginia" and "Eisner the Lyin' King."

After a yearlong battle, Disney retreated. "We got a political campaign against us the likes of which I've never seen," Eisner said after announcing Disney's retreat. He said the company was "killed day in and day out" by opponents and local media stories.

Determined not to be blindsided again, Disney has regrouped under Eisner's direction. Three years ago, the company added a well-connected lobbyist, former Maine senator and Majority Leader George J. Mitchell (1980-95), a Democrat, to its board of directors.

And under Padden, Disney will likely move away from its near-exclusive reliance on an in-house lobbying operation.

Padden said he would consider bringing a more diverse approach that will rely on both in-house lobbyists and outsiders. In 1997, ABC paid $300,000 to Timmons and Co. Inc., a firm with close GOP ties, to help Disney make its case on Capitol Hill last year.

"Preston Padden is not a bashful person. He will give the Washington office a higher profile," said James B. Hedlund, president of the Association of Local Television Stations. Padden headed the association as president in the 1980s before becoming an executive first for Rupert Murdoch's News Corp., then for ABC.

The Copyright Extension Fight

Under Padden, the company's sharply honed lobbying operation has begun a final push to promote the copyright term extension bill (HR 2589) on Capitol Hill this year.

Without copyright term extension, the company faces the potential nightmare of seeing its greatest treasures pass from corporate possession into the public domain.

The copyright for Disney's crown jewel, Mickey Mouse, will expire after 2003, 75 years after the appearance in 1928 of the Disney cartoon that launched Mickey's golden career, "Steamboat Willie."

In fast succession, copyrights will

Building Bridges Between Hollywood and Congress

Jack Valenti, Tinseltown's man in Washington, has an ear on both coasts and a pragmatic approach in tending to his wealthy clients.

"It's never personal. You stick to the issues," said Valenti, president since 1966 of the Motion Picture Association of America, which represents seven major movie studios. "That's one of the reasons I'm a survivor."

Now, Valenti, 76, a Democrat who was President Lyndon B. Johnson's press secretary, has assumed the role of a quiet broker in trying to work out a marriage of convenience between Democratic West Coast movie moguls and leaders of the Republican Congress.

The latest courtship ritual was a June 29 meeting of top movie studio executives and Speaker Newt Gingrich, R-Ga. Reps. David Dreier, vice chairman of the House Rules Committee, and Mary Bono, both Republicans from California, accompanied Gingrich to movieland.

Over a breakfast of eggs Benedict in a private dining room on the lot of Universal Studios in Studio City, Calif., Gingrich told a group of movie moguls that Republicans would "protect private property," whether it is movies or real estate.

Dreier said he and Gingrich stressed their commitment to issues important to Hollywood, including copyright protection of movies and music, and pro-business tax and trade policies. In return, Dreier said heads of a half-dozen studios agreed to support Republican fundraising efforts.

Gingrich Goes to Hollywood

Gingrich and Hollywood began a courtship soon after Republicans took control of Congress. He appointed the late Rep. Sonny Bono, R-Calif., as an emissary to Hollywood. After Bono's death in a skiing accident last January, Republicans turned to his wife, Mary, and Dreier to follow up. (*1998 CQ Weekly, p. 93*)

For its part, Hollywood badly wants help. It has faced long delays in key battles on Capitol Hill with other industries over a copyright term extension bill (HR 2589) and another bill to ensure copyright protection of software and compact discs (HR 2281). (*Copyright, 1998 CQ Weekly, p. 1953; House passage, p. 820*)

In the June meeting, Gingrich and Dreier offered to help promote both bills.

The executives who attended included Edgar Bronfman Jr., chairman of Seagram Co., parent of Universal; Ron Meyer, president of MCA Corp.; Frank Mancuso, chairman of Metro Goldwyn Mayer/United Artists; Terry Semel, chairman of Warner Brothers Studios; and John F. Cooke, executive vice president of corporate affairs for Walt Disney Co.

"It was a good meeting. They agreed to support some of our initiatives," Dreier said. "We are continuing to build bridges to Hollywood."

After breakfast, Bronfman escorted Gingrich onto the set of the movie "Ed-TV" to meet with director Ron Howard and actors Matthew McConaughey and Rob Reiner. The movie is about a video store clerk who agrees to let a television camera follow his life 24 hours a day.

Valenti said afterwards that both sides wanted closer communications. He said he had long encouraged industry leaders such as Michael D. Eisner, chairman of Disney, to make regular visits to Capitol Hill "to put a face with the name" and to adopt a bipartisan stance in dealing with lawmakers.

Privately, lobbyists for the entertainment industry describe a conflicted relationship with the Republican-controlled Congress.

They like what the party stands for when it comes to tax cuts, particularly lower capital gains tax rates, and measures aimed at increasing exports of American products. They re-

coil when Republicans start talking about a social agenda that supports family values and attacks gay rights and legal abortion.

Hilary Rosen, president of the Recording Industry Association of America, who attended the June 29 meeting, said the entertainment industry had "agreed to disagree" with Republicans on social issues, while backing parts of the Republican business agenda.

Money for the GOP

A new study by the Center for Responsive Politics shows that mixture of feelings in Hollywood toward Republicans. During the 1998 election cycle, the entertainment industry has directed campaign contributions to Democrats and Republicans roughly equally, both to individual campaigns and to soft money uses.

Meanwhile, individual contributions from executives and other employees in entertainment companies favor Democrats by a 9-to-1 ratio.

Andy Spahn, who manages political affairs for producer Steven Spielberg and his movie company, Dreamworks, said the individual contributions reflect the true colors of the people in the industry who are overwhelmingly Democratic, while the balanced giving by corporate political action committees reflects political reality.

Despite efforts by party leaders to embrace Hollywood, rank-and-file Republicans quietly grumble that Hollywood has a Democratic tilt and mainly employs key lobbyists with Democratic bloodlines.

Besides Valenti, other top guns include former Democratic congressional aides such as Richard Bates of Walt Disney Co., former executive director of the Democratic Congressional Campaign Committee. And despite the industry's attempts to appear bipartisan, many lawmakers still think they are dealing with Democrats.

"I sometimes wonder if the industry thinks we are still in the 1960s and President Kennedy is in the White House," said Rep. Scott Klug, R-Wis.

In one recent battle, libraries and universities found sympathy among Republican lawmakers skeptical of Hollywood's motives in promoting tougher copyright laws.

Valenti said there is unity in the industry on a plethora of issues involving copyright coverage for movies, compact discs, software and other forms of intellectual property. "These are treasures that need to be protected," Valenti said.

The latest battle pitted Hollywood against librarians over an amendment to HR 2281.

Klug said the battle provided a prime example of what will likely be a continuing problem for Hollywood: a lack of sympathy among Republicans.

Hollywood argues that the bill is an essential implementation of two international treaties to strengthen copyright protection for digitally produced works such as compact discs. But a sharp dispute broke out when libraries and universities argued that software and recorded movies and music deserved no more protection than books, which can be bought or lent for free to unlimited numbers of researchers and library patrons.

In the heat of the debate, Valenti argued that the tough position taken by the American Library Association would bring down the "entire fabric of intellectual property protection."

Klug's compromise amendment, adopted July 17 by voice vote by the Commerce Committee, called for a two-year delay in issuing federal regulations aimed at stopping copies from being made of digitally recorded material such as software and compact discs. It would permit regulators to grant waivers for lawful users of works covered by copyright. The amendment helped clear the way for passage of the bill. The House passed the bill by voice vote Aug. 4. (1998 CQ Weekly, p. 2182)

The battle left bruised feelings on both sides.

"When it comes right down to it,

Hollywood does not have much of a constituency. There are libraries and universities all over the country," Klug said.

The Battles Ahead

Hollywood will likely face more tough battles in Congress.

It remains under pressure to tone down sex and violence in movies and television programming.

In 1996, the industry was virtually forced to unveil a voluntary television rating system. A provision of

"You never know when you will need your adversary today to be your friend tomorrow," says Valenti, Hollywood's lobbyist in Washington.

the 1996 telecommunications law (PL 104-104) gave industry the option of imposing its own system or using guidelines established by the Federal Communications Commission.

Valenti failed in his efforts to convince Congress to apply the movie rating system to television.

The law also required the electronics industry to develop televisions with "v-chip" editing devices that allow viewers to block programming based on ratings. (1996 Almanac, 3-45)

Rep. Edward J. Markey, D-Mass, said the first big test of the ratings would likely come this fall, when the first televisions equipped with the v-chip are expected to hit the market.

Meanwhile, the industry faces continuing threats from potential pirates who would steal its wares, as well as continued criticism of sex and violence in movies and music.

While Hollywood sorts out its legislative agenda, the future of its ties with Republicans are hazy.

Before his death, Sonny Bono, Gingrich's handpicked ambassador, blamed the chilly relations with Hollywood's stars and media barons on years of mutual disdain.

"Members of Congress don't understand the industry," Bono remarked.

On June 25, four days before Gingrich's trip West to meet with studio executives, he, Dreier, Majority Leader Dick Armey, R-Texas, and Rep. Mark Foley, R-Fla., met with lobbyists for the entertainment industry to underscore their willingness to help promote legislation for Hollywood.

Valenti said the industry hoped to continue cultivating close relations with Republicans. Despite a Democratic pedigree, the former presidential press secretary said his clients relied on him to keep ties to both parties.

"I'm living out my days under the formula of Lyndon Johnson," says Valenti. "You never know when you will need your adversary today to be your friend tomorrow."

end for Pluto in 2006 and Goofy in 2008. Early in the next century, protections also will expire for Bambi, Dumbo, Donald Duck, Snow White and all the Seven Dwarfs.

Without copyright, Disney would collect no fees for the showing of classic movies such as "Fantasia," and other companies could freely use its characters in their movies and videos.

When he visited Capitol Hill in June, Eisner met personally with a number of lawmakers and insisted that the copyright term extension was vital to the company's future.

Despite the company's vaunted clout, Disney faces a tough fight in Congress, where a wide range of interests including consumer groups, libraries, restaurants and small businesses have raised questions about media companies' efforts to extend and toughen copyright protection.

Critics of the bill argue the companies already have earned plenty of money from classic movies and should now allow other companies to offer videos and other products based on these works when copyrights expire.

But Disney and Jack Valenti, president of the Motion Picture Association of America, say the copyright term must be extended by 20 years, to 95 years, to match a change adopted by the European Union. (*Story, p. 32*)

That would allow American companies to maintain their stream of revenue by collecting premium prices for works and keeping up with European rivals that already are able to claim 95-year copyrights. American copyrights currently last for the life of the creator of an artistic work plus 50 years, or, if the work was produced by a company, for 75 years.

Consumer Opposition

Consumer groups oppose the extension, charging that the original purpose of copyrights — to provide benefits to human creators of cultural works and nurture production of more works — has been lost. They say the biggest benefits of copyright extension will flow to large companies and investors.

"The bill is moving because it is supported by big entertainment companies like Disney," said Jamie Love, director of the Consumer Project on Technology, an advocacy group opposed to tougher copyright laws.

Adam Eisgrau, a lobbyist for the American Library Association, con-tended the bill would merely preserve Disney's premium prices.

"After 75 years, these classic movies belong in the public domain like the works of Shakespeare and Mark Twain. Works in the public domain are more accessible to more people at lower prices," Eisgrau said.

Disney replied in a statement portraying copyright extension as a matter of giving American entertainment the same rights that the European Union gave to European companies.

"It is important that the United States and its artistic talent not be disadvantaged in the worldwide market for creative properties," the company said.

Coble, the bill's sponsor, agreed with Disney, adding that it was important to ensure the financial health of companies that create jobs.

"We're working out a style for the office and an agenda. The two companies [ABC and Disney] merged two years ago, but the lobbying offices were kept separate. Now we are looking at combining resources."

— Preston Padden, Disney's Washington lobbyist

His copyright extension bill passed the House by voice vote March 25. But it remains bottled up in the Senate Judiciary Committee by opponents of a controversial House floor amendment. The House voted 297-112 to adopt an amendment by F. James Sensenbrenner Jr., R-Wis., to exempt most restaurants, bars and other small businesses from paying annual music licensing fees for piping in broadcasts from television and radio stations. The fees typically range from $200 to more than $1,000 a year, depending on the size of the business. (*1998 CQ Weekly, p. 820*)

The Sensenbrenner amendment would exempt most restaurants, if the rooms where sound speakers were located covered less than 3,500 square feet. Songwriters and music licensing societies want a narrower exemption covering restaurants with an entire floor space of less than 3,500 square feet.

Orrin G. Hatch, R-Utah, chairman of the Senate Judiciary Committee, said the bill will not move unless the exemption is removed or reduced. Sensenbrenner defended his amendment. "If they want to separate the two issues, it won't happen," Sensenbrenner said.

Public Sensitivities

Ronald G. Shaiko, a professor of government at American University who studies lobbying by companies, said Disney has had problems on Capitol Hill, such as the long delay in getting what it wants in copyright legislation, because the legislation lacks broad grass-roots support in many congressional districts.

"Disney has very important issues confronting it on Capitol Hill," Shaiko said. "And like other media conglomerates, it suffers from the lack of a large base of constituents, employees and consumers who could help win more support in Congress."

Disney faces an additional challenge in building political support because it is frequently a magnet for criticism from conservatives concerned about the company's portrayal of sex, violence and gay rights in its movies.

Recently, several members of Congress from New York criticized Disney for its comedy movie "Mafia!" which included crude portrayals of Italian-Americans.

"They peddle a crude, dirty, uneducated caricature to sell a movie, to make a buck," said Rep. Rick A. Lazio, R-N.Y. "It's time for them to be held accountable."

Eisner replied to a wide range of groups critical of particular Disney

Dollars From Disney: Top 15 Recipients in House and Senate

House		Senate	
Harman, Jane, D-Calif.	$7,500	Leahy, Patrick J., D-Vt.	$17,900
McCollum, Bill, R-Fla.	6,832	Boxer, Barbara, D-Calif.	17,469
Berman, Howard L., D-Calif.	5,750	Graham, Bob, D-Fla.	10,750
Coble, Howard, R-N.C.	5,000	Hollings, Ernest F., D-S.C.	8,500
Sanchez, Loretta, D-Calif.	4,750	Dodd, Christopher J., D-Conn.	6,500
Shaw, E. Clay Jr., R-Fla.	4,671	Reed, Jack, D-R.I.	6.250
Schumer, Charles E., D-N.Y.	4,000	McCain, John, R-Ariz.	6,000
Bliley, Thomas J. Jr., R-Va.	3,000	Hatch, Orrin G., R-Utah	6,000
Gephardt, Richard A., D-Mo.	3,000	Dorgan, Byron L., D-N.D.	5,113
Kennedy, Joseph P. II, D-Mass.	2.050	Johnson, Tim, D-S.D.	5,000
Matsui, Robert T., D-Calif.	2,000	Daschle, Tom, D-S.D.	5,000
Capps, Lois, D-Calif.	2,000	Wyden, Ron, D-Ore.	5,000
Goodlatte, Robert W., R-Va.	2,000	Breaux, John B., D-La.	4,000
Becerra, Xavier, D-Calif.	2,000	Torricelli, Robert G., D-N.J.	2,000
Rogan, James E., R-Calif.	1,750	Kerrey, Bob, D-Neb.	2,000

1997-98 contributions from Disney employees and PACs to Democrats	$438,674
1997-98 contributions from Disney employees and PACs to Republicans	$350,378
Total from Disney employees and PACs	**$789,052**

SOURCE: Center for Responsive Politics, 1997-98 election cycle

movies in a message to stockholders earlier this year. He said the criticism came from "groups that want to leverage our strength with the public for their own ends" and focus on Disney "because it is more effective than citing one of our competitors."

Shaiko said boycotts and angry special interest groups made it harder for Disney to win political backing for its causes.

But sheer size also draws attention to Disney. Sen. John McCain, R-Ariz., made Disney a target in 1997 when he took a jab at the company's policy of not subtracting the cost of stock options paid to Eisner from net income while listing them as a deductible expense on corporate tax returns.

He said the practice used by Disney was "exactly the kind of corporate benefit that makes the American people irate and must be eliminated."

The bill, S 576, cosponsored by McCain and Carl Levin, D-Mich., would have required companies to count executive stock options as an expense in financial statements in order to claim them as a tax deduction. It would have provided an exemption for companies that have broad-based stock option programs for employees. The Senate approved a resolution calling for a hearing on S 576. (*1997*

Almanac, p. 2-30)

S 576 was strongly opposed by a small group of senators who signed a letter circulated by Sen. Connie Mack, R-Fla. The letter charged that the McCain bill was "economically counterproductive and will deprive employees of the opportunity to share in the wealth they create."

Mack said he opposed the bill to help small high-tech companies, not Disney.

"Stock options are extremely important to start-up companies," he said. "My opposition was rooted in a philosophical point of view, not a company's specific perspective."

McCain said he believed Disney and other companies had quietly lobbied to help kill the bill.

Disney, McCain said, is an "800-pound gorilla. They don't really have to say much publicly. You know what they want."

Theme Park Interests

While Disney pursues its national agenda, including defense of its stock options policy, the company also pushes special legislation to help its theme parks.

Sen. Bob Graham, D-Fla., said the company has a wide range of needs, including occasional legislation to obtain

visas for animal trainers and other specialized employees for its theme parks.

The 1991 surface transportation law (PL 102-240) included $97.5 million in federal funding to construct a train powered by magnetic levitation from the Orlando International Airport to a busy intersection near the company's theme park and hotels in Orlando.

Disney was one of a group of local interests that supported the project, which was designed to zip tourists from the airport to Disney-owned businesses and other restaurants and hotels.

The plan was derailed, however, when the developers were unable to raise private financing for the project.

This year, the city of Orlando and civic groups won support for a light-rail train project. The 1998 surface transportation law (PL 105-178) provided $100 million for the project that will initially run in downtown Orlando.

Supporters of the project said Disney did not play a leading role in lobbying for it. But they said Disney had recently expressed interest in the project after it was included in the surface transportation law.

Looking to the Next Century

While trying to keep costs down at its theme parks and improving public transportation links for park patrons, Disney faces challenges on a broad range of other legislative issues.

Shaiko said entertainment and telecommunications companies will likely become lobbying powerhouses in the next century.

Love, the head of the Consumer Project on Technology, which opposes tougher copyright laws, said Disney was already in the first tier of companies lobbying on intellectual property issues.

"Intellectual property is where the big fortunes are going to be made in the next century. Pharmaceutical, entertainment and software companies will have the greatest stake in that new economy," Love said.

"They [Disney] are extremely good," said Robert Raben, an aide to Rep. Barney Frank, D-Mass., the ranking Democrat on the Courts and Intellectual Property Subcommittee. "They are well-informed, thorough. They know what they are doing." ◆

This Year's State Ballot Initiative Could Be Next Year's Federal Legislation

Interest groups use local issues, from private school tax credits to gay marriage, to build national momentum

Voters across the country will cast ballots Nov. 3 on state initiatives and referendums on such local issues as outlawing cockfighting in Arizona, banning horse meat in food in California and prohibiting billboards along roads in Alaska.

But many of the 235 proposals on state ballots this year also have national implications that some say could culminate in federal legislation in the near future.

Several proposals, such as campaign finance restrictions and efforts to end affirmative action, have already been shot down in Congress, but supporters hope a strong showing at the state level will put pressure on federal lawmakers to revisit the issues nationally.

"This year will really set the tone for the next two or three election cycles," said Dane Waters, president of the Initiatives and Referendums Institute, a nonprofit, nonpartisan group that tracks state ballot measures. "This election cycle is being watched quite a bit by various interest groups. A lot of these initiatives can be taken nationally."

Indeed, several interest groups are working for or against state measures, spending hundreds of thousands of dollars to encourage or prevent the issue from going national.

Some interest groups have become so concerned about the power of state initiatives that they are trying to pre-empt measures they fear will be placed on the ballot down the road. In Utah, for example, pro-hunting groups are backing a constitutional amendment to require a two-thirds vote of the people — rather than a simple majority — to adopt any initiatives to regulate wildlife hunting. Many states have adopted such hunting limits in recent years, and Utah hunters want to make sure it does not happen to them.

Some of the nation's most important legislative issues began as ballot initiatives — including the women's suffrage movement, which led in 1920 to the 19th Amendment granting women the right to vote.

California has a history of coming up with controversial proposals that spread across the nation, including 1978's Proposition 13 to limit taxes and spending.

Former U.S. drug policy chief William Bennett, left, shown outside the Colorado state Capitol in Denver, helps kick off an effort to stop a petition drive for a ballot proposal authorizing the medicinal use of marijuana byproducts. The rally took place in April.

The 1998 election cycle marks the 100th anniversary of the ballot initiative and referendum process. In the century since South Dakota first adopted the process, a total of 1,825 measures have been placed on state ballots, and 725 have been enacted.

Responding to Congress

One issue that is popping up in states across the country is the legalization of marijuana for medical use. The initiatives — on the ballot in Alaska, Arizona, Colorado, Nevada, Oregon and Washington — come in the wake of a non-binding measure (H J Res 117) that the House passed, 310-93, on Sept. 15. It puts Congress on record as opposing any state efforts to circumvent existing federal laws prohibiting the medical use of marijuana. (*Vote 435, 1998 CQ Weekly, p. 2532*)

A medical marijuana proposal is also on the ballot in the District of Columbia, but Congress has ensured that it will not become law this year. The catchall spending bill (HR 4328 – PL 105-277) enacted this month included language that prohibits the District from using federal or local funds to count the vote or certify the outcome.

Quick Contents

Several issues on state ballots this year already have been defeated in Congress, but supporters hope a strong showing at the state level will put pressure on federal lawmakers to reconsider.

Issues to be taken up by states in the wake of failed federal legislation include a ban on a procedure opponents refer to as "partial birth" abortion, tax breaks for parents who send their children to private schools, and a constitutional amendment to guarantee free religious expression on government property.

The House in June failed to muster the two-thirds vote needed to send a constitutional amendment on religious expression (H J Res 78) to the states for ratification. *(1998 CQ Weekly, p. 1530).*

In Alabama, voters will take up a state constitutional amendment that would prohibit the "burdening of the free exercise of religion unless government demonstrates that is has a compelling interest in doing so." Earlier this year, Alabama Republican Gov. Fob James Jr. threatened to bring in the National Guard to protect the right of a county judge to display a copy of the Ten Commandments in his court room.

If the referendum passes, Alabama will become the first state to enact such a measure.

Two states, Colorado and Washington, will take up bans on so-called partial-birth abortion, usually performed in the second or third trimester of pregnancy. Congress passed such a ban in 1996 and in 1997, but failed to override a presidential veto each time. *(1998 CQ Weekly, p. 2018; 1997 Almanac, p. 6-12)*

Jennifer Shecter of the Center for Responsive Politics said special interest groups often use state ballot measures to test the political winds. "It's a way of gauging public opinion before you finalize your legislative policy," she said.

Nicholas Sanchez of the Free Congress Foundation, a conservative think tank that tracks ballot measures, said many issues on state ballots this year carry national importance, but have been overshadowed by news of President Clinton's affair with White House intern Monica Lewinsky. "In most years, these kinds of initiatives would be drawing a lot of news, but now they're lost in other issues," he said.

One hot-button issue Sanchez predicts could spread across the country is "school choice," or whether tax dollars should be used to help parents send their children to private schools. Voters in Colorado will decide whether to amend the state constitution to pro-

vide income tax credits to parents who move their children from public to private schools.

The initiative has sparked opposition from the two national teachers unions, the American Federation of Teachers and the National Education Association. Both groups, along with the Clinton administration, have worked to kill congressional efforts to give tax breaks for private education, saying it hurts poor children by draining resources from public schools.

Congress cleared legislation (HR 2646) in June creating tax-preferred educational savings accounts that could be used to pay for private schooling, but Clinton vetoed it. *(1998 CQ Weekly, p. 2021)*

If Colorado approves the initiative, it will become the first state to establish a statewide tax system to help private schools. Backers of the initiative are telling voters it will give Colorado the "opportunity to lead the nation on school choice."

Deborah Fallin, press secretary for Coloradans for Public Schools, which is working against the measure, said her group fears the issue will spread across the country. "There is a danger," she said. "Colorado is being used as a testing ground. If they can pass it here, they can pass it somewhere else."

Polls have shown voters to be almost evenly split on whether to support the measure.

In Washington state, voters will take up another issue that has been hotly debated on a national level — affirmative action. Initiative 200 would prohibit state and local governments from discriminating against or granting preferential treatment to anyone based on race or gender. Proponents describe it as a civil rights plan. Opponents say it would abolish affirmative action programs in college admissions and government contracts.

Nationally, the GOP-led Congress has abandoned most efforts to kill affirmative action, fearing a political backlash. *(1997 Almanac, p. 5-7)*

Outside Money

The Washington state affirmative action measure has drawn attention from groups across the country, including the AFL-CIO, which is working with local unions to defeat it.

The AFL-CIO is also working hard against an Oregon measure that would prohibit public employee unions from

spending members' dues on political activities. The AFL-CIO and other labor groups have raised $2 million to defeat the measure, called "paycheck protection" by proponents.

Unions succeeded last June — after spending about $20 million — in helping to defeat a similar measure in California that was pushed by the conservative Americans for Tax Reform group, headed by Grover Norquist. The tax group spent about $400,000 on efforts to pass that measure. *(1998 CQ Weekly, p. 1287)*

"A threat to one of us is a threat to all of us," said Barbara Smith, campaign manager for the Oregon AFL-CIO committee working against the Oregon initiative. "When you knock off the public unions, private sector unions are next."

She added: "We hope by defeating this, it will not only put the nail in the coffin, but show that when union members mobilize, it makes a difference elsewhere."

Smith said that by mobilizing union members on the ballot initiative, the AFL-CIO hopes to energize support for pro-labor candidates running for office across the state.

Waters of the Initiatives and Referendums Institute predicted that as more state legislatures elect GOP majorities, unions will look to ballot initiatives to push legislation that they cannot get through the legislature.

Michael Kamburowski, a spokesman for Americans for Tax Reform, conceded that "a lot of people got cold feet" after the defeat of the California initiative, but he said his group will continue to push for similar measures elsewhere.

Five states — Wyoming, Washington, Idaho, Michigan and Ohio — currently have paycheck protection laws, and Kamburowski said as the measure "catches fire," it could put pressure on Congress to pass a federal law.

The House in March rejected a bill (HR 2608) that would have prohibited unions and corporations from making campaign contributions on behalf of union members or stockholders without their approval. *(1998 Weekly Report, p. 863)*

Gay Marriages

Another measure that is drawing the attention — and financial backing — of several national organizations is a proposal to ban same-sex marriages. It is on the ballot in Hawaii and Alaska.

In 1996, Congress passed — and Clinton signed into law — a measure (PL 104-199) that bars federal recognition of gay marriages but does not prohibit states from allowing such unions. (*1996 Almanac, p. 5-26*)

Leading the fight for the state measures, which would amend the state constitutions, are the Christian Coalition and the Mormon church. The Mormons have contributed $600,000 to the Hawaiian effort, and $500,000 for Alaska.

"The church leadership is strongly committed to doing all it can to preserve traditional marriage," said Don LeFevre, media spokesman for the church.

The national and state branches of the Christian Coalition also have spent tens of thousands of dollars on the campaign. In Hawaii, the Christian Coalition plans to advocate the measure's passage in a voters' guide that will be handed out to thousands of voters on Election Day.

Under Hawaiian state law, any group that contributes more than $1,000 to a campaign — for a candidate or ballot initiative — must register as a political action committee (PAC) and disclose all donors. The Christian Coalition, which keeps its donors secret, has filed suit against the Hawaiian Campaign Spending Commission asking for a temporary injunction against the state law, charging that it unconstitutionally limits its right to free speech.

On the other side of the issue, the Human Rights Campaign, the nation's largest gay political action group, is raising money across the country and running radio, television and newspaper ads in Hawaii to defeat the measure.

The Human Rights Campaign estimates that it will spend $1.1 million for the effort, and that overall spending by groups on both sides of the issue will make it the most expensive ballot campaign in state history.

"We find it frightening to think the extreme right would be running around the country trying to change states' constitutions," said David Smith, a senior strategist with the Human Rights Campaign. "It should be a wake-up call about the influence churches have on public policy."

Smith said polls currently show the referendum winning among voters. ◆

Highlights of State Ballot Measures

Abortion

Colorado: Would ban "partial birth" abortions, unless needed to save the life of the woman. Another ballot initiative would require parental notification for minors who seek abortions.
Washington state: Would outlaw "partial birth" abortions as "infanticide."

Affirmative action

Washington state: Would prohibit the state from discriminating against or granting preferential treatment to anyone based on race, sex, ethnicity or national origin in the operation of public employment, public education or public contracting.

Campaign finance

Arizona: Would grant public funding to candidates who gather a minimum number of $5 contributions.
Massachusetts: Would provide funding to candidates who agree to spending and contribution limits.

Gay marriages

Alaska: Would amend the state Constitution to define marriage as the union of a man and a woman.
Hawaii: Would amend the state Constitution to give the state legislature the power to reserve marriage for "opposite-sex couples."

Medicinal use of marijuana

Alaska: Would authorize doctors to prescribe marijuana to patients and for patients and primary health care providers to grow marijuana on the approval of a doctor.
Arizona: Would allow doctors to prescribe medicinal marijuana only if the federal government authorizes the medical use of marijuana.
District of Columbia: Would allow for the medical use of marijuana. Congress passed language prohibiting any funds — federal or local — from being used to count the votes for this measure.
Colorado: Would amend the state Constitution to authorize the use of marijuana for people suffering from "debilitating medical conditions." The Colorado secretary of state ruled that supporters failed to gather the appropriate number of signatures and, therefore, votes cast for the measure on Election Day will not be counted. Supporters have taken the issue to court.
Nevada: Would amend the state Constitution to allow the possession and use of marijuana for the "treatment or alleviation" of illnesses if prescribed by a doctor.
Oregon: Would allow the medical use of marijuana for debilitating conditions, such as cancer and AIDS.
Washington state: Would state that "the people of Washington find that some patients with terminal or debilitating illnesses" may benefit from using marijuana.

Religious expression

Alabama: Would amend the state Constitution to prohibit the government from "burdening" religious activities unless the government has a "compelling interest" in doing so.

School choice

Colorado: Would amend the state Constitution to grant tax breaks to parents who switch their children from public to private schools.

Union dues

Oregon: One measure would amend the state Constitution to prohibit public employee payroll deductions for political purposes. Another measure would amend the state Constitution to guarantee the rights of unions to use dues for political activities.

Industry seeks federal policy changes to help it cope with economic pressures

Is Big Oil's Profit Well Starting To Run Dry?

A quarter-century after the Arab oil embargo of 1973, one clear victor has emerged from the race for new oil riches: the U.S. consumer. While many service stations today offer dollar-a-gallon prices at the gas pump — the lowest inflation-adjusted level since economists began keeping records in 1920 — oil companies are hurting from global competition and lower profits caused by depressed crude oil prices. And they are looking to Washington for help.

On Capitol Hill, the oil industry lobby, ranging from conglomerates to independent drillers and refiners, is seeking legislation that would lower royalties it must pay for oil tapped on public land and tax credits for marginal operations. The industry wants backing for mega-mergers and an end to economic sanctions that lock American companies out of oil-rich nations such as Iran and Azerbaijan. *(1998 CQ Weekly, p. 2721)*

A broad new debate on oil policy is expected next year in Congress. It will center on demands from the domestic oil industry for help through a tumultuous era of corporate mergers and global competition.

The industry's problems, ironically, were precipitated by a boom in supply. Oil has been flowing from vast new oil fields stretching from the Caspian Sea to the Gulf of Mexico, producing lower prices and dramatically cutting the influence of any single nation on the cost of gasoline.

Energy Secretary Bill Richardson said he was working on measures within the administration to help out the oil industry. He said he hoped to promote relief for operators of marginal wells and a compromise with oil drillers who want to avert higher royalties for oil drilled on public lands. "I want to beef up the oil and gas section of our energy strategy," Richardson said in an interview on Oct. 6. "I would like to see legislation to help the domestic oil and gas industry."

Industry analysts predict oil companies will continue to face pressure from depressed prices. They note that prices have remained low despite the threat of potential conflict in the Middle East.

"There is an oversupply of petroleum in the world and in the U.S., compared to demand, causing prices to fall," said Trilby Lundberg, who publishes the Lundberg Letter, a newsletter that tracks gasoline prices. The glut has been even more marked, she said, because of a decline in demand for oil in Asia, which is now in a recession.

Rising Tide of Oil

Some economists in the 1970s projected that the world's oil might last only 30 years. But the current supply, estimated at just over 1 trillion barrels based on new discoveries, could last more than 40 years at the present rate of consumption. And the U.S. Geological Survey projects that reserves could increase sharply from discoveries using new technology.

These changes in the industry are setting the stage for a major review of energy policies established after the oil crisis in the 1970s.

The crisis came to a head in October 1973 when oil-rich nations in the Middle East cut back on production in retaliation against U.S. support for Israel during the Yom Kippur war. Industry experts said the crisis was com-

Twenty-five years after the Arab oil embargo, prices at the gas pump are at their lowest inflation-adjusted level in history. But the oil industry is pressing Congress for a broad new policy debate to deal with depressed prices, corporate mergers and political disputes that lock American companies out of oil-rich nations.

Cars line up in two directions on Dec. 23, 1973, in New York City to get gasoline rationed at the pump during the Arab oil embargo.

AP / MARTY LEDERHANDLER

plicated by gasoline rationing (PL 93 – 28). *(1973 Almanac, p. 867)*

Now, with oil shock fears fading into the distant past, the industry is arguing that federal assistance would help save American jobs. A shakeout that began in the 1980s has reduced jobs in the industry by about half, to 430,000.

New technology, mergers and off-shore production have cut into the domestic oil and gas industry work force.

And more job cuts loom as analysts predict an increasing number of mergers such as the planned marriage of British Petroleum Co. (BP) and Amoco Corp. The combined $110 billion company would cut 6,000 jobs and become the world's third largest oil giant after Texas-based Exxon Corp. and the Anglo-Dutch giant Royal Dutch/Shell Group.

Oil industry analysts are predicting sluggish results from the third quarter this year, possibly a 50 percent drop in earnings for many of the major oil companies.

Robert W. Gilmer, a senior economist at the Federal Reserve bank of Dallas, said the industry could be in the midst of a major restructuring, driven by concern about weak demand in Asia and low crude oil prices.

"Companies are just beginning to feel the pain. They are worried that the low prices will continue. And there's a fear that they will be left behind or gobbled up," Gilmer said.

The average spot price for the West Texas intermediate blend of crude oil fell from $22 a barrel in October 1997 to $12 in June, but has since recovered to about $15. On Wall Street, some financial analysts are predicting more mergers as oil companies race to cut costs and increase earnings.

In Congress, the industry's supporters say the pain of job loss and restructuring warrants a new look at ways to help oil companies.

"The oil and gas industry is struggling in a declining market," said Sen. Frank H. Murkowski, R-Alaska, one of the industry's strongest allies.

Political scientist Pietro Nivola, a senior fellow at the Brookings Institution, a Washington, D.C., think tank, said the industry appears to be motivated to make a strong push for federal assistance next year and will likely find sympathetic lawmakers.

"Oil companies have more influence when they can claim they are

Ken Knost, former mayor of Taft, Calif., stands near oil pumps west of town on Oct. 7, 1997. He said the government's sale of the Elk Hills oil reserve will be a boost to the entire area.

hard-pressed and in distress. The collapse in demand for oil is damaging the industry. And market conditions may help the industry make its case," Nivola said.

Oil Dependency

The quest for energy independence — once a high national goal under President Jimmy Carter — has been drowned in a sea of cheap oil.

The nation's reliance on foreign oil from many sources has dramatically increased, with foreign sources now satisfying nearly half of the nation's voracious thirst for oil, compared with 28 percent in 1972. The Energy Department projects dependence on foreign oil will continue to grow.

But that trend has been accompanied by dramatic changes in the oil industry. The Organization of Petroleum Exporting Countries, the 11-nation oil cartel that organized the oil embargo of 1973, once accounted for the lion's share of total U.S. oil imports in the late 1970s. Now, that share stands at 50 percent.

Some industry experts say there is little chance the oil powers of the Middle East will ever be able to dictate prices as they did in the 1970s because there are more major producers. And industrial nations are moving to cut consumption with conservation.

While reliance on Middle East oil

has declined, the industry continues to face challenges from foreign rivals and pressure from low prices.

Meanwhile, the oil industry remains a powerful lobbying force on Capitol Hill. The Center for Responsive Politics, which tracks campaign contributions to federal candidates, found the industry donated nearly $6 million during the 1997-98 election cycle to congressional candidates, and $4.8 million in unlimited so-called soft money to both political parties, three-fourths of it to Republicans.

Environmentalists and consumer groups say the industry's clout has diverted attention from conservation that is needed to reduce pollution and weaken the market power of the oil-rich nations.

"Oil companies see a Republican Congress and a weakened president, and they have to deal with low prices. They want to bring back tax credits and loopholes," said consumer activist Ralph Nader in an interview.

Faced with financial turmoil, the industry will enter 1999 with a strong desire to promote tax credits and favorable royalty rules. It was on the verge of winning key decisions in the closing weeks of the 105th Congress, as industry supporters successfully defended several pro-industry provisions in spending bills.

The industry won inclusion of a rider in the Senate version of the Interior

U.S. Oil Imports

U.S. reliance on imported oil has been rising since the 1960s and now accounts for about half of domestic oil consumption. While reliance on imported oil has increased, however, sources of imported oil have become much more diverse. The United States now imports larger amounts of oil from Canada, Mexico and other nations in the Western Hemisphere. The charts at right compare the oil imported from members of the 11-nation Organization of Petroleum Exporting countries and from non-OPEC nations and the percentage of oil imports.

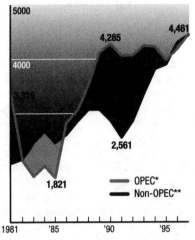

Percentage of Total Consumption

50%
46.5%
47.9%
40
30
27.3%
20
17.8%
1960 '65 '70 '75 '80 '85 '90 '95

OPEC and Non-OPEC Imports
(in thousands of barrels per day)

5000
4,285
4,461
4000
3,315
2,561
1,821
1981 '85 '90 '95

— OPEC*
— Non-OPEC**

*OPEC nations include Bahrain, Iran, Iraq, Kuwait, Qatar, Saudi Arabia, United Arab Emirates, Algeria, Nigeria and Venezuela
** Non-OPEC countries include Canada, Mexico, and the United Kingdom

SOURCE: U.S. Department of Energy

appropriations bill (S 2237) to delay for one year a hike in federal royalties on offshore oil. The battle was emblematic of the partisan and regional split over oil policy that will likely continue in 1999.

The jobs argument helped the industry build a strong case this year for delaying proposed federal rules that would require oil companies to pay more in royalties by basing them on higher market prices paid for crude oil instead of using the lower prices posted by each oil company.

In the fight to delay the rules, Democrats accused big oil companies of trying to get out of paying a fair royalty. They pointed to lawsuits filed by a number of states and by the Justice Department accusing oil companies of underpaying oil royalties. Many states backed the rules to increase income from their share of federal royalties.

In a floor debate on Sept. 16, supporters of the oil industry said it needed help to save jobs and relief for overly complex rules for the industry.

"We have oil prices at their lowest level in 11 years. And we have the best blue-collar jobs in America," Hutchison said. "We are talking about raising fees and taxes on the companies that are on their knees, with low prices, that are laying people off as we speak. It doesn't make sense."

Richard J. Durbin, D-Ill., disagreed.

"This is hardly an industry on its knees," he said. "And we are talking here about those who will come on our land, the taxpayers' land, the federal land, draw oil from our land to make a profit, who are unwilling to pay a fair share of that profit back to the taxpayers of this country."

Senate leaders pulled the Interior spending bill just before a vote on an amendment offered by Barbara Boxer, D-Calif., to strip the one-year moratorium from the new oil royalty rules from the bill. (*1998 CQ Weekly, p. 2494*)

The provision, and the rest of the Interior spending bill, was expected to be rolled into an omnibus spending bill. (*1998 CQ Weekly, p. 2723*)

But U.S. oil policy is still a work in progress. On May 1, President Clinton signed a supplemental spending bill (PL 105 – 174) that canceled a planned sale of 23 million barrels of oil in the Strategic Petroleum Reserve for $207.5 million. The industry argued the sale would sink prices in a flooded market. (*Supplemental, 1998 CQ Weekly, p. 1132*)

In August, the Interior Department decided to permit oil leasing in part of the pristine 23 million-acre National Petroleum Reserve in Alaska. The reserve was set aside in the 1920s to provide oil for the Navy in a crisis, but was kept off-limits to protect wildlife.

The administration concluded the industry had developed sound techniques, including accurate seismic testing and more compact drilling sites, to reduce the impact on the tundra.

Big Oil's Agenda

For the 106th Congress, Big Oil hopes to build on these victories, but will face strong opposition from the administration on key initiatives, such as the push to end sanctions on oil-producing countries such as Azerbaijan and Iran and a reduction in drilling prohibitions on other protected federal lands and on the California coast and portions of the Gulf of Mexico.

While the administration has supported opening the petroleum reserve in Alaska partially to drilling, it continues to strongly oppose proposals to open the state's Arctic National Wildlife Refuge.

In July, Murkowski unsuccessfully floated a trial proposal to permit seismic oil testing in the refuge. He is expected to promote a similar proposal in 1999.

Lawmakers hope to find common ground on other efforts to help operators of marginal domestic wells and exploration companies. Sen. Phil Gramm, R-Texas, said he would help lead efforts by the industry to promote a tax credit for operators of so-called marginal wells. Such wells produce small amounts of oil and may be forced to shut down when prices plummet.

Marginal wells account for a large share of the nation's 570,000 oil wells. The Energy Department estimates that about 16,000 marginal wells are abandoned each year.

Sen. Conrad Burns, R-Mont., said the industry could make a strong case for hardship. But he added that it would face competition from farmers, miners and other interests hard hit by a drop in Asian exports.

"Anybody that's producing a raw product today is not making any money," Burns said in an interview. "Asian flu has turned into Asian cancer." But, he predicted strong support for a proposal to allow royalty payments in oil instead of cash.

The plan would cut overhead for independent drillers. But critics argued it would force the government to wade into the oil storage and marketing business.

The administration has said it wants to phase out much of the government's oil stocks except strategic reserves. It trumpeted the Feb. 5 sale of a 78 percent stake in the Elk Hills Naval Petroleum Reserve for $3.65 billion to Occidental Petroleum Corp. (*1998 Weekly Report, p. 384*)

Merger Fears

While the industry promotes its agenda on Capitol Hill, consumer groups are urging lawmakers to scrutinize oil industry mergers.

The pending acquisition of the Chicago-based Amoco by BP, has fanned concern that the industry will be dominated by a few giant multinational companies.

On Main Street, the primary effect of big mergers could be consolidation of gasoline stations, similar to bank branch closures when banks combine.

"We need to know if consumers will have as many choices in their local communities; if not, will gasoline prices rise as a result?" said Senate Judiciary Antitrust Subcommittee Chairman Mike DeWine, R-Ohio, at a Sept. 22 hearing on the BP-Amoco merger.

"On a local level, we need to evaluate how this consolidation will affect regional refining and retail markets, as well as individual citizens and businesses," he added.

Critics warn giant companies will

A customer pumps gasoline in Warrenton, Va., on Oct. 6. Prices are at a record low.

be harder to regulate and result in even more job losses.

David Freitag, president of The Ohio Petroleum Retailers & Repair Association Inc., told DeWine's subcommittee that mergers could hurt retailers and motorists, too.

"At some point, competitive forces are reduced to the point that the consumer pays more," he said. "Independent dealers like me often feel like the guys who sweep elephant cages at the zoo. We try to do our jobs every day without getting stepped on by the oil giants."

A recent study by the National Petroleum News, an industry newspaper, found one of every five gasoline stations in the United States had closed since 1972. The decline has been linked to tighter environmental restrictions and a shift to bigger gas stations.

Giant oil companies contend that mergers are needed to help them cut costs and finance expensive new operations in remote locations including deep-water drilling sites in the Gulf of Mexico, and in remote countries with limited infrastructures such as Kazakhstan, once part of the former Soviet Union.

Philip K. Verleger, an industry ana-

lyst for The Brattle Group, said an oil mega-merger "would never have been approved" a quarter-century ago amid fears of market consolidation in oil companies and a small group of nations.

With oil now plentiful from diverse sources, he said fears have dwindled and mergers could cut costs and keep prices low.

Calls for Conservation

While Congress examines oil industry mergers, the industry faces potential attacks on other fronts, including proposals aimed at reducing oil consumption through taxes and caps on greenhouse gas emissions.

As part of the energy deregulation debate of 1999, environmental groups are planning to push for new legislation aimed at reducing greenhouse gas emissions by power plants fueled by natural gas, oil and coal.

Some environmentalists and economists have called for an energy tax to increase conservation and reduce reliance on foreign oil. But the idea has generated little support on Capitol Hill, where memories are still fresh of the short-lived Clinton administration proposal in 1993 for an energy tax. Lawmakers are not expected to back a new energy tax aimed at cutting emissions. (*1993 Almanac, p. 120*)

In the absence of such a tax, lawmakers are expected to consider other approaches such as tax incentives for conservation and support for alternative fuel such as ethanol.

The prospect of plentiful, cheap oil has prompted calls from taxpayer groups, environmentalists and budget hawks to curtail tax breaks and subsidies to sell reserve oil to raise revenue.

But industry analysts say the reserve keeps oil prices and OPEC in check. With oil prices low, Murkowski and Jeff Bingaman, D-N.M., argued not for a fire sale but for buying $420 million more oil for the reserve.

"There is nothing temporary about the glut," said Massachusetts Institute of Technology economist Morris Adelman.

"But we should be cautious. Things are unstable in the Mideast. And some unpleasant things could happen. The reserve keeps people from getting jittery, and politicians from getting stampeded," he added. ◆

Hoping To Fend Off Regulation, High-Tech Industry Steps Up Its Campaign Contributions

During a meeting at Microsoft's Redmond, Wash., headquarters in February, GOP Rep. W. J. "Billy" Tauzin of Louisiana offered company Chairman Bill Gates a little friendly advice: The high-tech industry needs to become more involved in the Washington political process if it wants to continue its growth without interference from policy-makers in the nation's capital.

Tauzin, chairman of the House Commerce Committee's telecommunications subcommittee, told Gates, "If you want to avoid infectious regulation, avoid the Federal Communications Commission becoming the Federal Computer Commission. . . . You will have to work with Congress. You have to form a partnership," Tauzin's spokesman Ken Johnson recalled his boss saying during the meeting.

Whether Gates was heeding the call of lawmakers like Tauzin or not, Microsoft, like many high-tech companies, is boosting its involvement in the political process by increasing its lobbying presence and political giving.

So far, Microsoft Corp. has topped the list of computer industry campaign contributors, with $574,099 from Jan. 1, 1997, through June 30, 1998. Its political action committee raised $318,020 in 1998 as of Aug. 31, compared with $59,750 during the entire 1995-96 election cycle. (*Chart, p. 44*)

While the industry still lags far behind more established sectors such as the telecommunications and entertainment industries, computer-related companies have given $5.4 million in total contributions from Jan. 1, 1997, to June 30, 1998. That is double the $2.8 million the industry gave during the same period in 1993 and 1994, the last midterm election cycle, according to the nonpartisan Center for Responsive Politics.

Some high-tech executives say increased giving is an outgrowth of its

AOL's Case says the 105th Congress did a good job dealing with Internet issues.

maturing as an industry.

"We can't afford as an industry to step back and say, 'Ah politics, we're purists. We only do great software,' " said Marcia Sterling, vice president for business development and general counsel for software maker Autodesk Inc. "We have a responsibility to be a voice in political decisions."

Increased attention to all things in Washington appears to have paid off for the industry.

High-tech companies got many of the legislative items they sought during the 105th Congress, including passage of legislation (HR 4328; PL 105-277) to impose a three-year moratorium on new Internet taxes and a measure (HR 2281) to expand copyright protection for digitally produced works such as computer software and compact discs. (*1998 CQ Weekly, p. 2817*)

"Congress made a lot of progress this session," America Online Chairman

Steve Case said Oct. 26 during a speech at the National Press Club in Washington, D.C.

Industry representatives insist that much of their success is due to the better relations they have built with members of Congress and efforts to educate lawmakers about the importance of their industry to the economy.

"I think the most important thing is that we have been effective at communicating why our core policy issues affect the current and future economy," said Robert Holleyman, president of the Business Software Alliance, a Washington-based software industry trade association.

The Valley Goes to Washington

The high-tech industry, particularly the new wave of entrepreneurs coming out of California's Silicon Valley and Seattle, had been criticized for ignoring the nation's capital and the power brokers who make policy on Capitol Hill.

But the industry quickly figured out the need for increasing its presence in Washington, as the number of bills that would have an impact in both positive and negative ways stacked up in the 105th Congress.

Many companies have been increasing their lobbying presence, most notably Microsoft, which is fighting a court battle with the Justice Department over allegations that the company has tried to leverage its overwhelming dominance in computer operating systems to expand into other markets. (*Antitrust, 1998 CQ Weekly, p. 2893*)

But even relatively new companies like Yahoo! Inc., a Santa Clara, Calif.-based Internet search service, are opening Washington offices in an effort to keep better tabs on policies that affect their bottom lines.

"It's just the basic evolution of an industry that's gone from being very sexy and up and coming to having arrived," said William Archey, the American Electronics Association's president. He said industry executives realized they need to be more aggressive.

Even though its political giving also has increased, the industry ranks 31st on a Center for Responsive Politics' comparison of contributors by industry during the current cycle. That is up from 39th in the 1995-96 cycle.

"They have enormous wallets," said Jennifer Shecter, an analyst with the Center for Responsive Politics. But "They're like oil in the Caspian Sea. They're untapped resources."

Ken Glueck, director of legislative affairs for software maker Oracle Corp., said the industry has yet to face a threat from Washington like the ones that have prompted other industries, such as tobacco companies, to give much more substantially.

"We are still an unregulated, unsubsidized industry," he said. "Where's the threat?"

TechNet's Influence

Nonetheless, Oracle belongs to a political action organization known as the Technology Network, which many observers credit with improving the industry's relations and influence in Washington. Its membership is made up of about 100 high-tech executives.

TechNet was launched in 1997 as an organized way for the industry to build closer relationships with policymakers in both parties. It grew out of the industry's efforts to fight off a 1996 California state ballot initiative that would have made it easier for shareholders to file lawsuits against companies in state courts.

Since its creation, TechNet, based in Palo Alto, Calif., has sponsored more than 120 fundraisers and briefings with high-tech executives and Washington policy-makers, including House Speaker Newt Gingrich, R-Ga., and Senate Majority Leader Trent Lott, R-Miss. TechNet has held 17 issue briefings with Vice President Al Gore.

Its political agenda in the 105th Congress was limited to a handful of issues, including passage of the Internet tax moratorium measure, legislation (HR 4328) to increase visas for high-skilled workers such as computer programmers, and a bill (S 1260) aimed at reducing class-action lawsuits against companies whose earnings do not meet expectations. Congress cleared all three measures this year. (*1998 CQ Weekly, pp. 2829, 2827, 2817*)

Top High-Tech Campaign Contributors

Following are the top high-tech contributors for the first 18 months of the 1997-98 election cycle. Donations include "soft money" and contributions from political action committees and individuals.

Company	Amount	Democrats	Republicans
Microsoft Corp.	$574,099 **	$191,403	$381,446
Kleiner Perkins Caufield & Byers*	328,863	219,363	109,500
EDS Corp.	280,646	119,468	161,178
Oracle Corp.	275,663	218,413	57,250
Gateway 2000	174,554	27,500	147,054
Cisco Systems	134,000 **	89,500	43,750
IDX Systems Corp.	133,750 **	122,250	11,000
JD Edwards	118,500	2,500	116,000
Sterling Software Inc.	107,800	0	107,800
CDB Infotek	103,000	0	103,000

* Silicon Valley venture capital firm that invests in high-tech companies
** Total includes contributions to third parties and others

SOURCE: Center for Responsive Politics

Michael Engelhardt, TechNet's vice president of public policy, said the group wants to raise $2 million to $4 million for political candidates this cycle. "As our CEOs have gotten involved in the process, they have recognized . . . [that they] should support politicians that get it," he said.

The group held fundraisers for members such as Sen. Patrick J. Leahy, D-Vt., who helped craft the digital copyright legislation; Rep. Christopher Cox, R-Calif., the House sponsor of the Internet tax moratorium measure; and Rep. Zoe Lofgren, D-Calif., who represents part of Silicon Valley.

Lofgren said she encouraged industry leaders who fought the state shareholder lawsuit ballot initiative to keep their operation up and running.

William M. Burrington, vice president for law and public policy at America Online, a TechNet member based in Dulles, Va., said his company is working with the growing high-tech industry in the Washington-area to become more organized and focused in its political activity.

Among the items industry representatives say they plan to focus on in the 106th Congress are bills to relax export restrictions on products such as encryption and to reduce potential litigation stemming from the Year 2000 computer glitch.

Following Success

Mark Buse, the Senate Commerce, Science and Transportation Committee's policy director, said political contributions have had little to do with the industry's success in Congress.

Many lawmakers are drawn to the industry's causes, he said. "They have an aura of good will, an aura of success," Buse said.

He and others say lawmakers are beginning to acknowledge the growing role the industry is playing in the economy and the increasing number of jobs it is generating nationwide.

"Everyone sort of looks at Silicon Valley" as the center of the high-tech indsutry, said Floyd Kvamme, a member of TechNet's executive committee and a partner in a Silicon Valley venture capital firm, Kleiner, Perkins, Caufield & Byers, which invests only in technology companies. "The fact is there are technology companies springing up all over the country."

Both Republicans and Democrats have worked hard to portray themselves as pro-tech lawmakers.

For example, Gingrich and other Republican leaders held a news conference at the Capitol with high-tech company representatives in early October to tout the GOP's role in moving measures supported by the industry through Congress.

Still, Republicans have received just over half the industry's contributions despite controlling Congress since 1995. Some observers say Democrats were much quicker to court the growing industry.

"To their credit, Bill Clinton and Al Gore were the first two politicians of either party who figured out the kind of political cachet that Silicon Valley" has, said Dan Schnur, TechNet's former Republican political director. "Republicans are trying to catch up." ◆

Government Institutions

The articles in this section provide insight into the workings of the major institutions of American government: Congress, the presidency, the judiciary, and the bureaucracy.

As the first article in this section suggests, the 105th Congress may be remembered as the Monica Lewinsky Congress. Its decision to open a formal inquiry against President Bill Clinton for covering up his affair with the former White House intern overshadowed its legislative accomplishments, which included a balanced budget but little else. Critics blamed Congress's lack of productivity—its failure to develop new tobacco policy, curb managed care abuses, eliminate loopholes in campaign finance laws, or liberalize trade practices—on its preoccupation with the Lewinsky inquiry and on midterm election campaigns, both of which diverted members' attention from pressing legislative business.

At the other end of Pennsylvania Avenue, the Lewinsky inquiry did more than simply hamper productivity. Some scholars asserted that embarrassing revelations about Clinton's relationship with Lewinsky had weakened the institution of the presidency, tipping the balance of power in Congress's favor. Others claimed that the inquiry, fueled by Independent Counsel Kenneth W. Starr's 445-page, sexually explicit report, had seriously compromised presidential authority over the executive branch. The extent to which these claims are valid is examined in a series of articles on the inquiry and the events leading up to the impeachment hearings. Included are profiles of the members of the House Judiciary Committee, charged with deciding whether Clinton committed impeachable offenses; a brief history of the independent counsel law, which, by shifting responsibility for policing the chief executive from Congress to an independent agent, has effectively skirted the system of checks and balances; and a chronology of the inquiry's newsworthy highlights.

The system of checks and balances is at the heart of another article in the section. Congress's antipathy toward the judiciary is nothing new, but its recent attacks on judicial nominees and sitting judges have been so fierce and protracted that former senator Alan K. Simpson and others have assailed them as a threat to the courts' independence and to the constitutionally mandated balance of power. On the other side of the issue, court critics, led by Rep. Tom DeLay, R-Texas, and Sen. John Ashcroft, R-Mo., claim that judges are the real threat to the system of checks and balances. By legislating from the bench, court critics say, activist judges have usurped the power of Congress to make laws. The article places the controversy in historical context, citing the long tradition of court bashing that originated in the early years of the Republic and continues to the present day.

The section concludes with a story about another embattled branch of government—the executive branch. The Census Bureau's decision to use large-scale statistical sampling in the 2000 census has spawned two lawsuits and raised the ire of Republicans in Congress, who disagree with the bureau's claim that sampling will improve accuracy. If the battle over sampling methods seems trifling, consider that census results help to determine how many government benefits are distributed (especially Medicaid funding) and form the basis for redrawing congressional and state districts. The high political stakes ensure that the census fight will continue into 1999 and perhaps right up until April 1, 2000, the day the count is scheduled to begin.

Congress

Decision on launching impeachment proceedings may top modest list of achievements

Clinton Case Overshadows 105th's Legislative Legacy

Leaders sputter at suggestions that this will be known as the 'Monica Congress.' But talk of impeachment has made the public pay special attention to an institution that does not always come off well when thrust into the spotlight. To political scientists, however, legislation still matters.

When the 105th Congress closes for business in the next week or two, its legacy will be neatly divided into two distinct categories. There is Monica, and there is everything else.

This is the Congress that, with an indispensable assist from a booming economy, balanced the budget. It will also be remembered for failing to write a new national tobacco policy, curb abuses by managed health care bureaucrats or plug loopholes in campaign finance laws.

But indisputably, Congress' public image and its place in the civics books will be determined by its historic decision to start down the road toward impeaching a president — not by its legislative record.

With echoes of Watergate in the air, the House is expected to vote during the week of Oct. 5 to open a formal inquiry against President Clinton for covering up his affair with former White House intern Monica Lewinsky.

A resolution to do so should pass easily, as even the White House has virtually conceded defeat. At the same time, congressional leaders from both parties are trying to measure this session by the more traditional yardstick of what it did in the legislative arena. In a preview of this fall's campaign, Democrats are lambasting Congress for giving short shrift to policy in order to hound Clinton. Republicans counter that Clinton's problems have made it far more difficult to broker legislative deals. (*1998 CQ Weekly, p. 2647*)

What is clear is that, since forging the budget deal with Clinton in July

1997, Congress has largely been stuck in neutral. A major effort to combat teenage smoking died in the face of a multimillion-dollar ad campaign by tobacco companies. Proposals to liberalize trade have gone nowhere. Battles over abortion and family planning tied up $17.9 billion in credits for the International Monetary Fund and other foreign policy programs.

In their initial assessments of this session, historians and political scientists have concluded that little has been achieved of major significance, in part because both parties were fine-tuning campaign themes for November. "It is a pretty short list of accomplishments," said David R. Mayhew, a political scientist at Yale University who has for years analyzed the effectiveness of Congress.

Still, there were bipartisan successes. The Senate voted to open the doors of the North Atlantic Treaty Organization, and compromises were forged to significantly increase funding for educational programs for pre-schoolers and college students.

Holding forth in the hallway near his office recently, Senate Majority Leader Trent Lott, R-Miss., pronounced himself satisfied with the record of this session. He extolled last year's balanced-budget deal. And in the next breath he underscored his support for public works programs, lauding this year's budget-busting, $216 billion transportation bill. (*Budget, 1997 Almanac, p. 2-3; transportation, 1998 CQ Weekly, p. 1385*)

'Monica Congress'?

GOP leaders bristle at the notion that Congress' legislative record has been submerged by the Clinton-Lewinsky affair. "The president's behavior brought the Monica Lewinsky issue to the Hill, Congress didn't," said Sen. Larry E. Craig of Idaho, a member of the Republican leadership. "It is grossly

unfair to suggest in the final hours of this session that this is a Monica Congress."

But Republicans and Democrats also assert that, outside of declaring war, impeachment is the gravest task Congress can undertake. The House vote could label this session as the Impeachment Congress, although no final decisions on punishment are likely to be made until the 106th Congress.

More important, the drive toward impeachment will expose members of Congress to intense public scrutiny and political risk. It will take lawmakers from the relative comfort and obscurity of the legislative arena and place them in the position of judging a popular president on his personal behavior, truthfulness and fitness for office — as the whole world, or at least CNN, watches.

Already, the national debate over whether and how Clinton should be punished for his misbehavior has prompted people to pay closer attention to Congress, and many do not like what they see. The widespread public belief that the first phase of this process was handled by Republicans in a partisan manner has resulted in a sharp drop in Congress' approval ratings.

"In every scandal, we're all tarred with the brush," said Arizona Republican Sen. John McCain. "I worry about the effect on the institution, no doubt about it."

Relaxed Schedule

Much still has to get done before the books can be closed on this session. Partisan infighting has snarled a pile of appropriations bills, which is likely to delay adjournment past the Oct. 9 date set by leaders.

In addition to the spending bills, other measures could become law before Congress departs, including a rewrite of banking regulations and a proposal to impose a moratorium on taxes aimed at Internet commerce.

But since January, there have been strong indications that this session would probably not produce much historically significant legislation. The relaxed, election-year schedule set by GOP leaders made it difficult to gain any traction.

From the first of the year through the end of March, Congress' biggest feat was renaming Washington's National Airport after former President Ronald Reagan. (*1998 Weekly Report, p. 317*)

Politicians from both parties struggled to cope with an unfamiliar economic environment, in which decades of debate over the budget deficit have given way to the politics of surplus.

"That's been the biggest historical change this year," said Sen. Joseph I. Lieberman, D-Conn. On Sept. 30, the government ended fiscal 1998 by reporting its first surplus since 1969, which Clinton promptly trumpeted as validation of his economic policies.

Early on, the president placed Republicans on the defensive with his admonition — made during his State of the Union address — to "save Social Security first." Even with the session winding down, Republicans have still not resolved deep internal divisions over whether to use the surplus for tax cuts or heed the president's plea.

Those differences helped doom prospects for last-minute Senate passage of an $80 billion tax-cut package.

Playing Defense

While Republicans have been unable to enact most of their initiatives, they have played a suffocating defense. In June, Senate Republicans — aided immeasurably by Big Tobacco — killed the teen smoking bill. (*1998 CQ Weekly, p. 1669*)

In many ways, that was the most stinging defeat of the year for the administration and Democrats, because Clinton had sought to use higher cigarette taxes to finance new programs, including tax credits for child care expenses.

"It wasn't scandal that killed those initiatives, it was the defeat of the tobacco bill," said Robert D. Reischauer, a senior fellow at the Brookings Institution.

Republicans also have successfully held up Democrat-backed bills to overhaul the campaign finance system and impose new restrictions on managed care plans. Adamant GOP opposition

What Congress did, clockwise from top: Leaders celebrated when Clinton signed a bill to balance the budget in 1997; opening NATO membership let new nations join; the Starr report on Clinton ignited an impeachment inquiry; Rep. Bud Shuster led the fight for more spending on federal highway and transportation programs.

had long ago rendered those measures — which both passed the House in some form — as legislative long shots.

Once the Lewinsky scandal exploded anew in August — after the president's unprecedented testimony before a federal grand jury — GOP senators had an easier time shelving the two bills. Mc-

Cain, who cosponsored the campaign finance bill with Russell D. Feingold, D-Wis., marveled at how little attention last month's Senate debate on that issue garnered.

"It became a perfunctory exercise," he said. "It would have been a far, far different debate."

Beyond the impact of the scandal, both parties learned this year just how difficult it is to galvanize public opinion at a time of economic prosperity.

Throughout the summer, Democrats shifted their strategy and tactics to try to gain a political foothold. After the tobacco bill went down, they focused on education and managed care. They also championed measures to boost aid for drought-stricken farmers.

What Congress didn't do, clockwise from top: Enact Clinton's 'patients' bill of rights' or other legislation to regulate managed care; put tough curbs on the cigarette industry over the objections of tobacco-state lawmakers such as Rep. Howard Coble, R-N.C.; renew trade powers for the president; pass campaign finance laws after investigations in the House headed by Dan Burton, R-Ind., and in the Senate, where Buddhist nuns were called to testify.

The elections will largely determine whether they struck a chord with voters, but Republicans for the most part did not feel enough heat to compromise.

Yet Republicans found that the public, outside of the party's base of conservative activists, was not clamoring for tax cuts, particularly if they are financed with part of the surplus.

"The public likes a lot of these things," Lieberman said. "But even if the Clinton-Lewinsky scandal hadn't emerged, I doubt if much would have gotten through. Life is just so good for most people right now."

First Step

As lobbyists and staffers jammed into the Capitol's first floor Sept. 28 to monitor the progress of conference committees meeting on spending bills, one might never have believed that Congress was on the brink of a historic impeachment debate.

But while deals were being cut over farm commodities and other issues, the House Judiciary Committee was closeted in the Rayburn Building — with a bank of cameras standing outside — debating impeachment procedures.

Lawmakers know that, with the House vote looming, they are about to make history. But the timing of the vote at the end of the session allows them to cast it as a single, discrete act — just the initial step in what could be a long process.

Still, it will be a process in which individual lawmakers and the institution itself will be on the spot. The electoral fallout could cost some Democrats their jobs in November.

Many Republicans, fearing a political backlash if the proceedings are seen as partisan, are counting heavily on Judiciary Committee Chairman Henry J. Hyde, R-Ill., to muffle the raucous ideology on his committee.

In the end, this can be a chance for Congress to distinguish itself at a time of crisis, as during its dignified and uplifting debate over going to war against Iraq in 1991. (*1991 Almanac, p. 437*)

But often when the spotlight has been turned on it, as with the Clarence Thomas confirmation hearings in 1991, and the government shutdown of 1995-1996, Congress has embarrassed itself. If it ends up focusing on the intimate details of Clinton's sex life or tries to run a still-popular president out of office, Congress may again become the object of national derision. ◆

Independent counsel's inquiry could affect the very nature of government

Starr Power: What the Probe Means for the Presidency

President Clinton's court setbacks on issues of privilege have caused legal scholars to conclude that the balance of power is tipping toward Congress. The outcome could be dramatic. But the commotion surrounding this long-anticipated constitutional crisis disguises the remarkable changes that have already occurred in our system of government as a result of the Clinton investigation.

As President Clinton prepared for his scheduled Aug. 17 grand jury testimony about his relationship with Monica S. Lewinsky, the nation and Congress were beginning to focus on the implications of possible impeachment hearings.

The United States, many constitutional experts are concluding, now has a somewhat different form of government than it did when Independent Counsel Kenneth W. Starr embarked on his investigation four years ago. Power has been shifted away from the presidency to the Congress, the authority of presidents over the executive branch has been lessened and new areas of case law have been created where negotiations and Founding Fathers' precepts of checks and balances were sufficient before.

This spring and summer, courts in Washington and Arkansas have adjudicated questions of executive privilege, attorney-client privilege and "protective function" privilege involving the president's bodyguards. The loser in almost all of these rulings has been Clinton; the winner has been Starr.

The rulings were triggered by subpoenas not from a congressional committee but from Starr's grand juries. But if history is any guide, they will have a significant impact on the relationship between the executive and legislative branches.

While searching for Clinton's vulnerabilities in the course of the investigation, Starr has, in essence, found the vulnerabilities of the presidency that can be exploited by the Congress.

The Supreme Court's first, and only, significant foray into the area of executive privilege, *United States v. Nixon,* not only forced the release of secret White House tapes in the Watergate case, it emboldened future Congresses to issue subpoenas to future administrations. The most recent rulings are expected to stimulate a similar response.

"Rulings against the president like these are catnip to congressional investigators," said Charles Tiefer, law professor at the University of Baltimore and a former Democratic House counsel. "Their claws will be out to play with a weakened presidential mouse."

Regardless of whether the fault for this turn of events belongs to Starr himself, to the independent counsel statute (PL 103-270) or to a recalcitrant president — an issue that is hotly disputed among lawyers and partisans — there is widespread agreement that this is not a healthy development. It has occurred without debate or forethought.

"So much of this is terra incognita," said A.E. Dick Howard, law professor at the University of Virginia. "We're creating all this precedent, and clumsily, I'm afraid."

"This is certainly going to have a long-term impact," said Theodore B. Olson, a senior Justice Department official under President Ronald Reagan.

Seeing Silver Lining

To be sure, some conservatives see a silver lining in the president's troubles — one with implications that go far beyond the immediate future of the Clinton presidency.

Presidents in general have grown too powerful, and we expect too much out of them, says Robert H. Bork, former appellate judge, Supreme Court nominee and Nixon administration official, whose firing of special prosecutor Archibald Cox in 1973 was cited by Democrats as the rationale for creating independent counsels in 1978.

Bork said the country would be well-served by a president more along the lines of what the late Sen. Paul Tsongas, D-Mass. (1979-1985) proposed during his 1992 presidential bid. When asked how he was going to solve the nation's problems, he often admonished people that he was neither a father figure nor a national Santa Claus.

"This begins to demystify the presidency, and I'm not sure that's all bad," Bork said.

But many presidential observers insist that an inflated presidency has hardly been a problem in the post-Watergate years. In fact, there is growing sentiment that Congress should take steps to enhance the legal privileges of the presidency in the wake of Starr's probe.

Senate Judiciary Committee Chairman Orrin G. Hatch, R-Utah, for example, plans to examine whether Congress should create by statute a protective-function privilege such as the one that the Clinton White House failed to prove in court. Other privileges will probably be examined as well.

Political Disputes and the Courts

Perhaps as important as the nature of the court rulings that brought about these changes is the mere fact that there were any rulings at all. The new precedents remove flexibility and discourage negotiated agreements, legal experts say. They create ambiguities, rigidity and the potential for further rulings. They erode something known as the "political question doctrine," a body of jurisprudence that says courts

NEWSMAKERS PHOTO / RANDALL LINKS

should stay out of political disputes.

In a case known as *United States v. The House of Representatives of the United States*, the Reagan administration sought in 1982 to clarify and bolster the doctrine of executive privilege in light of a congressional subpoena of environmental policy documents.

U.S. District Court Judge John Lewis Smith Jr. would have none of it. The case, he concluded, demanded a political accommodation rather than a new body of case law: "Courts have a duty to avoid unnecessarily deciding constitutional issues."

But 16 years later, the Starr investigation has forced the courts to do precisely what Smith was trying to avoid: rule on what privileges (exemptions from subpoenas) the president and his aides are entitled to.

Without the institution of the independent counsel, which has been enacted in four different incarnations since 1978, it is unlikely any of these issues would have been raised.

Nevertheless, the impact comes as something of a surprise to many members of Congress who favored the law. Until very recently, only a handful of conservative thinkers, such as Bork, were convinced that the inde-

pendent counsel posed dangers for the presidency.

Unlike conventional prosecutors, independent counsels have unlimited resources and an easy opportunity to expand their probe in any direction they see potential wrongdoing. Independent counsels can pursue any path, as long as they bring their evidence to Congress for impeachment consideration.

Presidents are not afforded the privileges and protections that members of Congress have. Members, for instance, are protected by the "speech and debate" clause of the Constitution from prosecution or subpoenas for anything they say in official proceedings. And courts have given them wide latitude in resisting grand jury subpoenas.

Presidents are immune from civil cases connected to their official acts as president, as a result of the 1982 *Nixon v. Fitzgerald* ruling. And in criminal cases, presidents have been protected by their control of the branch of government that prosecutes, at the federal level at least, and by the belief among most constitutional experts that a sitting president cannot be indicted, a proposition that has

Secret Service agents who protect President Clinton were compelled to testify before a grand jury on July 21, after a White House claim of "protective privilege" was rejected by the court.

Bork, Longtime Critic of Counsels, Takes a New Contrarian Stand

No one has made more of a career out of criticizing the concept of independent counsels than Robert H. Bork, the former judge, Solicitor General and unsuccessful nominee to the Supreme Court.

His firing of special prosecutor Archibald Cox in 1973 is credited (or blamed) for prompting the creation of the statute, first passed in 1978 and reauthorized three times since. His message has been that he acted appropriately, the Justice Department is capable of handling allegations of administration wrongdoing and the statute is unconstitutional on grounds of separation of powers.

Some of his predictions about independent counsels have bordered on prescient. In a 1993 article in Commentary magazine, for instance, he said the statute encourages independent counsels to bring cases that ordinary prosecutors would not.

That is precisely what Independent Counsel Kenneth W. Starr's detractors say he has done by launching a criminal probe into perjury charges stemming from a non-relevant portion of a civil case that was dismissed.

With all that has transpired in the probe of the president by Starr, one might think Bork would feel a sense of vindication, perhaps animated with glee at seeing the party that created the independent counsel law forced to live with its consequences.

Actually, that is not Bork's response. Ever the iconoclast, he is now rethinking his opposition to the statute. "I was against the statute when it was popular," he said. "Now that it is unpopular, I am beginning to go the other way."

What has changed his mind is Attorney General Janet Reno's decision, so far at least, not to appoint an eighth independent counsel during her tenure, this one to probe alleged campaign finance abuses by the Clinton-Gore re-election team in 1996. This has shattered Bork's confidence that the Justice Department

"I was against the statute when it was popular," says former judge Robert Bork. "Now that it is unpopular, I am beginning to go the other way."

can be counted on.

He has not firmly come down in the camp of supporters of the statute yet, but Bork says he is no longer sure what he thinks. "This leaves me in a quandary," he said.

In 1993, Bork's assertion that independent counsels might go further than ordinary prosecutors was met with great umbrage by defenders of the statute. "That remarkable statement is a sweeping denigration of all past and future independent counsels," said James C. McKay.

McKay's indignation may have stemmed from the great restraint he showed as an independent counsel. He declined to indict Edwin Meese III, attorney general during the Reagan administration, even though the top two Reagan-appointed officials in the Justice Department's criminal division were pushing for it.

In 1993, Bork noted that Lawrence E. Walsh, the independent counsel who investigated the Iran-contra matter, began poking into the sex lives of his targets and witnesses when other tactics got him nowhere. "What conceivable relevance could that infor-

mation have?" he wondered.

Today, he is not troubled by the apparent centrality of President Clinton's sex life in Starr's investigation. The sex would be inexorably linked with whatever perjury or obstruction of justice presentation he might make to Congress, he said.

This type of reassessment of the independent counsel statute has been fairly common. As the circumstances, and control of the White House have changed, so have a number of minds. Cox and Senate Judiciary Committee Chairman Orrin G. Hatch, R-Utah, have come fairly close to swapping positions. Cox says the law needs major revisions, while Hatch, like Bork, is warming to it.

Democratic lawmakers who played a major role in one or more of the statute's reauthorizations say they are shocked at how it is being used now and how frequently it is being invoked.

Republicans ask why Democrats were not so shocked at the treatment of several aides to President Ronald Reagan — the election-eve indictment of former Defense Secretary Casper W. Weinberger in 1992, the extraordinary pressure brought down on Assistant Secretary of State Elliot Abrams, or the essentially political dispute that formed the core of the investigation of Justice Department aide Theodore B. Olson.

In addition to the people who have changed positions are those who maintain their original stance but do not let that get in the way of their views on the current state of affairs.

Olson, for instance, who took his opposition to the statute all the way to the Supreme Court in 1988, still advocates its total repeal. But he is also a big fan and personal friend of Starr, and a critic of Clinton.

As long as the statute is on the books, he said, it should be enforced. And yes, he said, perjury in a civil case is a potentially impeachable offense.

never been tested.

In Starr, however, Clinton faces a prosecutor over whom he has no control, and who is not concerned by lack of precedent on whether a president can be indicted.

Furthermore, if, as anticipated, Starr's report to Congress is based on Clinton's actions in connection with Paula Jones' sexual harassment suit (whether Clinton lied under oath about his relationship with Lewinsky or encouraged others to do so), the report would be tied to the president's only traditional legal vulnerability short of impeachment — a civil case not related to his official duties.

Privilege Setbacks

So far, Clinton's efforts to fend off Starr through assertions of privilege have been a dismal failure. His claims of executive privilege have gained no traction, having been rejected by U.S. District Court Judge Norma Holloway Johnson.

Executive privilege is an assertion that high officials of the executive branch need to be able to hold candid conversations — without fear of having to divulge their content — to do their job effectively.

Clinton has done only slightly better in the courts on attorney-client privilege, a protection recognized in common law as far back as Elizabethan England, and "protective function" privilege, something never formally articulated until Starr subpoenaed White House Secret Service agents.

The protective function privilege, and attorney-client privilege as it applies to government lawyers, have both been rejected at the appellate level. Clinton's only real victory to date has been a Supreme Court ruling that former White House aide Vincent W. Foster Jr.'s discussions with his private attorney can remain confidential after his death. The Foster issue, however, dates to an earlier part of Starr's probe and is unrelated to the Lewinsky matter.

The vulnerabilities of the presidency Starr has uncovered will surely arise again the next time there is a criminal investigation, experts say. But they quickly add that the larger impact of these court rulings will be on the president's authority over his own executive branch, and over his ability to resist subpoenas from Congress.

The *United States v. Nixon* ruling

on executive privilege, which both defined and limited the president's executive privilege, helped spawn a generation of congressional probes into administrations. Even though the ruling's principal limitation on executive privilege pertained to providing relevant facts for criminal trials rather than congressional inquests, Tiefer argues that subsequent Congresses have gained leverage from the ruling merely by asserting that criminal misconduct is a central focus of their inquiries.

The probe of intelligence agencies by Sen. Frank Church, D-Idaho (1957-81), in the 1970s was an early example of this, he argues. Since then the practice has gained momentum. A pre-Nixon Congress probably would not have so aggressively pursued Reagan's Environmental Protection Agency administrator, Anne M. Burford, to the point of citing her for contempt of Congress when she refused to comply with a subpoena. And a pre-Nixon Congress probably would not have been in the state of perpetual conflict with the White House that has typified the last three years.

The new rulings offer Congress more avenues for taking on the president. Tiefer predicts they will encourage Congresses to dig deeper into the inner workings of the White House, demanding to know of events on an hour-by-hour, even minute-by-minute basis.

"Congressional committees used to have to build a substantial case of presidential involvement in wrongdoing

before they could get much leverage on the White House," Tiefer said. "With Ken Starr's legacy, congressional committees will have a strong club with which to beat the president."

Rulings Not Questioned

Legal scholars offer relatively little criticism of the actual court rulings. The executive and protective-function privilege rulings in particular strike many experts as persuasive. But taken together, they raise serious issues.

"Each ruling may be correct," said Howard. "But it seems to me that the cumulative effect of these decisions makes it increasingly difficult for the president to operate in a separation of powers context."

In the same way, the rulings foreshadow more difficulty for the president as he tries to function within his own branch. If a president cannot count on candid advice from his advisers, legal experts say, he probably will have a harder time asserting control of the vast executive branch.

Presidents routinely use their most trusted White House advisers to imbue the federal bureaucracy with their policy objectives. They do this through centralization of the decision-making process and control of the flow of information, among other things. A hamstrung White House would presumably mean more decisions could be made further down the chain of command, sometimes by bureaucrats or officers less than sympathetic to the goals of the administration.

Independent Counsel Kenneth W. Starr's determination to litigate subpoenas for White House material has precipitated what many think is a shift in the balance of power.

To some degree, Clinton could have avoided the legal downside of this investigation of the presidency by not challenging subpoenas so often. But by giving in to the demands of Starr and Congress, he has set precedents, as well.

No president has ever agreed to directly answer a prosecutor's questions in response to a subpoena, as Clinton was scheduled to do Aug. 17. No president has complied with so many congressional subpoenas — the result of inquiries into the 1994 Whitewater land deal and many other allegations.

If presidential advisers know they can be forced to testify — either as a result of a court order, or because a president does not have the power to stand up to a congressional subpoena — they may be more inhibited in what they say in the future, Clinton's lawyers say.

Rulings Spawn Rigidity

Over and above the restrictive nature of the court rulings against Clinton in this case is the question of whether the country would be better off without rulings of any kind. Most legal experts argue that presidential privileges, while raised here in the context of a criminal case, are really more of a separation-of-powers issue.

As such, according to legal experts, it would have been best if they had been left undecided and constantly argued over by the legislative and executive branches as they try to advance their policy and political agendas. The court-established precedents create a kind of rigidity and a necessity for further rulings. "It was kind of unhealthy to have these things undecided," said Cass Sunstein, law professor at the University of Chicago.

Had these subpoenas been brought by a congressional committee, the courts probably would have been able to follow the example of Judge Smith and stay out. But since they were brought by a grand jury, the courts have been forced to hand down rulings formerly thought to be in the realm of the political question doctrine.

Not only is it unfortunate that the courts are being drawn into these questions, said Sunstein, but it is equally troubling that they are being pulled in-

to such a highly charged political environment. Sunstein notes that some of the rulings have split along party lines, with the judges appointed by Democrats favoring Clinton and those appointed by Republicans forming majority opinions limiting his options.

While Sunstein is not saying the rulings are necessarily partisan, he is worried about the inferences that could be drawn from them. "You don't even want the appearance of that," he said.

Conservatives and liberals differ on who is to blame for these circumstances.

Liberals tend to blame Starr for what they consider to be an overzealous prosecution. Since he began his investigation of the Ozark Mountains land deal known as Whitewater, he has cut a fairly wide swath through Arkansas, turning upside down the lives and careers of people only remotely connected with Clinton. Yet he has turned up little or nothing to prosecute.

Only after three and a half years of looking and changing focus many times did he stumble upon a possible crime in the Paula Jones case. And even this — possible perjury in a portion of a deposition that is not material in a civil case that has been dismissed — strikes many critics as a something of an overreach in prosecution.

"This is horrifying conduct," said Larry Pozner, president of the National Association of Criminal Defense Lawyers, referring to the ever-widening scope of the Starr probe. "No matter what side of the aisle you sit on."

Olson and other conservatives, meanwhile, argue that the problem lies not with Starr, who is merely doing the job he was hired to do, but in Clinton's response. Olson said none of this would have happened had the Clinton White House not insisted on waging war against the independent counsel's office.

And, of course, if the evidence shows that he did have an affair with former intern Monica S. Lewinsky and did perjure himself, conservatives will be able to make the case that none of this would have happened

had the president told the truth or behaved more responsibly in the first place.

Conservatives also point to a kind of moral diminution of the presidency that may be at least as important as the legal diminution since it extends well beyond official Washington.

"This whole thing is so damaging," Olson said. If Starr finds the president lied, under oath and in front of the American people, "it would be hard to explain to your children how important it is to tell the truth."

Congress Is Wary

Even members of Congress who might benefit from the legal and moral diminution of the presidency seem wary of recent developments. The House voted Aug. 6 to place new ethical guidelines on all federal prosecutors, including independent counsels, a sign that many lawmakers are growing wary of the powers of prosecutors. (*1998 CQ Weekly, p. 2176*)

And when the independent counsel statute comes up next year for reauthorization, few Republicans or Democrats are likely to defend it in its current form. The main debate will be between those who want to scale it back dramatically and those who want to eliminate it outright.

For many constitutional experts, the Starr probe has been a lesson on the delicate balance between the branches of government that will be discussed for many years to come.

Howard argues that the independent counsel is the wrong institution, at the wrong time, in the wrong place. He suggests the remedies put in place to prevent a repeat of the abuses by the Nixon White House may not be what is needed today.

He makes an analogy between the independent counsel's pursuit of the president and the tendency of some military officers and diplomats who assume the current war will be like the previous one.

"There is something like that happening in the Clinton-Starr context," he said. "We remember the imperial presidency of 25 years ago. We remember an administration that was genuinely abusive of power." ◆

As it takes up the Starr report, Congress is sure to find its own judgment on trial

The Weighty Why and How Of Punishing a President

Quick Contents

Against the backdrop of a national dialogue on crime, punishment, sin and redemption, Congress now faces the huge responsibility of finding a penalty appropriate to the misdeed. Because the consequences of a mistake would be profound, few people expect a quick answer.

Matching a suitable punishment with a given crime has been something of a preoccupation among the leading lights of Western thought. German philosopher Georg W. F. Hegel once observed: "Injustice is done at once if there is one lash too many, or one dollar or one cent, one week in prison or one day, too many or too few."

Hegel, of course, was not addressing the indiscretions of national leaders, and the punishment of horsewhipping is not one Congress is likely to contemplate for President Clinton. But his observation about the importance of proportionality has a saliency today as Congress begins its inquiry into Clinton's affair with former White House intern Monica Lewinsky and his accompanying lies.

Now that it has received what Independent Counsel Kenneth W. Starr said may be evidence of four impeachable offenses — perjury, obstruction of justice, witness tampering and abuse of power — the House is about to begin a national dialogue on crime and punishment. The importance of the deliberations is every bit as great for Congress and the nation as for Clinton. If Congress gets it wrong, exacting a penalty that is seen as either too lenient or too severe, the consequences will be profound. It will set a precedent for future presidents and future Congresses, go down as a black mark in American history, and precipitate an angry and emotional response from the citizenry.

"Their wrath will fall upon those who jump to judgment prematurely," Sen. Robert C. Byrd, D-W.Va., cautioned in a Sept. 9 floor speech. *(Byrd, p. 56)*

No one knows how soon Clinton's punishment will be determined, but the debate could easily linger into next year. After considering the evidence against Clinton, members on both sides of the aisle could coalesce around a belief that Clinton should be — must be — impeached and expelled from office if he does not resign.

The nation went through this process in 1974, and the system showed how it can work. The vice president becomes president and declares that our national nightmare is over — or words to that effect — and the na-

tion adjusts. The St. Louis Cardinals' Mark McGwire finishes the season with 70 home runs. Some cuddly new toy becomes the latest rage at Christmas. Life goes on.

Conversely, there could be a consensus around some lesser punishment: censure or reprimand, perhaps negotiated with the White House in a sort of presidential plea bargain. Congress may even decide that Clinton needs a year of round-the-clock humiliation by talk show discourse on the nature of his sexual indiscretions. It could sentence him to time served.

But such a consensus resolution may not be in the cards. At least as likely is a long and drawn-out process — what Byrd referred to as "a yawning abyss." Even when completed, it may leave bitterness and a sense that justice was not completely served.

A lengthy and cumbersome process without a clear resolution could result if the assertions in the report fall into the many gray areas of contemporary thinking on impeachment. There is virtually no precedent for consideration of such a report and little guidance from the Constitution.

Within minutes of the delivery of Starr's report Sept. 9, the principle that reasonable people can disagree was evident as Democrats and Republicans differed over the rules governing release of the report and the powers the Judiciary Committee will have in conducting its inquiry. *(1998 CQ Weekly, p. 2391)*

No matter what the outcome, it is hard to imagine a complete sense of closure in the current political climate. If Clinton survives the episode and continues to serve with or without formal rebuke, his sternest critics will no doubt argue that justice was not served and that the nation's highest officeholder had gotten away with breaking laws and bringing shame to the presidency.

On the other hand, if he is forced out of office — either by resignation or impeachment and conviction — such treatment will likely leave a reservoir of bitterness among his supporters. Even if they conclude that he has to go, they will always reserve a special enmity for Starr.

Luck of the Draw

The four areas of possible impeachment in the report stem from the Monica Lewinsky affair, which Starr did not even get to until three years into his investigation. He was originally charged with examining the Whitewater land dealings Clinton engaged in while governor of Arkansas. Starr expanded his investigation to include the suicide of White House lawyer Vincent W. Foster Jr., the "travelgate" and "filegate" episodes, and several other issues.

This strikes many prosecutors — including some who have served as independent counsels in the past — as an overly broad probe.

Because of the breadth and duration of Starr's inquiry, Clinton supporters could argue that the fate of his presidency was determined by the personality of the person who happened to be selected as independent counsel. If Clinton's wounds were entirely self-inflicted, the decision to expose them was not.

Clinton lawyer David Kendall said the charges contained in report were embarrassing to the president, but fell far short of impeachable offenses.

"This private mistake does not amount to an impeachable action. A relationship outside one's marriage is wrong — and the president admits that," Kendall told reporters Sept. 11.

AP PHOTO / SCOTT APPLEWHITE

Clinton, shown Sept. 10 at a speech to science and technology students, had spent part of the day apologizing to Democratic lawmakers, members of his cabinet and others for the Lewinsky episode.

'Reaping the Whirlwind'

Excerpts of the Sept. 9 floor speech of Sen. Robert C. Byrd, D-W.Va.:

"The pressure on the Congress is escalating. Talk of impeachment is in the air, along with suggestions of resolutions of reprimand and censure. Some have even suggested that we ought to get on with impeachment and get this thing behind us.

"There had to come a time sooner or later when the boil would be lanced. The problem is that with the lancing a hemorrhaging may be only one of those continuing symptoms of an even greater lancing, perhaps even an amputation, that still lurks in the shadows up ahead.

"There is no question but that the president himself has sown the wind and he is reaping the whirlwind. His televised speech of Aug. 17 heaped hot coals upon himself — coals causing wounds that continue to inflame and burn ever more deeply. Coming as the speech did so soon after the president's appearance before the grand jury, his words were ill-timed, ill-formed and ill-advised. . . .

"In this instance, the president himself has by his own actions and his own words thrown the first stone at himself, and thus, made himself vulnerable to the stoning by others.

"What a sorrowful spectacle!

"To maintain that presidents have private lives is, of course, not to be denied. But the Oval Office of the White House is not a private office. It is where much of the business of the nation is conducted daily. . . .

Byrd (shown June 25), an authority on congressional history, called for calm.

"Former President Nixon, in an earlier tragedy for the nation and for all of us who were here and lived through it, tried the same thing — delay, delay, delay and counterattack, attack, attack. . . . Time seems to be turning backwards in its flight. And many of the mistakes that President Nixon made are being made all over again.

"As we find ourselves being brought nearer and nearer, as it would seem, to a yawning abyss, I urge that we all step back, and give ourselves and the country a little pause in which to reflect and meditate before we cast ourselves headlong over the precipice. To say we ought to get on with impeachment and get this thing behind us is a bold thing to say. But boldness to the point of cavalierness can come back to haunt us. . . .

"I also suggest that putting this thing behind us is not going to be an easy thing to do. If Congress reaches that stage of voting on articles of impeachment, it is going to be a traumatic experience for all of us, both here in this city and throughout the country. . . .

"There is a constitutional process in place. We should let it work. It is my suggestion that everyone should exercise some self-restraint against calling for impeachment or censure or for the president's resignation. Who knows? I may do that before it's all over. But not now. . . .

"Let us, as senators, remember that if the House ultimately votes to impeach this president, then we all should be careful not to attempt to influence the other body — and when I say we all, I have reference to ourselves and to the executive branch and to the media. . . .

"We must not compromise any final decision by rushing to judgment in advance. I trust that we all will weigh carefully in our own minds and hearts the possible consequences to the nation of our words and actions and judgments if that duty ultimately should beckon us. . . .

"And so I respectfully urge everyone in this town to calm down for a little while and contemplate with seriousness the impact that our actions may have on the well-being of the nation — your children, my grandchildren, our children, our grandchildren — and the paralysis we may be spawning if we continue to be mesmerized with each new rumor and each new titillating whisper."

"It is not a high crime or misdemeanor."

In trying to resolve what type of punishment is suitable for Clinton, Congress has virtually no road map, especially when it comes to dealing with the personal indiscretions of a president.

High Crimes, Misdemeanors?

This would be only the third time impeachment has been seriously considered. In 1868, President Andrew Johnson was impeached on highly politicized charges. He avoided conviction in the Senate by one vote. In 1974, after the House Judiciary Committee voted in favor of impeaching him, President Richard M. Nixon resigned. Neither involved questions of personal conduct.

The Constitution hands the power to impeach to the House and to convict to the Senate — acknowledgements that the process of removing the nation's highest elected official from office is more political than legal.

Other than assigning the task to Congress, the Constitution gives little guidance on what might constitute impeachable offenses. Article II, Section 4 lists "treason, bribery, or other high crimes and misdemeanors."

Just what constitutes these offenses is an open question. Scholars are divided between those who believe the phrase applies only to official conduct and those who would include any serious criminality evidenced by the breaking of existing law. Alexander Hamilton, in Federalist Paper No. 65, gave what might be the broadest definition: "violation of some public trust."

In its 1974 Watergate inquiry, the House Judiciary Committee set a precedent that criminality alone is not grounds for impeachment. The offense must constitute a serious abuse of power. (*1974 Almanac, p. 903*)

That committee adopted three articles of impeachment, for obstruction of justice, abuse of power and contempt of Congress. Two other articles were rejected because they did not fit the committee's definition of impeachable offenses. One dealt with Nixon's conduct of the Vietnam War and was rejected on the grounds that it amounted to a policy dispute with partisan overtones. A second dealt with tax evasion. The committee decided that although it was an indictable crime, it was not a serious abuse of power.

In reaching this conclusion, the committee drew on previous impeachment resolutions on Johnson and other federal officials. A report compiled by the committee noted that prior impeachments "placed little emphasis on criminal conduct." It went on to conclude that: "In an impeachment proceeding, a President is called to account for abusing powers that only a President possesses."

This precedent could generate considerable debate about Clinton's set of circumstances. Any lying he may have engaged in during the Paula Jones deposition or his own appearance before Starr's grand jury Aug. 17 could be dismissed by some as non-impeachable offenses, even if they concluded that criminality occurred.

For that matter, some members might argue that Starr's entire 18 boxes of documents refer to nothing more than unofficial (though perhaps illegal) attempts to prevent embarrassing private conduct from being made public.

Barney Frank, D-Mass., the second-ranking Democrat on the committee, is the leading proponent of the private-conduct argument. He says the appropriate response for behavior like Clinton's is a rejection by voters. Since Clinton is prohibited by the Constitution from seeking a third term, Frank is afraid the voters may turn to impeachment as their only option.

"I'm afraid people will fight to impeach him to satisfy" their desire to punish him for his conduct, said Frank. "That's not what impeachment is for."

Other House members might conclude that this precedent is too limiting; that the president is sworn to uphold the Constitution, and breaking laws is not consistent with that mission. Bill McCollum of Florida, for instance, is one of many Republicans in recent days to insist that he is not willing to cavalierly dismiss lying in a civil deposition as a minor offense.

Speaker Newt Gingrich, R-Ga., appeared to take something of a middle road, saying that criminality alone was sufficient grounds for impeachment, but only if it was widespread. In late August, he said Congress would look for "a pattern of felonies," not merely a "human mistake."

Alternatives to Impeachment

Because of the ambiguities of impeachment doctrine, some members, particularly in the Senate, have suggested the use of a resolution of censure or reprimand. Sens. Robert F. Bennett, R-Utah, and Joseph I. Lieberman, D-Conn., have discussed censure with their colleagues, although both say it is premature to publicly discuss it.

This approach has allure in the Senate, where, unlike an impeachment, it could be done without waiting for the House. It would also hold attraction for Democrats looking for a way to protect their president from an impeachment debacle. Sen. Barbara Boxer, D-Calif., said Sept. 9 that a resolution of censure could pass the Senate unanimously.

Here, too, there is little guidance from history. Censure and reprimand are both primarily vehicles for punishing errant members of Congress. The two vary somewhat in severity and have different functions in the two chambers. Censure is considered the stricter of the two, although the distinction has little relevance to a president. In the House, censure means losing any leadership post or committee or subcommittee chairmanship. It also denies the member from formally responding to the charge on the floor. In the Senate, a reprimand can be voted on by a single committee — normally the Ethics Committee — and delivered to the full chamber as a fait accompli. A censure must be voted on by all senators.

The only precedent for presidential censure was the case of Andrew Jackson, who was censured by the Senate in 1834. The move was blatantly political, was denounced by Jackson, and was reversed after Jackson's Democrats regained the majority. (*1998 CQ Weekly, p. 566*)

What a censure would mean for Clinton is an open question. Though it contains no sanction other than a verbal rebuke, it is not meaningless.

"It is a serious and emphatic expression of condemnation and disapproval," said Byrd. "Censure by the Congress is a major blot on the record and reputation of a public official."

Indeed, it is possible that censure might not allow Clinton to put his troubles behind him but could precipitate demand for his resignation, followed by massive desertion.

"It depends on the context and tone of the censure message. If it were strongly worded and expressed a total lack of confidence, that would really disable the president," said Thomas Sargentich, law professor at American University. "If, on the other hand, a censure motion were written by friends, saying we really disapprove of your behavior, but we still want to work with you, that is a different ballgame."

For that reason, Clinton is already receiving some unsolicited advice that he would be best advised to try to negotiate some kind of language, perhaps even agreeing to extra conditions, such as paying a fine or restitution.

"If there is a political plea bargain out there he can strike with the Republicans — short of selling out the party and the presidency — he ought to grab at it," said John Pavia, adjunct professor of law at Quinnipiac College in Hamden, Conn. ◆

Starr Report Hits Capitol Hill, Drawing Outrage and Trepidation

As independent counsel presents 11 possible grounds for impeachment, lawmakers look homeward for guidance

For the benefit of cameras, Capitol police officers transfer file boxes containing the independent counsel's report from the back of one vehicle to another Sept. 9 on the east side of the Capitol, setting off a scramble to react and release portions.

Lawmakers reacted to the release of the long-anticipated report detailing President Clinton's illicit relationship with Monica Lewinsky with disgust, shock, outrage — and a wary eye to public opinion.

The documents from Independent Counsel Kenneth W. Starr, containing lurid details of White House liaisons, charged Clinton with perjury, obstruction of justice, witness tampering and abusing the power of his office in an effort to cover up an extramarital affair with the former intern.

It leveled 11 specific charges of wrongdoing against Clinton, including lying under oath, working with Lewinsky to conceal information about their relationship, and attempting to improperly influence the grand jury testimony of his personal secretary, Betty Currie.

In an effort to prove the president was untruthful when he testified in a civil deposition that he had never had sex with Lewinsky, Starr outlined their relationship at a level more suited to a pulp novel than a sober, legal report.

Based on testimony from Lewinsky, Starr said the former intern performed oral sex on the president nine times. Among the encounters were instances when Clinton was talking on the telephone to House members — a gesture of disrespect toward Congress that is not likely to go over well.

One of those involved, Sonny Callahan, R-Ala., chairman of the Appropriations Foreign Operations Subcommittee, said he could recall talking to the president about the deployment of U.S. troops in Bosnia. "If it is true that my name is somehow mentioned in this report, I can say unequivocally and without hesitation that I had no knowledge I was sharing the president's time or attention with anyone else," he said in a statement.

Asserting that the president knowingly and willingly violated the law and encouraged others to do so, the independent counsel said Congress was forced to consider issues far beyond a private, personal transgression.

"When such acts are committed by the president of the United States, we believe those acts 'may constitute grounds for impeachment,'" the report said. (*1998 CQ Weekly, p. 2378*)

A Political Decision

Members appeared dumbfounded by the speed with which Starr's investigation had concluded and uncertain what to do next. Like the American public, lawmakers were angered by Clinton's behavior but unsure whether his alleged transgressions were serious enough to merit the wrenching step of launching impeachment hearings.

"This could be a make-or-break weekend for the president," said Rep. Peter T. King, R-N.Y., as lawmakers left Washington on Sept. 11 with Starr's report in their briefcases.

With seven weeks until the midterm elections, one thing was clear: Not only Republicans but many Democrats were unwilling to go out on a political limb for a president they did not trust long before the Lewinsky scandal. *(1998 CQ Weekly, p. 2383)*

A senior Senate Republican aide said that a key factor in what happens next will be what Democrats heard during their weekend swings at home.

The decision whether to proceed to impeachment hearings or take some other action against Clinton, such as a censure, is in the end, a political, not a legal, determination. Congress' future course depends on whether the report produces an outcry from a public that, to date, has seemed as ambivalent as Congress — personally offended but leery of drastic measures.

The White House immediately began a counteroffensive, with Clinton's attorneys asserting that Starr had carried out a witch hunt, spending millions of dollars to rummage through Clinton's private life.

"This is personal and not impeachable," said Clinton's private attorney, David Kendall. "The amount of lurid, graphic detail here far exceeds any legal justification."

Earlier Friday, at a prayer breakfast, Clinton apologized for the first time to Lewinsky and her family. "I don't think there is a fancy way to say that I have sinned," he said.

But if a newly contrite Clinton, who spent the week begging forgiveness from lawmakers, his Cabinet and the public, was looking for signs that Democrats would rally 'round in his time of need, he did not find many.

Just hours after the prayer breakfast, the House passed a resolution (H Res 525) that authorized the public release of the report and laid out procedures for handling other evidence given to Congress by Starr. The resolution passed 363-63, with 138 Democrats voting yes.

Rep. James P. Moran, D-Va., said he was shocked by the number of Democrats who voted for the resolution. "Anxiety, nervousness, fear — all of those emotions play a role. And this [vote] was the easy one," he said.

Those Democrats who did speak out on the floor accused Republicans of reneging on a bipartisan deal worked out with House Speaker Newt Gingrich, R-Ga., that was to govern release of the thousands of pages of supporting materials delivered to the House on Sept. 9.

Others complained that the decision not to give the White House an advance copy of the report was unfair. Just a handful of liberals, including leaders of the Congressional Black Caucus, ventured so far as to defend the president.

Some Republicans who read portions of the report professed shock.

"We do not expect our presidents to lie under oath. We do not expect them to commit perjury," said Senate Judiciary Committee Chairman Orrin G. Hatch, R-Utah. "What I've read thus far bothers me greatly."

Charles T. Canady, R-Fla., chairman of the House Judiciary Committee's Constitution Subcommittee, said the report is "quite disturbing. . . . I believe there is evidence of perjury and obstruction of justice."

But he added that the Judiciary Committee cannot "rubber stamp" the report and must conduct its own review before deciding whether to proceed with an impeachment inquiry.

The Findings

The independent counsel's investigation began four years ago as a review of a questionable Arkansas land deal. It was later expanded to cover the 1995 firing of White House travel office personnel and improper White House use of confidential FBI files. The report before Congress deals solely with Clinton's relationship with Lewinsky. *(Whitewater, 1995 Almanac, p. 1-57)*

Lawmakers had hoped to avoid such a situation. Gingrich last month said the House would likely seek evidence from all of Starr's investigations before deciding whether to proceed with an impeachment inquiry. The Speaker at that time said a "pattern of felonies" would be needed for the House to act.

In the report, Starr said it was his original desire to send up all findings at once, but as the information about the Lewinsky matter became overwhelming, it was apparent that delay "would be unwise." Decisions about what steps to take, if any, on the other matters are to be made "at the earliest practical time," it said.

The report leveled charges against Clinton in four areas:

• **Perjury.** It said Clinton, both in a civil deposition in a sexual harassment lawsuit brought by former Arkansas state employee Paula Corbin Jones and in testimony before a federal grand jury, lied numerous times about the nature of his relationship with Lewinsky and efforts to conceal their affair.

During that Jones deposition, Clinton denied that he had had a sexual relationship with Lewinsky. Clinton's legal team in their rebuttal said those statements were based on an ambiguous definition of sex.

To make the case that there could be little confusion about whether sex had taken place, Starr includes graphic descriptions of the physical relationship. Based on testimony from Lewinsky, White House personnel, official logs and transcripts, the report detailed encounters between Lewinsky and Clinton from Nov. 15, 1995, to Dec. 28, 1997.

Lewinsky said that while the two never had intercourse, she performed oral sex on the president nine times and that Clinton touched her breasts and genitals during some of their encounters. The report also said government-conducted DNA tests proved that semen stains on a blue dress owned by Lewinsky matched a blood sample taken from Clinton.

The report also said the two had engaged in sexually explicit conversations over the telephone on 10 to 15 occasions.

Clinton's lawyers said Starr had focused on the lurid details solely to humiliate Clinton: "The principal purpose of this investigation and the report is to embarrass the president and titillate the public."

The report further said Clinton was untruthful when he said he couldn't recall whether he had ever been alone with Lewinsky and or had exchanged gifts with her.

That leaves Congress faced with an earnest desire to muster up the dignity required by the historic situation — and the necessity of digging into the salacious details of the Starr report.

• **Obstruction of justice.** The Starr report said there was an understanding with Lewinsky to lie under oath in the Jones case. Lewinsky originally signed an affidavit denying that she had sex with Clinton. After a grant of immunity from Starr, she changed her story.

Starr charged that Clinton and Lewinsky also had an understanding to conceal gifts they had given each other instead of turning them over to lawyers in the Jones suit. He also said Clinton had not been truthful about discussions with his friend, lawyer Vernon Jordan, who tried to help Lewinsky find a job in New York.

He further charged that Clinton attempted to impede investigators by helping Lewinsky look for a job in New York, at a time when she would have been a witness harmful to him if she had testified in the Jones case.

Presidency

Kendall denied that Clinton had tried to get Lewinsky a job in order to influence her testimony in the Paula Jones case: "Ms. Lewinsky was never offered a job at the White House after she left — and it's pretty apparent that if the president had ordered it, she would have been."

• **Witness tampering.** Starr charged that Clinton improperly tampered with a potential witness by attempting to in-

fort to hinder, impede and deflect possible inquiry by the Congress."

What's Ahead

The report now launches Congress and the country on a politically perilous journey.

While there are some members who served in the House during the 1974 Watergate impeachment hearings, most lawmakers are heading into uncharted

reneging on an agreement that only House Judiciary Committee Chairman Henry J. Hyde, R-Ill., and ranking Democrat John Conyers Jr. of Michigan would review boxes of supporting documents before they were released to the public.

Democratic Rep. David R. Obey of Wisconsin complained of "blatant disregard to fairness." Noting that he had served in Congress during Watergate, Obey said, "The reason, in the end, that the congressional process worked is that this was seen by the minority — then the Republicans — as being fundamentally fair to them."

Hyde insisted the debate on the first resolution did not presage partisan wrangling in the Judiciary Committee: "We won't be out on the floor where they can get some mileage out of it. This was spin, this morning. . . . Their idea of bipartisanship is that we surrender on everything."

Democrats seemed willing to fight procedural, though not personal, battles for the president. But even then, only to a point. One great fear, beyond the impact on the November elections, is that any proceedings on the Lewinsky matter could stretch on for months.

Senate Minority Leader Tom Daschle, D-S.D., has publicly broached the idea of a lame-duck session after the elections to quickly dispose of the issue.

"I don't think it's responsible for this Congress to leave on Oct. 9 [the target adjournment date] and expect this matter to be held over the country for the next three or four months without any action," Daschle said.

The White House appeared poised to mount a two-track counterattack against Starr and congressional Republicans: While Clinton apologizes repeatedly for his actions — and even admits that his first nationally televised mea culpa was not contrite enough — his lawyers and political aides denounce the report as factually flimsy and unnecessarily graphic.

In his original address to the nation, Clinton admitted that he had an improper relationship with Lewinsky but quickly turned to a denunciation of Starr and his lengthy investigation. After negative public reaction — and private confrontations with leaders of his own party and even his Cabinet members — Clinton has not repeated those attacks, instead talking about the biblical injunction to forgive one's enemies. ◆

Clinton lawyer David Kendall is mobbed by the media after meeting with House Judiciary Committee members Sept. 10 to discuss the release of Starr's report and its review.

fluence the testimony of Currie, his secretary.

Starr said that Currie facilitated many of the meetings between Clinton and Lewinsky. She also collected gifts that Lewinsky said had come from Clinton after they were sought by subpoena.

On Dec. 28, 1997, Currie drove to Lewinsky's Watergate apartment and collected a box containing the gifts. She later turned them over to Starr.

The White House asserted that Currie said she was asked by Lewinsky to hold the gifts and that Clinton never asked Currie to get them.

• **Abuse of constitutional authority.** Starr said it was an abuse of power for Clinton to lie about the relationship to Congress and the public in January 1998; to promise to cooperate with the investigation and then refuse six invitations to voluntarily testify and invoke executive privilege; and to lie again in testimony in August.

It was, Starr said, "all as part of an ef-

territory. Even for those who were then in the House, history is not a reliable guide to what lies ahead.

This is the first time Congress has faced the possibility of an impeachment inquiry based on the findings of an outside, independent counsel. The independent counsel is itself a relatively recent creation of Congress, a response to the Watergate scandal.

"This is a sacred process. This goes to the heart of our democracy," said House Minority Leader Richard A. Gephardt, D-Mo. "This is not politics. This is not spinning. This is not polling. This is not a lynch mob. This is not a witch hunt. This is not trying to find facts to support our already reached conclusions. This is a constitutional test."

But it was clear during debate on the rule to release the report, and from comments afterward, that Congress is going to have a tough time rising above partisanship.

Democrats accused Republicans of

Panel Votes to Release Clinton Video After 'Vigorously Partisan' Debate

Republicans push for maximum disclosure of evidence; Democrats say president's enemies are trying to build momentum for impeachment

Republicans by now had hoped to be gaining bipartisan approval for their handling of Independent Counsel Kenneth W. Starr's report to Congress on President Clinton's affair with Monica Lewinsky.

Instead, they now face the possibility of taking on one of the Constitution's most difficult tasks in an atmosphere of partisan acrimony.

This mood was illustrated by the rancorous, closed-door meetings of the House Judiciary Committee Sept. 17 and 18. The committee voted along party lines to release on Sept. 21 the videotape of Clinton testifying before the grand jury Aug. 17 and approximately 2,800 pages of printed material. (*1998 CQ Weekly, p. 2391*)

"It was strongly partisan, vigorously partisan," said Chairman Henry J. Hyde, R-Ill. "I prefer that it would go more smoothly."

What particularly disappointed members of both parties is that all of this quarrelling preceded the first real step — a formal vote of the House to initiate impeachment proceedings.

Republicans say the process has been driven by a belief that the public should know as much of the case against Clinton as possible. Democrats, however, say Republicans have designed the process solely to embarrass the president and sway public opinion.

"The public is not sufficiently anti-Clinton now," said committee member Barney Frank, D-Mass., characterizing the GOP's strategy, "This is designed to build up support for impeachment."

Republicans argued they were just trying to do their constitutional duty and examine the evidence supplied by Starr. They said they were complying with the spirit of a resolution (H Res 525) passed with bipartisan support Sept. 11 ordering Starr's material to be released no later than Sept. 28. (*1998 CQ Weekly, p. 2530*)

"There was a general view among Democrats not to reveal anything, and a general view among Republicans to reveal as much as possible," Hyde said.

Nor was the rancor limited to the closed-door session. Democrats and Republicans en-gaged in a hostile exchange after the on-line magazine Salon published a story on a long-ago affair Hyde, who was married, had with a married woman. Speaker Newt Gingrich, R-Ga., and other members of the House Republican leadership asked FBI Director Louis J. Freeh to investigate whether any White House official was involved in leaking the story. The White House responded that anyone who was found to be involved would be fired, and attacked the letter to Freeh as an attempt by Republicans to use the story "for their own partisan interests."

The partisan disputes are only likely to continue as the process unfolds and Congress decides whether to formally commence an impeachment inquiry.

The committee still has to consider the release of enormous amounts of other materials. It will then turn to the issues of how to conduct an impeachment inquiry. That will address such questions as how to issue subpoenas, grant immunity and cite recalcitrant witnesses for contempt. It is still uncertain whether the committee would rely solely on Starr's evidence or seek testimony from Clin-

With the Judiciary Committee split in a bitter partisan dispute over the release of evidence from the Starr report, Republicans risk losing the crucial support of Democrats as they move forward in deciding whether to begin a formal impeachment inquiry.

Hyde, shown Sept. 11, presided over a deeply divided House Judiciary Committee on Sept. 18, as members decided to release videotaped testimony by President Clinton.

Legal Experts Say Perjury Charge Poses Greatest Peril to Clinton

Of the four grounds for impeachment enumerated by Independent Counsel Kenneth W. Starr, perjury strikes most legal experts as the most troublesome for President Clinton.

It also shows how the impeachment process differs from a criminal proceeding. Assertions by Clinton's attorneys that his statements under oath were technically not perjury might hold up in a court of law, where legalistic quibbling is commonplace.

In the court of public opinion, however, there is less tolerance for what Senate Minority Leader Tom Daschle, D-S.D., called "semantic tap-dancing" by the president and his lawyers.

The problem for Clinton is that he has to defend himself in both of these courts.

Daschle and other Democrats are clearly ambivalent about exploring whether the statements qualify as perjury. On Sept. 14, Daschle publicly advised Clinton to stop "hair-splitting over legal technicalities."

"It simply stands in the way of what we need to do: Move forward and let common sense guide us in doing what is best for the country," Daschle said in a statement at a news conference with House Minority Leader Richard A. Gephardt, D-Mo.

But Republicans may not want to drop the issue so quickly. It is clearly the one that resonates most with the public. While polls show that most Americans oppose impeachment, pollsters caution that might change if it is demonstrated that Clinton committed perjury.

In all likelihood, the Republican-controlled House Judiciary Committee will want to examine what Clinton said during his January deposition in the Paula Jones sexual harassment lawsuit and again during his grand jury testimony on Aug. 17. And even if it decides this qualifies as perjury, Congress will have to then determine whether it is an impeachable offense.

White House counsel David E. Kendall Sept. 10 after meeting with Rep. Henry J. Hyde.

A Question of Interpretation

Both questions lend themselves to varying interpretations. Perjury is a criminal offense defined as knowingly giving false testimony in a legal proceeding when testimony is relevant to a material issue in the proceeding. The nation's founders set the standard for an impeachable offense as treason, bribery or "high crimes or misdemeanors."

If Congress wants to consider whether Clinton's testimony formally fits the definition of perjury, it would have to examine whether the statements were untrue, whether Clinton knew them to be and whether they were relevant to a material issue.

The first two lend themselves to an inquiry that could be highly embarrassing to the president. Some or all of the graphic descriptions of sex could be transformed from words on a page to live testimony.

The third — whether the testimony involved is a relevant issue — is unresolved in the case of the Jones deposition. In the case of Starr's criminal probe, it would be relevant, but by then Clinton was admitting inappropriate contact with Lewinsky.

The Jones case was dismissed in April by U.S. District Court Judge Susan Webber Wright. Prior to that, she had determined that the testi-

mony pertaining to Clinton's relationship with Lewinsky was not crucial to Jones' sexual harassment suit. Her ruling came on a motion by Starr to halt the discovery process in the Jones case because it could interfere with his probe. She halted only the discovery related to Lewinsky.

Clinton supporters and a number of sympathetic legal scholars have taken this to mean his testimony does not relate to a material issue. Wright, however, still could decide that it does, and cite Clinton for contempt of court. In a footnote to a ruling on an appeal by Jones, she cited this possibility.

The other possible legal development is that the 8th Circuit Court of Appeals could reverse Wright's ruling and reinstate the Jones case.

The larger question is whether perjury — especially this perjury, if it qualifies as such — would constitute an impeachable offense. Perjury was grounds for the impeachments of two federal judges in 1989: Alcee L. Hastings (now a Democratic House member from Florida) and Walter L. Nixon Jr. What was an impeachable offense for a judge could also be for a president, says Joseph diGenova, a former federal prosecutor and independent counsel who probed the State Department's actions in the Bush administration. (*1989 Almanac, p. 229*)

"A prosecutor would bring this case in a minute," said diGenova. "Of course it's impeachable."

But others argue that it is one thing to commit perjury to hide official misconduct — which both Hastings and Nixon were accused of — and another to commit perjury about an extramarital affair.

"You need to consider the level of turpitude and the excuse, so to speak, which is that he was lying to protect his privacy and his family," said Mark M. Hager, law professor at American University in Washington.

ton, Lewinsky and others — and endure the embarrassing details again.

The House now appears likely to take a vote, before adjourning, on convening a formal inquiry. If it approves such an inquiry, the committee may hold hearings in a special session after the election. The committee could report articles of impeachment to the 106th Congress next year.

Comparisons With Watergate

As they move through the process, lawmakers of both parties refer to the only precedent they have — Watergate — and in that they have a selective memory.

Ranking Democrat John Conyers Jr. of Michigan, the only current member who was on the committee in 1974, remembers his fellow Democrats allowed Nixon's attorneys to review and rebut all materials before they were released. (*Watergate, 1974 Almanac, p. 903*)

"In 1974, we kept the records for seven weeks, going over them before there were any releases. This time we've dumped process and fairness on its head. . . ." he said.

But Republicans remember that Watergate was not without its partisan sparring over procedural issues.

"I was there in 1973-74, and if that was bipartisan I would really like to see partisanship," said Senate Majority Leader Trent Lott, R-Miss.

In Watergate, Congress was not dealing with a report like Starr's, which Democrats contend is both overreaching and overly salacious. In March 1974, Watergate special prosecutor Leon Jaworski sent a 60-page "road map" and 800 pages of grand jury testimony and documents in what was referred to as a "bulging brief case."

Unlike Starr's 445-page report, the road map contained no narrative of events. Nor did it have any discussion of possible grounds of impeachment. It was merely an index to the most pertinent portions of the grand jury documents.

The Watergate-era Congress was also slower in releasing the material it received. Much of Jaworksi's report did not see the light of day until it was published at the end of August 1974. The committee did release material over the spring and summer of 1974, but the bulk of that came from its own investigation.

These types of differences have been central to Democratic claims of unfair-

ness.

"I have to say with great remorse, and great disappointment, that we have here a Salem witch hunt, and I will not participate," said Rep. Sheila Jackson-Lee, D-Texas.

Jackson-Lee said Starr's material and the way it is being handled completely ignore principles of "due process" accorded defendants in a criminal proceeding.

This was a distinct minority position when the House voted 363-63 on Sept. 11 to release Starr's report. But as members read the report, heard from constituents and contemplated the release of more sexually explicit material, the initial bias toward openness was receiving a second look.

"I was so stunned by the graphic nature of it that I spent a good bit of the weekend wondering if I had cast the right vote," said David R. Obey of Wisconsin, a senior Democrat. "I'm not sure I would have voted to release that report if I had known the vulgarity," added John P. Murtha, D-Pa.

Constance A. Morella, R-Md., suggested that Clinton's videotaped testimony not be publicly released, saying it would only generate anger and fan partisan flames. "I think it would shed more heat than light," she said.

But Judiciary Committee Republicans argued they had little choice after the overwhelming vote to release the documents. "I would only remind you that 363 members voted to release this material," said a GOP committee aide.

The vote gave the panel the authority to withhold material, but little guidance on what grounds to use.

Some Republicans are also pushing to have the committee's inquiry go beyond issues related to Clinton's affair with Lewinsky. An inquiry dealing only with matters related to a sexual relationship has always made Gingrich uncomfortable.

He suggested earlier this summer that Starr send Congress material that he compiled on the Whitewater land deals, the White House's improper use of FBI files on Republicans and personnel changes in the White House travel office. When Starr provided nothing on these fronts, House Republicans immediately considered adding these matters to the impeachment inquiry on their own, using materials gleaned by the House Government Reform and Oversight Committee.

But expanding the probe faces skep-

ticism not only from Democrats, but from some Republicans, who wonder if it would only complicate matters.

"That's within our purview, but the mechanism for this is more difficult," said committee member Asa Hutchinson, R-Ark. "What is in front of us is the Starr report."

Overriding Public Opinion

The Republicans' apparent determination to move toward impeachment against the polls represents something of a change in the GOP's attitudes.

Throughout their nearly four-year tenure at the House's helm, Republicans have often relied extensively on public opinion. Many of their most prominent policies — to overhaul welfare, balance the budget and cut taxes and spending, for example — have been justified at least partly on the grounds that they are the public's will.

But impeachment, some leading Republicans contend, is a serious, constitutional question that ought to be determined more by one's conscience than public opinion.

They have tended to discount the current polls, which show that while the scandal has ruined Clinton's personal standing and trustworthiness, about two-thirds of those surveyed still approve of his job performance. And about two-thirds say he should not be impeached.

To some extent, Republicans are anticipating a change in public attitudes as it digests the Starr report and its implications. "The impact of this still hasn't settled on the American people," said E. Clay Shaw Jr., R-Fla.

Many Republicans also report hearing a much more negative reaction to Clinton at town hall meetings in their districts and in phone calls. "That goes right in the face of what they see in the polls," said Michael Franc, vice president of government relations at the Heritage Foundation, a conservative think tank.

While some Republicans — particularly Majority Whip Tom DeLay, R-Texas, and a number of Judiciary Committee members — have expressed a strong resolve to move forward with an inquiry, others are reserved, especially in their public comments.

"There is no shortage of American people today that are eager for the chance to step up and yammer on this subject," said Majority Leader Dick Armey, R-Texas. "I think I have an

Points of Contention

Independent Counsel Kenneth W. Starr's report, released Sept. 11, contains 11 counts of alleged wrongdoing by President Clinton arising from his illicit affair with former White House intern Monica Lewinsky. The counts could be grounds for impeachment. Clinton's lawyers issued a point-by-point rebuttal Sept. 12. Following are the key issues in dispute:

ALLEGATION	STARR FINDINGS	CLINTON REBUTTAL
Perjury: Clinton lied about his relationship with Lewinsky in his Jan. 17, 1998, deposition in a sexual-harassment lawsuit filed by former Arkansas state employee Paula Corbin Jones.	Clinton denied having a "sexual relationship," a "sexual affair" or "sexual relations" with Lewinsky. She later testified to 10 sexual encounters.	The president's "good faith and reasonable interpretation" is that oral sex was not covered by the "special" definition presented by Jones' lawyers.
Perjury: Clinton lied again about Lewinsky when he testified on Aug. 17, 1998, before Starr's grand jury.	Clinton admitted an "inappropriate intimate relationship" but denied perjuring himself in his deposition in the Jones case. He contended oral sex was not covered by the definition offered by Jones' lawyers.	". . . False testimony provided as a result of confusion or mistake cannot as a matter of law constitute perjury."
Perjury: Clinton lied in the Jones case when he said he could not specifically recall being alone with Lewinsky or giving her gifts.	Clinton lied three times about time spent alone with Lewinsky, in one case repeating a "cover story" that she may have brought him "papers to sign."	Clinton did not deny meeting alone or exchanging gifts with Lewinsky; he simply could not recall specifics — and Jones' lawyers did not press him.
Perjury: Clinton lied about his conversations with Lewinsky regarding her testimony in the Jones case.	Clinton said "I'm not sure" that he discussed with Lewinsky her testimony in the Jones case beyond making jokes; she said they discussed it three times.	Differing recollections "cannot possibly support a perjury charge."
Obstruction of justice: Clinton concealed evidence of his involvement with Lewinsky, including gifts and an "intimate note" she sent him.	There is "a reasonable inference" that Clinton tried to conceal the gifts he gave Lewinsky by having his secretary retrieve them.	"This claim is wholly unfounded and simply absurd." The president "frequently exchanges gifts with friends" and did not try to conceal his gifts to Lewinsky.
Obstruction of justice: Clinton and Lewinsky agreed to lie about their relationship, and he instructed her to file a false affidavit in the Jones case.	Clinton and Lewinsky had an understanding that they would lie about their affair, and he knew her affidavit in the Jones case would be false.	"The use of 'cover stories' to conceal such a relationship, apart from any proceeding, is not unusual and not an obstruction of justice."
Obstruction of justice: Clinton tried to find Lewinsky a job in New York while she was a witness in the Jones case.	Hoping to ensure Lewinsky's silence, Clinton "devoted substantial time and attention" to help her find a private-sector job.	"There is no suggestion he ever ordered or directed anyone to assist Ms. Lewinsky or . . . give her special advantages," and his help was "insubstantial."
Perjury: Clinton lied about his conversations with lawyer Vernon Jordan regarding Lewinsky.	Clinton said he had not discussed Lewinsky's testimony with Jordan, but Jordan said they "absolutely" had talked about it.	"This allegation is a fabrication" because the testimony does not support Starr's version of events.
Obstruction of justice: Clinton attempted to influence the grand jury testimony of his secretary, Betty Currie.	Clinton improperly tried to influence her testimony by discussing his deposition with her the day after he gave it.	The charge is unfounded because "Currie was not a witness in any proceeding at the time he spoke with her."
Obstruction of justice: While Clinton refused to testify before the grand jury for seven months, he continued to lie to aides who were to testify.	Clinton's repeated denials of an affair — and the distribution of untrue "talking points" to his staff — caused top aides to mislead the grand jury.	Clinton "simply repeated to aides substantially the same statement he made to the whole country" in January; he did not attempt to corruptly influence them.
Abuse of power: Clinton's lies, refusals to testify for seven months and claims of executive privilege amounted to failure to "faithfully execute the laws."	Clinton's public denials, refusals of six invitations to testify before the grand jury and claims of executive privilege violated his oath of office.	Starr over-reached in an attempt to "transform personal misconduct into impeachable official malfeasance," especially when Clinton relied on legal advice.

obligation to hold my counsel."

Phil English, R-Pa., said that while Starr made a powerful case for impeachment, Clinton deserves a chance to respond. "I'm trying to puzzle this through," English said. "I'm not trying to draw any conclusions."

A House GOP leadership aide said that Republicans will move slowly, but deliberately, in the impeachment process. "We're going to move gingerly, one step at a time," he said, acknowledging that "our position is not without risks."

Republicans have strong incentives to "let this thing play out," said Roger Davidson, a professor of government and politics at the University of Maryland. "Public opinion hasn't jelled yet. And their core constituency would be furious if they thought that Republicans were somehow letting Clinton off the hook."

DeLay has promised to quash any attempt to forestall impeachment proceedings by censuring Clinton, saying such a punishment would be meaningless. However, that option may eventually gain popularity if Clinton's job approval ratings remain firm.

Democrats Go Slow

Democrats are also feeling their way. Most do not take solace in Clinton's relatively lofty job approval figure. They, too, figure that his support is soft and his presidency could easily implode with additional revelations.

The vast majority of Democrats are extremely critical of Clinton's having had an affair with Lewinsky and his misleading statements afterward, though uncertain whether the Starr report warrants an impeachment inquiry. But Clinton has never had close ties with congressional Democrats, especially those in the House, and they have not rushed to defend him.

For example, a majority of Democrats voted to publicly release the heart of Starr's report Sept. 11. (*1998 CQ Weekly, p. 2391*)

Members of the Congressional Black Caucus and some liberal stalwarts have demanded that Clinton be treated fairly. But many Democrats have been circumspect, wary of being seen as defending Clinton.

With the dearth of moderate Democrats on the Judiciary Committee, Republicans have to look elsewhere to find bipartisan support for impeachment. Moderate Democrats and those in competitive districts may be the

most receptive to calls for resignation or impeachment, though most have held their fire so far.

Charles W. Stenholm of Texas, a conservative Democrat, said there is enough evidence to launch an impeachment inquiry. But he is uncertain whether Clinton ought to be impeached. He said he would judge cautiously, saying that his constituents want him to "act like a juror that they would want deciding their fate."

Tim Roemer, D-Ind., a moderate who blasted Clinton for his "reckless-

ness" and "cavalier attitude with the truth," said lawmakers are proceeding carefully because "there are people all over the board back home." But Clinton's actions will not be easily dismissed, Roemer said, because "forgiveness to most Americans is not just to move on and forget about it."

Murtha, who took office in February 1974, in the midst of the Watergate scandal, said he has more immediate concerns than the possibility of impeachment, namely, "Can the president govern?" The first test, he said, is whether Clinton "has the ability to stand up to the pressure of a tax cut." (*1998 CQ Weekly, p. 2477*)

As long as Clinton can retain a favorable job approval rating and demonstrate that he has the capacity to govern, Murtha added, "as one of the senior Democrats, I wouldn't call on him for anything."

One Democratic aide said confidently that the impeachment threat has bound Clinton more closely than

ever to congressional Democrats. "He can't make any deals with Republicans that we won't bless," the aide said.

Finding the political turf unsettled, many lawmakers in safe seats are concluding that there is comfort in hewing closely to their political base. Those who fail to do so are feeling the heat.

James P. Moran, D-Va., has been so outspoken in his criticism of Clinton that, he joked, "I'm basically making a safe Democratic district very competitive." He said he was asked not to speak at one gathering of local Democrats in

Christopher Cox, R-Calif., center, talks to reporters after a Sept. 16 news conference on the release of President Clinton's videotaped grand jury testimony.

his suburban Washington district and booed when introduced at another.

By the same token, Mark Souder, R-Ind., has drawn the ire of some of his constituents for saying he is unsure whether Clinton ought to be impeached. Souder, a member of the GOP's feisty Class of '94, is no Clinton ally. His votes are consistently conservative, and in February he called for Clinton's resignation.

But after reading Starr's report, Souder decided the case for impeachment based solely on the Lewinsky affair is inconclusive. Souder said he would vote to launch a formal impeachment inquiry and would welcome expanding it to include allegations on such matters as campaign finance abuses.

That is not tough enough for some of Souder's constituents. "A lot of our people want him impeached — then for the inquiry to start," said Souder, surprised at suddenly being accused of being a Clinton sympathizer. "It's 'Fire! Aim! Ready!' " ◆

Ten Worth Watching on the Judiciary Committee

Howard L. Berman, D-Calif.

Many of the 37 members of the House Judiciary Committee have already declared their intentions on determining a punishment for President Clinton's misdeeds in the Monica Lewinsky affair. And as expected, their positions are determined in large measure by their partisanship: Republicans favor impeachment, Democrats are looking toward some lesser sanction.

But there is a group of members from both parties who have been more careful in stating their views. While they may have condemned the president's actions, they have not stated what sanction they are ready to support.

Most of that group is made up of younger members of the committee, including its newest GOP member, Mary Bono of California, the widow of former committee member Sonny Bono. Bono has said little about the conclusions of Independent Counsel Kenneth W. Starr's report — although, according to a local newspaper account, when her 7-year-old daughter, Chianna, asked if it had "any bad words" in it, the congresswoman replied, "Too many bad words for you to read."

Here are 10 Judiciary Committee members who are worth watching as the process unfolds in the weeks and months ahead:

Age: 57. Profession: Lawyer. Elected: 1982. Joined panel: 1983.
As the fourth-ranking Democrat on the committee, his silence on the Lewinsky matter has been deafening — though his reticence is in keeping with his reputation and his responsibilities. Berman is ranking Democrat on the Ethics Committee. If there is a vanguard of Democrats joining with Republicans to vote for impeachment, Berman is likely to be in it.

Asa Hutchinson, R-Ark.

Age: 47. Profession: Lawyer, prosecutor. Elected: 1996. Joined panel: 1997.
A former U.S. attorney for western Arkansas, he prosecuted Clinton's brother Roger on drug charges. Republicans and Democrats alike respect his deliberative manner. Hutchinson says he was "personally offended and deeply saddened" by Starr's report, but cautioned the committee against a rush to impeachment "until having made a thorough review of all evidence."

Zoe Lofgren, D-Calif.

Age: 50. Profession: Lawyer, professor. Elected: 1994. Joined panel: 1995.
As an aide to former Judiciary Committee member Don Edwards, D-Calif. (1963-95), she helped draft an article of impeachment against Richard M. Nixon. Viewed as a reliable Democrat, Lofgren says impeachment requires "a destruction of the constitutional form of government, and all we've got is, the president had a girlfriend and lied about it."

Ed Pease, R-Ind.

Age: 47. Profession: College administrator, lawyer. Elected: 1996. Joined panel: 1997.
As chairman of the Indiana Senate's Judiciary Committee, he was instrumental in reforming state sentencing guidelines. He has called for lawmakers to keep an open mind on the Clinton charges. After spending hours reviewing Starr's supporting materials, he said, "We begin with the presumption that everything should be released."

Mary Bono, R-Calif.

Age: 36. Profession: Restaurant owner. Elected: 1998. Joined panel: 1998. Bono, who holds a degree in fine arts, is the only GOP woman on the committee, as well as its youngest member. She has been reserved in her statements on the scandal, though she expressed disappointment that Clinton attacked Starr in his initial televised confession and said she was offended by the behavior described in Starr's report. But Bono said the details were necessary to support Starr's charges of perjury.

Rick Boucher, D-Va.

Age: 52. Profession: Lawyer. Elected: 1982. Joined panel: 1983. More comfortable delving into complexities of intellectual property law than engaging in partisan battles, he has declined to comment on details of the Starr report. He says committee members should "carefully review all the information and do so while keeping counsel before rendering decisions. . . . It is the national interest that must motivate these decisions, not partisan interest."

Lindsey Graham, R-S.C.

Age: 43. Profession: Lawyer. Elected: 1994. Joined panel: 1998. In 1997, this former Air Force prosecutor was a key player in the effort to depose House Speaker Newt Gingrich, R-Ga. While critical of Clinton's policies, Graham has been quiet about his conduct in the Lewinsky affair. "Evidence will be the determining factor in deciding whether the House goes forward with a fuller inquiry."

James E. Rogan, R-Calif.

Age: 41. Profession: Lawyer, prosecutor, state judge. Elected: 1996. Joined panel: 1998. Earlier this year, Rogan reviewed the history of congressional investigations of the executive branch for GOP leaders. He says he was probably the last person in Washington to read Starr's report. "I am trying to do it the old-fashioned way," going through the report and two White House rebuttals page by page to compare them with grand jury testimony and other documents.

Steven R. Rothman, D-N.J.

Age: 45. Profession: Lawyer, former surrogate court judge. Elected: 1996. Joined panel: 1997. His is likely to be a critical vote. Rothman has called Clinton's behavior "morally wrong," but he has promised to give the evidence a thorough review before making judgments. "I intend to consider the evidence as it is presented to me on the merits, as any juror would who is committed to giving an impartial verdict. This is not a partisan assignment," he says.

Charles E. Schumer, D-N.Y.

Age: 47. Profession: Lawyer. Elected: 1980. Joined panel: 1983. Having won his party's nomination to challenge Sen. Alfonse M. D'Amato, R-N.Y., Schumer's actions will be closely scrutinized in coming weeks. He has called Clinton's behavior "morally very wrong" but not necessarily criminal. And he has called on Congress and the public not to rush to judgment. Schumer attended a New York City fundraiser with Clinton on the eve of his Sept. 15 primary victory.

Independent Counsel Law Then and Now: Enough Irony for Both Parties

As Congress wends its way toward a presidential impeachment inquiry, it is worth noting a couple of important milestones. The 20th anniversary of the passage of the independent counsel law falls this month, as does the 25th anniversary of the event that precipitated it: the "Saturday Night Massacre" firing of Watergate Special Prosecutor Archibald Cox.

The ironies here are unavoidable. A scandal begets a law that begets (at least in part) a new scandal. A law created largely by Democrats comes back to haunt them. A system that may not have been broken then surely is now.

When historians look back on the current scandal they may well dub it "Nixon's Revenge." As president, Richard M. Nixon's attempts to attack his critics only backfired. His order that Cox be fired, far from saving his presidency, actually hastened its demise.

But in the years after Nixon left office, Democrats — it now appears to a growing number of people — seriously overplayed their hand. It was not enough that Nixon had resigned from office in great humiliation, or that Democrats scored big in the 1974 congressional elections, or that they regained the presidency in 1976. They had to prevent a Nixon from ever happening again. They had to come up with a highly complex — some would say quintessentially liberal — scheme for policing evil out of government.

Before 1978, when the independent counsel law (PL 95-521) was enacted, the system for limiting government corruption was based on the Founding Fathers' precepts about separation of powers, and checks and balances. While admittedly imperfect, the system dealt well with the most egregious abuses of office. It gave all prosecutorial power to the executive branch, which was kept in line through congressional pressure, judicial rulings and public opinion.

Since 1978, corruption in high office has been policed by an independent agent, divorced from any of the three branches, and more or less free to root out malfeasance where he sees fit.

The Democrats still in Congress who were involved in drafting the original statute and its various rewrites defend the law by arguing that it has been corrupted by Kenneth W. Starr. They point to the lengths to which Starr went to uncover evidence of criminality by Clinton.

But this argument overlooks the fact that, with the possible exception of alleged leaks of grand jury material, Starr has not done anything that the statute prohibits. Nowhere does it say he should exercise restraint, or put his decisions in broad perspective. Nowhere does it say he should not make the strongest case he can, given the evidence he has. Nowhere does it say charges related to sexual conduct or lying in a deposition for a dismissed civil case are not worthy of pursuit.

A more telling reaction to Starr comes from Democrats who have left office and have the luxury of public remorse. They have become something of a mea culpa caucus.

"I was a member of the Judiciary Committee then [in 1978]," said former Rep. Don Edwards, D-Calif. (1963-95). "I'm sorry I didn't pay more attention. It's a flawed law, and we are now paying the price."

"I don't know if anyone cares about old white males admitting their lack of foresight. But that's what we are," said Charles Tiefer, a former House deputy Democratic counsel who helped defend the statute when it was being challenged in court by Republicans.

The independent counsel statute, of course, is not solely responsible for the current state of affairs. The list of contributing factors is long. It includes the Supreme Court's decision that Paula Jones' sexual harassment suit could proceed while Clinton was in office. It includes U.S. District Judge Susan Webber Wright's decision that Monica Lewinsky was a suitable subject for pre-trial discovery in the Jones case. And, most important, it includes the conduct of Clinton, who could have spared himself and the nation considerable pain had he acted more decently to begin with or more truthfully in his Jones deposition.

But, for better or worse, the nation would not be in this situation today under the old system, in which special prosecutors were appointed on an ad hoc basis only when there was a public outcry for one.

Now it is the Republicans' turn. It would seem they are looking at a golden opportunity to overplay their hand. The public could judge them very harshly if it concludes they pushed the impeachment issue too far.

For much of the statute's 20-year history, Republicans have been the chief critics of the law as well as of the persons who have served as independent counsels, most notably Iran-contra investigator Lawrence E. Walsh. Now they are using the statute, which is up for reauthorization next year, as the rationale for an inquiry and defending Starr against attacks from Democrats. House Judiciary Committee Chairman Henry J. Hyde, R-Ill., insists that Democratic criticism of Starr is part of an effort to deflect attention from Clinton's misdeeds.

He and other Republicans would like to push forward with their inquiry without having to constantly evaluate Starr's actions. Perhaps they should look at the situation Democrats are now in and remember the old admonition: Be careful what you wish for, because you just might get it.

Scandal Chronology

SEPTEMBER 5–OCTOBER 30:

SATURDAY, Sept. 5: Newspapers report that House Government Reform and Oversight Committee Chairman Dan Burton, R-Ind., a chief critic of President Clinton, acknowledges fathering an illegitimate child years ago while a member of the state legislature.

He blames the White House for inspiring a media investigation of his personal life and vows he will not back off his probe of campaign finance irregularities. The White House denies any role in the media's focus on Burton.

MONDAY, Sept. 7: Amid rumors that its delivery is imminent, Clinton lawyer David Kendall asks Independent Counsel Kenneth W. Starr to give the White House an advance copy of his report to Congress, arguing that it should be provided out of "fundamental fairness." Starr later refuses.

TUESDAY, Sept. 8: A Clinton appearance at an elementary school in Silver Spring, Md., is boycotted by the state's Democratic governor, Parris N. Glendening, who also disinvites Clinton from an October fundraiser for his re-election campaign.

WEDNESDAY, Sept. 9: On the day the House returns from its summer recess, Clinton meets privately with leading Democratic House members to apologize and discuss priorities for the remaining weeks of the session. At the first bipartisan meeting on the matter, House leaders agree that the Judiciary Committee will lead the review of Starr's report and conduct the likely hearings that could lead to a vote on articles of impeachment.

Then, while Clinton appears at fundraising events in Florida and expresses public regret in more direct terms than he has to date, Starr's report and accompanying evidence are delivered to the Capitol.

THURSDAY, Sept. 10: Clinton has private meetings with leading Senate Democrats and members of his Cabinet to voice his contrition. In response to a question, he promises the senators there will be no further surprise disclosures about his conduct.

Speaker Newt Gingrich, R-Ga., instructs House members to follow "proper decorum" when they speak about the president on the House floor, including abstaining from the use of "language that is personally

offensive toward the president."

Clinton lawyers travel to Capitol Hill to meet with Judiciary Committee members of both parties to discuss the process the House will follow. Republicans reject their plea for time to review the report before its release.

The House Rules Committee by voice vote approves a resolution (H Res 525) authorizing the Judiciary Committee to take custody of Starr's report and to make portions of it publicly available.

FRIDAY, Sept. 11: The House adopts the resolution, 363-63. The report, containing lurid details of the president's encounters with former intern Monica Lewinsky, is posted on the World Wide Web.

At a White House prayer breakfast, Clinton again apologizes for the pain he has caused to his family, friends, staff and the American people — and, for the first time publicly, to Lewinsky and her family.

Kendall sends to Capitol Hill Clinton's first attempt at rebutting the allegations contained in Starr's report.

SATURDAY, Sept. 12: A day after Independent Counsel Kenneth W. Starr's report is released, President Clinton's legal team issues a 42-page rebuttal that says the report "is so loaded with irrelevant and unnecessary graphic and salacious allegations that only one conclusion is possible: Its principal purpose is to damage the president."

SUNDAY, Sept. 13: On television talk shows, House Minority Whip David E. Bonior, D-Mich., and other Democrats do not rally to Clinton's defense. Rather, they make it clear that Congress is almost certain to pass some sort of rebuke.

MONDAY, Sept. 14: Senate Minority Leader Tom Daschle, D-S.D., and House Minority Leader Richard A. Gephardt, D-Mo., issue statements criticizing the president's lawyers for their defense strategy; Daschle calls it "hair-splitting."

Clinton travels to New York City for a speech to the Council on Foreign Relations and three Democratic fundraising events, including a Broadway show, which raise a total of $4 million. He makes no direct references to the scandal.

(Continued on next page)

TUESDAY, Sept. 15: Members of the House Judiciary Committee begin debating whether to release a videotape of the president's Aug. 17 grand jury testimony.

White House Chief of Staff Erskine Bowles and Deputy Chief of Staff John D. Podesta attend several meetings on Capitol Hill and attempt to reassure Democratic lawmakers upset with Clinton's legal strategy. The White House hires additional advisers, including Gregory B. Craig, director of policy and planning at the State Department. Craig will be special counsel coordinating the White House's response to Congress.

Speaker Newt Gingrich, R-Ga., announces that the House will not formally adjourn this year, to allow the Judiciary Committee to work past the target adjournment date of Oct. 9, if necessary.

The White House confirms media reports that the president has asked three ministers to provide him spiritual guidance through prayer meetings and Bible study.

WEDNESDAY, Sept. 16: At a joint press conference with Czech President Vaclav Havel, Clinton insists he will not resign: People "want to put it behind them. . . and they want me to go on and do my job. . . . That is the right thing to do."

Confirming a story in an on-line magazine, House Judiciary Committee Chairman Henry J. Hyde, R-Ill., admits to having had an adulterous affair three decades ago. The White House denies any involvement with the emergence of the story.

THURSDAY, Sept. 17: The House Judiciary Committee meets privately to further discuss the release of Starr's evidence, but after hours of debate does not agree to immediately release the grand jury videotape. Clinton's lawyers complain that Starr's office refused to agree to destroy the videotape after it had been viewed by all grand jury members. "The only purpose of preserving this videotape . . . was to ensure its public release and embarrass the president."

A group of House Republicans asks the FBI to investigate allegations that White House aides are behind the media reports of the affairs of Hyde and other GOP lawmakers.

FRIDAY, Sept. 18: While Clinton travels to Boston for party fundraisers, the House Judiciary Committee votes to release the videotape and other materials.

SATURDAY, Sept. 19: President Clinton thanks the Congressional Black Caucus for "understanding the true meaning of repentance and atonement." Rep. Maxine Waters, D-Calif., tells Clinton the caucus, which she chairs, "will be the fairness cops" during the investigation of his affair with Monica Lewinsky.

MONDAY, Sept. 21: The House Judiciary Committee releases videotape of Clinton's Aug. 17 grand jury testimony, as well as more than 3,000 pages of Clinton's and Lewinsky's testimony. The president's four-hour appearance is broadcast on all major TV networks. White House spokesman Mike McCurry says the "rank partisanship that led to the . . . release of these materials, most of which are irrelevant, is regrettable."

Clinton receives a standing ovation from the U.N. General Assembly before his annual address, which focuses on combating global terrorism. He also attends a New York University round table with world leaders. Clinton does not comment on the videotape.

TUESDAY, Sept. 22: In a letter to the House Judiciary Committee, Clinton's lawyers complain that Independent Counsel Kenneth W. Starr's report is a "one-sided and unfair manipulation of the evidence and the law." They cite the omission of Lewinsky's statement that "no one ever asked me to lie, and I was never promised a job in return for my silence." Starr's office insists that no evidence supporting the president was intentionally omitted.

Former Sen. Bob Dole, R-Kan., who lost to Clinton in 1996, says the president sought his help to generate support among Republicans on Capitol Hill, but Dole declined.

At Emory University, former President Jimmy Carter, a Democrat, says, "I have deplored and been deeply embarrassed about what has occurred" in the scandal.

At a White House reception, South African President Nelson A. Mandela says Clinton "has my full support in everything that he does."

WEDNESDAY, Sept. 23: After meeting with House leaders from both parties, Speaker Newt Gingrich, R-Ga., announces that there will be no immediate deal for censure and a fine for the president.

In an interview on NBC's "Today" show, former GOP President George Bush says that the office of the presidency is "strong . . . and I'm afraid for now it's been diminished." He declines to comment further on the Clinton scandal.

THURSDAY, Sept. 24: House Judiciary Chairman Henry J. Hyde, R-Ill., announces that his committee will likely send a resolution recommending an impeachment inquiry to the House the week of Oct. 5. Hyde adds that "there is no precedent for censuring a president. The Constitution doesn't provide for it."

Clinton tells party loyalists that "adversity is our friend" and that Democrats should be optimistic about the midterm elections.

FRIDAY, Sept. 25: A *New York Times*/CBS News poll shows that 54 percent of the respondents disapprove of the House Judiciary Committee's handling of the Clinton matter.

Reports say lawyers for Clinton and former Arkansas state employee Paula Corbin Jones are negotiating a settlement of her sexual harassment suit.

As Clinton heads to party fundraisers in Illinois and California, the committee meets to decide how to handle nearly 60,000 pages of additional testimony.

SATURDAY, Sept. 26: At a Reform Party convention, Ross Perot says President Clinton is "mentally and emotionally unstable" and has "a defective brain."

SUNDAY, Sept. 27: Clinton winds up a three-day fundraising trip in Texas.

TUESDAY, Sept. 29: Media outlets report that liberal organizations, including People for the American Way and the AFL-CIO, are planning ad campaigns critical of GOP handling of the scandal. Several Democrats express concern that the campaigns will divert funds away from candidates.

White House Chief of Staff Erskine Bowles promises Democratic lawmakers that the White House is not supporting the ad campaigns and will encourage supporters to donate money to candidates rather than pro-Clinton efforts.

Senate Majority Leader Trent Lott, R-Miss., says that he thinks "bad conduct is enough . . . for impeachment."

WEDNESDAY, Sept. 30: House Judiciary Committee Chairman Henry J. Hyde, R-Ill., says the draft resolution for an impeachment inquiry "follows the Watergate resolution word for word."

THURSDAY, Oct. 1: Ranking Judiciary Committee Democrat Rep. John Conyers Jr. of Michigan asks the committee to "limit both the time and scope of the inquiry . . . and lift the cloud which hangs over the nation."

Clinton's lawyers reportedly offer former Arkansas state employee Paula Corbin Jones $700,000 to settle her sexual harassment suit, first filed in 1994.

FRIDAY, Oct. 2: Judiciary Committee Democrats present a resolution proposing to limit the inquiry to the Lewinsky affair, hold hearings before voting on a formal inquiry, and conduct proceedings in two phases beginning Oct. 12.

Nearly 5,000 additional pages of evidence compiled by the independent counsel's office are released, including transcripts of tapes that Linda Tripp secretly made of conversations with Monica Lewinsky.

SUNDAY, Oct. 4: In an op-ed piece in the *New York Times*, former President Gerald R. Ford recommends that the House act with "dispatch" in conducting an impeachment inquiry and that President Clinton receive "a harshly worded rebuke as rendered by members of both parties."

MONDAY, Oct. 5: The House Judiciary Committee votes along party lines, 21-16, to recommend that the House begin formal impeachment proceedings. The GOP resolution (H Res 581) resembles the 1974 Watergate resolution, with no limits on the length or scope of the inquiry.

Committee Democrats propose two alternative resolutions requiring that "impeachable offense" be defined before hearings start and place a time constraint on the inquiry. Both are defeated by party-line votes.

David P. Schippers, the committee's majority counsel, outlines 15 impeachable offenses, four more than Independent Counsel Kenneth W. Starr did in his referral.

White House lawyers petition the Supreme Court to hear an appeal of the July court decision that denied attorney-client privilege claims regarding communications between Clinton and White House deputy counsel Bruce Lindsey.

Clinton lawyer David Kendall asks Attorney General Janet Reno to release material Starr's office used to gain permission to investigate the president's relationship with former White House intern Monica Lewinsky.

(Continued on next page)

WEDNESDAY, Oct. 7: At a news conference with Hungarian Prime Minister Viktor Orban, Clinton says House Democrats should "cast a vote of principle and conscience" on whether to approve an impeachment inquiry.

THURSDAY, Oct. 8: The House votes, 258-176 (including 31 Democrats), to start a formal impeachment inquiry against Clinton. A proposal by Democrats to end the inquiry by Dec. 31 and limit its scope is rejected, 198-236.

After the vote, Clinton says his fate "is not in my hands. It is in the hands of Congress and the people of this country — ultimately in the hands of God."

SUNDAY, Oct. 11: Appearing on CBS, White House special counsel Gregory B. Craig says that President Clinton's actions are not an impeachable offense as defined "throughout history, and we lower that standard at our peril."

MONDAY, Oct. 12: In New York City, Clinton attends fundraisers for Democratic gubernatorial candidate Peter Vallone and Senate candidate Charles E. Schumer, a member of the House Judiciary Committee. House Majority Whip Tom DeLay, R-Texas, says Clinton's appearances at the two events for Schumer — which raise about $1 million — are "unseemly" and amount to "jury tampering." Clinton skips a trip to Florida to return to budget negotiations in Washington.

TUESDAY, Oct. 13: Clinton visits a Maryland public school accompanied by several Democratic lawmakers and Gov. Parris N. Glendening, who tells Clinton, "We are proud of you and Vice President Gore." A month earlier, Glendening had canceled a fundraiser with Clinton because of the scandal.

A court brief filed by lawyers for former Arkansas state employee Paula Jones says evidence in Independent Counsel Kenneth W. Starr's report to Congress warrants the reinstatement of her dismissed sexual harassment lawsuit against Clinton. By denying his affair with former White House intern Monica Lewinsky in a deposition last January, Clinton "unlawfully interfered" with the Jones case and caused it to be "tainted by perjury," the brief argues. But settlement negotiations continue.

Residents of the Watergate South apartment building,

which has often been surrounded by TV cameras, receive notes of apology "for the inconveniences of the past nine months" from departing neighbor Lewinsky.

WEDNESDAY, Oct. 14: House Judiciary Committee Chairman Henry J. Hyde, R-Ill., says the impeachment inquiry will focus on perjury, witness tampering and obstruction of justice — narrowing the list of charges recommended by committee aides — and will ideally finish by a self-imposed year-end deadline. Hyde says committee lawyers will be meeting with Clinton's lawyers on Oct. 20 to discuss parameters of the inquiry.

The House Oversight Committee votes, 7-0, to give the Judiciary Committee an additional $1.2 million from a reserve fund to conduct the impeachment inquiry.

Media outlets report that in 1994 Starr gave a lawyer representing Jones unpaid advice about the feasibility of a sexual harassment lawsuit against a sitting president. But Starr did not disclose these conversations to the Justice Department in January 1998 when he sought permission to expand his investigation to include accusations of perjury and witness tampering by Clinton in the Jones lawsuit. Clinton's lawyers argue this shows a conflict of interest, and the Justice Department says this information will be included in a review of Starr's practices.

THURSDAY, Oct. 15: Clinton and congressional Republicans announce a budget deal for fiscal 1999.

Hyde tells a Chicago Bar Association lunch that chairing the investigation has been a thankless task. "I would trade it for a Hershey bar," he says. "Anyone who wants it can have it."

FRIDAY, Oct. 16: Clinton and the first lady travel to Chicago for party events, including a fundraiser for Sen. Carol Moseley-Braun, D-Ill., who is in a competitive race for re-election.

SUNDAY, Oct. 18: A handwritten note from President Clinton expressing repentance for his affair with former White House intern Monica Lewinsky and seeking forgiveness from his home church, Immanuel Baptist in Little Rock, Ark., is read from the pulpit by the Rev. Rex Horne.

Appearing on Fox TV, Senate Judiciary Committee Chairman Orrin G. Hatch, R-Utah, says "there is no bipartisan consensus on impeachment." While he believes there is enough evidence on which to impeach Clinton, Hatch says he "cannot name one [Senate] Democrat" who would vote for conviction.

MONDAY, Oct. 19: U.S. District Judge Susan Webber Wright releases 724 pages of previously classified materials related to the sexual harassment case brought by former Arkansas state employee Paula Corbin Jones. The documents reveal an effort by Clinton's legal team to expose Jones' sexual history. Wright dismissed the case April 1.

New York literary agent Lucianne Goldberg says she and her son, Jonah, will testify to a Maryland grand jury probing Linda Tripp's secret records of conversations with Lewinsky.

Clinton rejects a $2 million deal to settle the Jones case, half of which would have come from New York real estate magnate Abe Hirschfeld.

In his first public speech since leaving the White House, former spokesman Mike McCurry says Clinton had been "exasperatingly stupid in his personal life."

TUESDAY, Oct. 20: The same three-judge panel that moved in 1997 to send the Jones case forward hears arguments in St. Paul, Minn., on whether the case should be reinstated.

Newspapers report that military officials, responding to public criticism of Clinton by military personnel in newspapers and magazines, have issued warnings that "contemptuous words" against the president are prohibited under military law.

WEDNESDAY, Oct. 21: Lawyers from the House Judiciary Committee and the White House, including Clinton special counsel Gregory B. Craig, emerge from a two-hour meeting with few differences resolved, fueling speculation that a year-end deadline for the House inquiry may not be met.

FRIDAY, Oct. 23: Culminating nine days of talks and a marathon overnight negotiating session, participants in the Middle East peace negotiations at Maryland's Wye River plantation reach a land-for-peace compromise. Clinton spends a total of six days at the talks and cancels four political fundraising trips in hopes of brokering a compromise between Israeli Prime Minister Benjamin Netanyahu and Palestinian Leader Yasser Arafat.

MONDAY, Oct. 26: U.S. District Judge Susan Webber Wright releases a second set of documents from former Arkansas state employee Paula Jones' sexual harassment suit against Clinton, including a motion filed by her lawyers to prohibit Clinton's lawyers from introducing evidence concerning Jones' sexual history.

TUESDAY, Oct. 27: Rep. John Conyers Jr., D-Mich., ranking member of the Judiciary Committee, asks Independent Counsel Kenneth W. Starr for evidence used to persuade the Justice Department to allow his investigation to expand to include Clinton's affair with former White House intern Monica Lewinsky.

The Republican Party launches a $10 million negative ad campaign that focuses on the Clinton sex scandal.

Former House Judiciary Chairman Peter W. Rodino Jr., D-N.J. (1949-89), says Clinton's actions do not "rise to that level where we have to consider it to be a ground to remove" him from office.

WEDNESDAY, Oct. 28: More than 400 historians issue a statement saying that if the impeachment inquiry continues, it "will leave the presidency permanently disfigured and diminished."

At a news conference with Colombian President Andres Pastrana, Clinton says he has tried "to atone" for his mistakes and undergone "inner changes."

FRIDAY, Oct. 30: U.S. District Judge Norma Holloway Johnson finds "a prima facie violation" of grand jury secrecy rules by Starr's office in the Lewinsky probe. ◆

The latest struggle over the bounds of judicial power is being waged on several fronts

Indicting the Courts: Congress' Feud With Judges

American political history includes a long tradition of attacking the judiciary, but legal scholars on both ends of the political spectrum are concerned that Congress has brought the conflict to a new level. When lawmakers hold up confirmations, assail sitting judges and limit their power, experts say, it upsets the balance of power envisioned by the Founding Fathers.

It is hard to imagine former Sen. Alan K. Simpson worrying what others might think of him. Here, after all, is a man who proudly calls himself an "old geezer" and penned a book entitled "Right in the Old Gazoo." But the one-time lawyer wonders: What if he were starting out and wanted to be a judge, rather than a politician? Would he be confirmed? What dirt would today's senators have on him?

"Good God," he muses. "I represented murderers, insane people, a guy who bit someone's ear off. What would they do with that?"

The question is not altogether academic. Simpson says he has seen many would-be judges of today turned into "gargoyles" by a process that has gotten out of hand.

Simpson, who served from 1979-97, is one in a host of former lawmakers, judges and academics who are alarmed by what they see as an increasing hostility on the part of Congress toward the federal judiciary. Fierce attacks on judicial nominees, they argue, are but one front in an extraordinary, escalating war of wills between the legislative and judicial branches of government. This war is being driven in considerable part by politics and mistrust. But it shows more fundamental differences as well, over such matters as the proper balance in a democracy between the rule of law and the rule of popular sentiment, and the proper role and scope of government in general.

Three broad areas of confrontation are at the center of this conflict:

• **Confirmations.** The Senate has turned the process of confirming federal judges into a political sideshow for the two parties to curry favor with their hard-core supporters. In some cases, this has meant distorting the nominees' records. In others, it has meant quietly holding up whole blocks of nominees for months or years at a time. Many Republicans trace this trend to the villainization of Robert H. Bork by Senate Democrats, when they defeated his Supreme Court nomination in 1987. Most Democrats argue that the atmosphere is much worse now that the tables have turned. There are 73 vacancies on the 845-member federal bench. The number passed 100 last year. It is not uncommon for nominees to wait two or three years for confirmation. (*Bork, 1987 Almanac, p. 271*)

• **Attacks on sitting judges.** A number of judges, ranging from District Judge Harold Baer Jr. of New York to District Judge Thelton E. Henderson of California, have come under virulent criticism from members of Congress. House Majority Whip Tom DeLay, R-Texas, has called for widespread impeachments, and individual members have launched rhetorical broadsides: "There is no doubt in my mind that there is a special place in hell for a number of federal court judges . . . " Rep. Jack Kingston, R-Ga., declared in a May 4 floor speech on school prayer.

• **Jurisdiction.** In the past several years, Congress has passed bills to prevent federal judges from hearing cases that could undermine policies advocated by conservative lawmakers. Specifically, they have prevented judges from hearing cases involving prison conditions or appeals from immigrants about to be deported.

At the same time, it has forced the courts to participate in a cause very popular in Congress — prosecuting crime at the federal level. This intrusion into an

Considering today's highly charged political atmosphere, Simpson wonders what might have happened if he had aimed for a federal judgeship.

area previously left to state courts has loaded the federal dockets, crowding out other important cases.

The courts' harshest critics argue they are merely preventing the worst judicial abuses. Simpson and his compatriots say such attacks on the judiciary threaten its very independence and ultimately could upset the system of checks and balances envisioned by the Founding Fathers.

"The erosion of the independence of the judiciary is not something absolutely dramatic," said Sheldon Goldman, a political scientist at the University of Massachusetts. "It's an incremental thing. It's a cancer on the American constitutional framework. Someday we may wake up to find a very different United States."

A Long Tradition

Attacking the judiciary is an old tradition in American politics. The biggest actual threats to the courts came in the early years of the republic, the Civil War era, and during Franklin D. Roosevelt's New Deal, when he demanded the chance to pick six additional Supreme Court justices.

Sharp verbal criticism of the federal judiciary has been particularly popular among presidents and members of Congress with a populist bent. The notion of an unelected group of powerful jurists serving for life, and accountable to virtually no one, has been an irresistible target for politicians ranging from President Andrew Jackson to Wisconsin Sen. Robert M. LaFollette Jr. (1925-47), leader of the Progressive movement in the 1920s. A few Supreme Court rulings — most notably the landmark 1954 desegregation case *Brown v. Board of Education* — have produced an avalanche of hostility to the federal courts.

Today's generation of court critics is led by DeLay in the House and John Ashcroft, R-Mo., in the Senate. While the Democrats held up some Republican judges and passed legislation unpopular with the third branch, most legal scholars agree that the relationship between Congress and the courts has deteriorated since the GOP took control in 1995.

Many Republicans see some sitting judges as arrogant, unresponsive to the public and prone to "activist" rulings that overstep their constitutional role of applying, rather than creating, the law.

"There is an activist judge behind each of most of the perverse failures of today's justice system," DeLay said in a floor speech April 23. "When judges legislate, they usurp the power of Congress. When judges stray beyond the Constitution, they usurp the power of the people."

One of the most often-cited examples is Missouri District Court

Judge Russell Clark, who forced $1.8 billion in tax increases in Kansas City to fund court-ordered improvements to inner-city schools.

Also cited are several judges who have struck down public referendums that won popular majorities, such as a California vote to limit affirmative action (Proposition 209) and a 1992 Colorado proposition to limit civil rights protections for homosexuals. Judges who are considered soft on crime are highly unpopular with conservatives, as are those who impose a rigid church-state separation.

Much of the criticism of the courts centers on their interpretation of the Constitution. For instance, when Rep. Ernest Istook, R-Okla., is asked why Republicans are so quick to propose amendments to the Constitution, he responds that the courts do it all the time. Istook, sponsor of a proposal (H J Res 78) that would expand rights of religious expression, argues that the Supreme Court has perverted the First Amendment through a series of church-state rulings in the past three decades.

DeLay argues that such rulings indicate the judicial branch has exceeded its authority. "The system of checks and balances so carefully crafted is in serious disrepair and has been for years," he said.

Others criticize the expansive role of government advocated by some judges. Judge Clark's rulings in Kansas City have been attacked not just for their activism but for their liberalism. The notion of transferring almost

Datafile

Confirmations in the Clinton Era

President Clinton's nominees for district and circuit courts were confirmed at a quick pace when Democrats controlled Congress but slowed after Republicans took control.

• In the 103rd Congress, 141 nominations were received; 127 were confirmed.

• In the 104th Congress, 105 nominations were received; 73 were confirmed.

• In the 105th Congress, as of June 1, 108 nominations were submitted; 61 were confirmed.

Source: Congressional Research Service

Cuomo at a news conference June 9 to announce the formation of a new group, Citizens for Independent Courts.

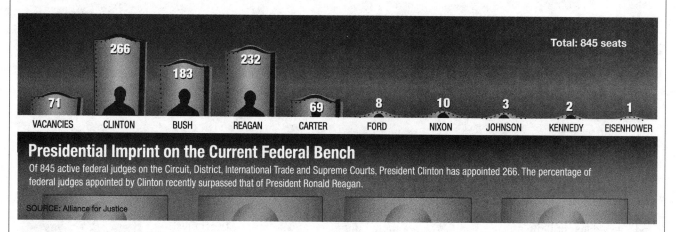

Total: 845 seats

VACANCIES	CLINTON	BUSH	REAGAN	CARTER	FORD	NIXON	JOHNSON	KENNEDY	EISENHOWER
71	266	183	232	69	8	10	3	2	1

Presidential Imprint on the Current Federal Bench

Of 845 active federal judges on the Circuit, District, International Trade and Supreme Courts, President Clinton has appointed 266. The percentage of federal judges appointed by Clinton recently surpassed that of President Ronald Reagan.

SOURCE: Alliance for Justice

$2 billion to inner-city schools strikes many conservatives as an exercise in social engineering reminiscent of President Lyndon B. Johnson's Great Society or of the New Deal.

In essence, many Republicans see themselves using pressure on the courts to undo what Roosevelt may have done in part through pressure in his day. Even though Roosevelt's bid to "pack" the Supreme Court failed because Congress would not allow it, it apparently had an impact.

For reasons that are still being debated by legal scholars, the Supreme Court began a shift to the left not long after the episode in 1937. Initially, this appeared to be driven by a switch in positions by sitting members, though by 1941, the trend had been accelerated by a string of seven Roosevelt appointments in just four years.

This shift represented the beginning of a major expansion of the federal government's size and function. Subsequent courts championed integration, and later busing; created a limited constitutional right to abortion; took officially sanctioned prayer out of schools; and made other rulings opposed by conservatives.

Today's criticisms of the federal judiciary are not merely an inside-the-Beltway spat between two branches. They have broad resonance among religious conservatives, libertarians and populists.

Sitting judges are a regular target of conservative talk radio shows. Blocking pending nominees is also a popular topic. President Clinton has already appointed almost a third of the federal bench, and he will get more opportunities as judges retire. *(Chart, this page)*

Supporters of a more independent judiciary argue the judiciary is being dragged into a fight between the two other branches. Furthermore, they argue, it is Congress, not the courts, that is

jeopardizing the balance of power envisioned by the Constitution.

Out of Balance

The judicial branch "is beyond comparison the weakest of the three departments of power," Alexander Hamilton wrote in Federalist Paper Number 78. ". . . It can never attack with success the other two; and all possible care is requisite to enable it to defend itself against their attacks."

That the judiciary is the weakest branch is evident in Article III of the Constitution, which makes its very existence subject to the good will of the two other branches. The Senate could strangle it by refusing to confirm judges. The president could do the same by not nominating any. Congress could refuse to fund it, or even abolish all but the Supreme Court, which is created by the Constitution.

Last year, DeLay proposed widespread impeachments, naming three district court judges he thought were ready to be taken on immediately: Henderson, who blocked California's referendum limiting affirmative action; Baer, who dismissed key evidence in a drug case; and Fred Biery, in Texas, who refused to seat a Republican sheriff and county commissioner because of controversy over absentee ballots.

In Tennessee, the ouster of District Court Judge John T. Nixon has become a crusade of victims' rights advocates. His decisions blocking executions has enraged them to the point of bringing a judicial misconduct suit and persuading the state legislature to pass a resolution asking Congress to impeach him.

Baer's case may be the most illustrative because of the 1996 presidential campaign and its aftermath. GOP candidate Bob Dole made Baer, and his evidentiary ruling, the centerpiece of his criticism of Clinton appointees. Not

wanting to be outflanked, Clinton joined the criticisms.

Under attack from both sides, Baer reversed his decision. Regardless of the merits of his original ruling, and his switch, champions of an independent judiciary are horrified by the possibility that a judge changed his opinion under political pressure.

"After taking a battering in the press for some days, he reviewed his decision and altered it," said former New York Democratic Gov. Mario M. Cuomo. "He altered it into a form that was acceptable to the people who were criticizing him. . . . And no one but God knows exactly why he did that."

Cuomo has joined with Simpson and a number of other former lawmakers and legal experts to form a group called "Citizens for Independent Courts." The group will argue that granting the courts considerable autonomy is in the nation's best interest.

The judiciary is designed to be the only branch of government that does not respond to political pressure. The Constitution gives judges lifetime tenure so they can make rulings based solely on the law, as informed by their legal education and experience. If parties in lawsuits believe that rulings are made on the basis of polls, popular sentiment or political pressure, it undermines judges' authority, said William S. Sessions, a former district judge and FBI director from 1987-93.

"Having judges rule on the basis of law is a tremendous advantage to society," Sessions said.

Another function of a strong and independent judiciary is to check the excesses of the other two branches. When Roosevelt attempted his court-packing scheme, he was, in essence, trying to take over all three branches of government. Thanks to huge Democratic majorities in both houses of

Congress after the 1936 election, he had control of two but mused over a recalcitrant court that blocked many of his early legislative proposals. He looked at the three branches not as autonomous entities striving to check each other, but as a team of horses that should function together, with the president as driver.

"Two of the three horses are pulling in unison," he said in a radio address advocating his plan. "A third is not."

The courts routinely rule on congressional and presidential powers and prerogatives. The Supreme Court has recently struck down a number of public laws on the grounds that they represented an overstepping of congressional authority. A unanimous court in 1974 forced President Richard M. Nixon to release his White House tape recordings, precipitating the end of his presidency. And Judge Norma Holloway Johnson has ruled against President Clinton, who sought to shield his aides from having to testify in the ongoing investigation by Independent Counsel Kenneth W. Starr. (*1998 CQ Weekly, p. 1686*)

Defenders of the courts say the judiciary needs its independence to serve as a counterweight to the other branches. Attacking it, they say, could come back to haunt conservatives.

"A true conservative would want to maintain the independence of the judiciary, because it is the last best break on a runaway executive," said Sen. Patrick J. Leahy, D-Vt.

A New Level

After being virtually shut down in 1996 and 1997, the pace of confirmations has picked up this year, partly because of some pointed complaints from Chief Justice William H. Rehnquist (who even took the unusual step of attending a Democrats-only luncheon in the Senate). Also, Senate Judiciary Committee Chairman Orrin G. Hatch, R-Utah, has been willing to stand up to pressure from other committee members who want to block the nominees.

Certain courts have been hit harder than others by this slowdown. The San Francisco-based 9th Circuit Court of Appeals, which has a reputation for liberalism and a knack for being reversed by the Supreme Court, had 10 open slots out of 28 at the end of last year. This shortfall of judges has meant lengthy delays in trials, and considerable haste when they do come up, said Chief Judge Proctor Hug Jr. Struggling to keep up

with his caseload, he has had to bring some judges out of semi-retirement and import others from other regions.

"We have made superhuman efforts," said Hug. "I have pleaded with our judges to take more than they otherwise would. I've noticed there is a real burnout level in the judges. There's a feeling we just need more time with these cases."

A debate rages over whether these types of holdups are merely Republicans retaliating for the Bork affair, or whether they are so widespread that they represent an entirely new level of partisan judicial politics.

Democrats tended to go after high court judges such as Bork and a select few lower court judges. Their strategy was to publicly attack them to build enough votes to defeat the nominations.

"Before my eyes, they turned [Bork] into a gargoyle — a sexist, racist, invader of the bedroom, violator of women," said Simpson. "That was repugnant to me."

Republican senators who were elected in 1994 have not had a crack at a Clinton nominee to the Supreme Court yet. But in lower court positions, their main strategy in the past three years has been to hold up scores of nominees, preventing them from even coming up for a floor vote. Groups such as the Judicial Selection Monitoring Project, a division of the conservative Free Congress Research and Education Foundation, have mounted a full court press against Clinton nominees.

"We want to make sure that the Senate does not underestimate how strongly the American people feel about standing up to judicial activism," said project director Thomas L. Jipping.

The Senate has responded to this pressure not so much by defeating nominees as delaying them. If and when nominations do reach the floor and are openly debated, they usually pass with relative ease. For instance, Margaret M. Morrow, a corporate lawyer from Los Angeles, saw her nomination to a district court judgeship held up for nearly two years amid intense criticism that she was an activist in waiting. When she finally got a vote Feb. 11, she was approved 67-28.

"You have extremely good people who are held in limbo for year after year," said Leahy. "If you are a woman

FRED O. SEIBEL / RICHMOND TIMES DISPATCH

or a minority, you are held longer. It may be coincidental but it's what happens. It's demeaning to the court, and it's demeaning to the Senate."

Issues of Jurisdiction

Starting when the Democrats controlled Capitol Hill, but picking up considerably under Republican rule, Congress has been keen to tell the courts what they can and cannot rule on.

The 1996 immigration bill (PL 104-208), for instance, contains a section saying certain deportation orders issued by the Justice Department are "not reviewable in a court of law." A similar provision, included in a portion of the 1996 omnibus spending bill, was designed to limit prison inmates' ability to file grievance cases in federal courts (PL 103-134). Another measure (PL 104-132) would significantly limit the ability of prisoners to use habeas corpus appeals to federal judges to question the constitutionality of their convictions. These appeals are often used by death row inmates to have their executions delayed or blocked entirely. (*Immigration, 1996 Almanac, p. 5-3; prison litigation, p. 10-5; anti-terrorism death penalty, p. 5-18*)

Not surprisingly, these types of limitations enrage civil rights groups, which say Congress is imposing its ideology on the courts by preventing them from ruling on certain issues.

"When Congress selectively removes particular issues, then it is in effect prescribing the outcome," said Nadine Strossen, national president of the

American Civil Liberties Union.

Limiting the jurisdiction of federal judges was the purpose behind a bill (HR 1252) the House passed April 23. In its original form it would have prevented any judge from issuing an order that forced a local jurisdiction to raise taxes. It also would have allowed civil litigants to reject the first judge assigned to them. (1998 *CQ Weekly, p. 1074*)

Although these two provisions were dropped, the measure still included jurisdictional limits and an overall tone expressing a lack of confidence in the courts. It would strengthen provisions in earlier laws limiting federal court involvement with prison crowding issues. And it would further limit habeas corpus appeals.

The bill would also attempt to protect public referendums from judges such as Henderson by stipulating that they could be struck down only by a three-judge panel. The measure would take a swipe at the judiciary's ability to police itself by requiring that judicial misconduct cases be automatically transferred to another part of the country. (The provision arose from the Nixon case in Tennessee, after judges there quickly dismissed a misconduct case against him.)

At the same time that Congress has limited federal court involvement in liberal causes, it has greatly increased its role in dealing with crime. As Congress has passed numerous bills creating new federal offenses, it has not only increased the workload for the Justice Department and the FBI but also for the federal courts that must now hear all these cases. Since criminal defendants have a constitutional right to a speedy trial, this onslaught of cases means important civil cases are often put on the back burner or not heard, because the litigants do not think it worth the wait.

Rehnquist has sharply criticized congressional treatment of the judiciary.

This trend has not only come under attack from liberal groups, which see it as more evidence that Congress is attempting to legislate judicial output by dictating input. It has also been sternly criticized by Rehnquist.

In a May 11 speech, the chief justice complained bitterly about expanded federal authority in pending juvenile crime legislation (HR 3, S 10). Rather than focus the burden on the courts (which he has cited before), Rehnquist spoke in terms designed to capture the attention of congressional Republicans. He said the juvenile crime bills are hardly conservative, because they involve a vast expansion of the federal government's role in crime fighting. Indeed, he said, they represent a fundamental violation of federalist principles developed by some of the party's brightest lights — namely Abraham Lincoln and Dwight D. Eisenhower.

He suggested Congress was unwittingly erecting a government not unlike the highly centralized system in France.

"How much of the complex system of legal relationships in this country should be decided in Washington, and how much by state and local governments?" he asked. "Do we really want to move forward into the 21st century with the prospect that our system will look more and more like the French government?"

A 'Three Bowler' Issue

Criticizing judges and nominees is fairly easy. And passing bills limiting their jurisdiction wins plaudits from conservative groups. In contrast, advocates of a more independent judiciary, such as Cuomo and Simpson, find themselves dealing with a very dry and complicated issue when they start talking.

Charles Geyh, a professor at Case Western Reserve University in Cleveland and a consultant to the American Judicature Society, an organization of legal professionals, calls it a "three-bowler" issue. This means that even if he can get a newspaper writer to tackle the issue, it usually results in little more than a series of sleep-induced splashes.

"Your face falls into the cereal bowl three times before getting through the article," he said.

Be that as it may, defenders of an independent judiciary say it is vital that the issue be raised. Judges do not feel it appropriate to publicly defend themselves, their rulings or the institution they represent. Rehnquist's comments are considered by many to be extraordinary, even though they are couched in measured and legalistic terms.

Because judges usually steer clear of political debate, it is vital that someone speak up on behalf of the judiciary, said Sessions.

"We should be very concerned about this," he said. "It is very easy in this day and time to destroy a perfectly valid judge. Similarly, it is possible to attack the judiciary broadly and take away respect for the rule of law." ◆

From courts to congressional committees, battles rage over the 2000 count

Census: A Political Calculation

As famed as the Bureau of the Census is for collecting the statistical strands of American life, it has never tabulated one important detail — the number of angry words exchanged over how the head count is conducted.

Even without an official tally, the number is immense. And the fight over the 2000 census may become the most bruising in recent history. That is no small achievement given the level of controversy surrounding almost every census since the first one in 1790.

Nearly two years before the next count is to begin, the battle over the 2000 census has already spawned two lawsuits, delayed passage of a disaster relief bill in 1997 (PL 105-18) because it contained a rider prohibiting the Census Bureau from using statistical sampling, and, in recent weeks, fueled an increasingly abrasive stream of words over the bureau's plan for conducting the census. Many believe the fight will continue even beyond April 1, 2000, when the count is to officially begin. *(1997 CQ Weekly, p. 1362)*

"It shouldn't be a surprise to anyone that the census is contentious because it's at the core of political representation. But the tenor of the debate has become more harsh," said TerriAnn Lowenthal, an independent consultant on census issues and former staff director of a House oversight panel on the 1990 census. The latest twist occurred June 24 when a House Appropriations subcommittee approved a bill that would stop funding for the Census Bureau on March 31, 1999, unless a dispute is resolved over how the census will be conducted. *(1998 CQ Weekly, p. 1769)*

The agency proposes using statistical sampling on a large scale for the first time to improve the accuracy of the count. Critics, including many Republicans, vehemently oppose such a step, arguing that it would not necessarily improve accuracy and that the numbers could be manipulated. So broad are the differences that cen-

Clinton visits a Houston clinic that operates a Women, Infants and Children program. He was at the clinic June 2 for a tour and a discussion about census accuracy.

sus officials are concerned the stalemate could directly affect the census by disrupting funding and distracting bureau officials with political concerns.

Commerce Secretary William M. Daley urged the House on July 8 not to allow political differences over the use of statistical sampling to interfere with the census, though he conceded that the battle lines are so hardened that his plea will likely be ignored.

"The success of census 2000 absolutely requires that there be no interruption in full funding," Daley said, noting that important preliminary work will begin this fall.

"This kind of living with a sword over the Census Bureau's head does not lend well to long-term planning. ... If Congress is going to have a fight and vote over what method ought to be used ... they should not hold hostage the census," Daley said.

And he said that if Congress failed to heed his warning, he would recommend that President Clinton veto not just the Census Bureau's $4 billion spending plan, but the entire fiscal 1999 $33 billion appropriations bill

for the departments of Commerce, State and Justice that contains the funding for the decennial count.

Republicans, most of whom oppose a census using sampling, are unlikely to be swayed by such threats. "It's very irresponsible to use a plan that is unproven and which has failed in the past," said Rep. Dan Miller of Florida, chairman of the House Government Reform and Oversight subcommittee on the census, who holds a doctorate in marketing and statistics.

Miller, like many of his Republican allies, objects to sampling on several levels. It is unconstitutional, he said, and it is too complicated to carry out on a large scale. Most important, it can be manipulated for political gain by a Democratic administration, he said.

"This should not be a partisan issue," Miller said. "But it is the administration that wants to make a change after 200 years that will benefit them."

History of Controversy

By now, however, the Census Bureau should be accustomed to living under a sword that has been dangling precariously for more than 200 years.

In 1792, George Washington issued the first presidential veto in history because he disagreed with the way Congress decided to apportion itself based on the 1790 census which put the population at 3.9 million.

According to the General Accounting Office, the experience in 1790 set the stage for the next two centuries.

"Ever since George Washington questioned the results of the first census in (1792), the accuracy of any given census has been in question," said a GAO report issued in May. "The questions have always been legitimate: The census has never counted 100 percent of those it should, in part, because American sensibilities would probably not tolerate more foolproof census-taking methods."

There are ways to ensure a better count using traditional practices, experts say, but Americans, not to mention Congress, would never accept the conditions that would have to be imposed. The census could be made precise if people were required to register with the government. Or, the country could follow the example set by Turkey, where a 14-hour mandatory curfew was imposed in December 1997 so census canvassers could easily count people.

Chronic Undercount

Doubts and disputes about the census have surfaced with regularity every 10 years, with much of the attention focused on the size of the undercount.

As the GAO report pointed out, "The debates over the years about methods of apportionment focused on mathematics, but the crux of the matter was political power."

The pressure became even more acute in 1911 when Congress set the number of representatives at 435. After that action, a gain of representation in any one state came only at the loss of representation in another.

Concerns about the accuracy of the census crystallized in 1941 when the number of men turning out for the wartime draft was considerably higher than the number anticipated by the 1940 census.

There have been more recent controversies, too. Several states and cities sued the government in 1991 when Commerce Secretary Robert A. Mosbacher refused a Census Bureau request to adjust the 1990 census to compensate for an undercount. The case ended in 1996 when the Supreme Court ruled against the suit. (*1996 Almanac, p. 5-52*)

But this year, criticism has spilled beyond questions of how the count will be conducted to the motives of key officials to charges of racism from both sides.

The fights, says historian Margo J. Anderson of the University of Wisconsin at Milwaukee, "are structural to the process. The decision over how to count can be dressed up as science over politics, but the bottom line is, one side usually ends up with the advantage."

The struggle for advantage is being played out in full fury in the House where Democrats support the proposal as the best way to count every American, including minority populations that traditionally have been undercounted.

Embarrassed by missing an estimated 4 million Americans in the 1990 census, the Census Bureau recommended that statistical sampling be used in 2000 to ensure a more accurate count. Under the bureau's proposal, at least 90 percent of the people in every census tract (a geographic area) would be physically counted.

Sampling would then be used to fill in the statistical holes. Census officials insist sampling is a valid approach that will yield a more accurate census at a lower cost. Republicans, however, claim the technique is unconstitutional and open to political manipulation.

"It is a very risky approach," Miller said, voicing concerns by some statisticians that the Census Bureau may not have enough time to develop a fail-safe sampling program.

The Senate, meanwhile, has shown no interest in the debate.

"We represent the same amount of people, no matter how they count them," said Sen. Judd Gregg, R-N.H.

Money and Politics

The view is far different in the House, where the fight is being fueled by two of the most powerful forces in Washington — money and politics.

Census results help determine how $180 billion annually in federal spending is distributed through 20 grant programs, including such impor-

Up in Smoke

A 1921 fire that started in a storage room of the Commerce Building on Pennsylvania Avenue wiped out or damaged much of the 1890 census.

When the smoke cleared on Jan. 10, 1921, it was a disaster for historians.

Officials determined that about 25 percent of the completed census surveys had been destroyed, and half of the remaining surveys had been damaged.

Although the 1890 data had been analyzed by statisticians, the original questionnaires were irreplaceable. It was the first time questions had been asked about such issues as race, homeownership, ability to speak English and service in the Civil War.

The questionnaires were stacked outside a vault containing other census records. But as fate would have it, they were directly in the path of firefighters.

The cause of the three-alarm fire was never determined. Many suspected it was caused by a cigarette.

The disaster heightened awareness among researchers and historians of the need for formal archiving procedures to prevent destruction of valuable documents. The public furor that ensued over the Commerce building fire led to the 1933 construction of the National Archives building to protect national documents.

In 1938, the Census Bureau took other steps to protect the census, copying completed questionnaires onto microfilm.

The microfilmed records are open to the public after 72 years, a waiting period that became law in 1978 (PL 95–416). (*178 Almanac, p. 815*)

While the National Archives felt access to the schedules would benefit historians, the Census Bureau wanted to preserve the confidentiality of all those surveyed.

tant ones as Medicaid and educational assistance to poor children.

And, most important for the political landscape, the results form the basis for redrawing boundary lines for congressional districts as well as those for state legislatures.

The Census Bureau, Miller said, "is one institution of government that should be above politics. Most elected officials in this country are dependent on a fair and accurate census, and if people don't trust it, it is a real threat to our democratic process."

With such high stakes comes sharp rhetoric.

One particularly acerbic display occurred June 23, when Miller derided Kenneth Prewitt, Clinton's choice to head the agency, as an academic who is ill-equipped to manage the logistics of the massive undertaking.

"The bureau needs a Gen. [H. Norman] Schwarzkopf, not a Professor Sherman Klunk, to save the census," Miller said on the House floor. "So why did the president nominate an academic? Because of politics."

That same day, Loretta Sanchez, D-Calif., proclaimed on the House floor:

"The Republican leadership of the House fails to match their rhetoric in favor of a colorblind America with deeds. . . . We who oppose government-sanctioned racism will not be silenced by these attacks. We will stand in this well as long as it takes to shed light and bring honest debate about the merits of an accurate census. . . . Race became an issue by those who have turned this process into a fight over raw political power."

Two weeks earlier, on June 11, when a Republican-sponsored court challenge to the bureau's plans for the 2000 census was heard in U.S. District Court in Washington, D.C., Democrats had first unleashed their own tough talk.

"Shame on Newt Gingrich and other Republican extremists who want to pursue another racially exclusionary and inaccurate census in the year 2000," said J. Gerald Hebert, counsel to the Democratic Congressional Campaign Committee.

Driving the fight is the bureau's plan to break from tradition by using statistical sampling on a large scale to augment the physical count of the population.

Without sampling, supporters say, the 2000 census will be less accurate

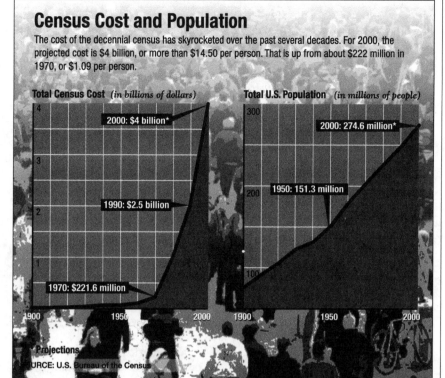

Census Cost and Population

The cost of the decennial census has skyrocketed over the past several decades. For 2000, the projected cost is $4 billion, or more than $14.50 per person. That is up from about $222 million in 1970, or $1.09 per person.

than the one conducted in 1990, which was the most inaccurate in decades. The 1990 census, which cost $2.6 billion, earned the dubious honor of being the first census in modern history to be less accurate than the one preceding it.

The 2000 census, by comparison, is projected to cost $4 billion if sampling is used. That is nearly twice the $2.6 billion spent in 1990 and four times the $1.1 billion cost in 1980. With costs so high, census officials say they feel pressure to deliver the most accurate count possible.

"You could end up spending $4.7 billion and have a worse census than you had in 1990," Daley said.

Counting Heads

The Census Bureau, backed by the National Academy of Sciences, proposed to increase accuracy by augmenting the traditional count with statistical sampling. Under the Census Bureau's proposal, most Americans would be counted the traditional way by tabulating surveys returned in the mail and follow-up interviews by census-takers for those who did not respond.

Even with such arduous work, census officials and other experts say it is impossible to count everybody using those methods.

Sampling would use the information gained from physically counting at least 90 percent of the people in a given census tract and project the remaining population. The accuracy of the projections would be buttressed by a separate survey of 750,000 households nationwide.

That approach has been deemed scientifically valid by the National Academy of Sciences, the General Accounting Office and the Commerce Department's inspector general.

But House Republicans, led by Speaker Gingrich, R-Ga., filed a lawsuit in U.S. District Court in Washington, arguing that sampling is illegal because the Constitution requires an "actual enumeration" every 10 years.

A second lawsuit was filed with a special three-judge federal panel in U.S. District Court in Alexandria, Va., on behalf of several plaintiffs led by Matthew Glavin, president of the Southeastern Legal Foundation of Atlanta. Both cases are pending.

When the Constitution was written, Maureen E. Mahoney, a lawyer representing House Republicans, told a special three-judge panel at the U.S. District Court in Washington on June 11, "The word 'enumerate,' in every dictionary at the time, said to count one-by-one or reckon singularly."

In other words, Mahoney said, the

Constitution requires the census to be based on a physical counting of the population and not statistical extrapolation.

No matter what the court rules, an appeal to the Supreme Court is a virtual certainty, Republicans and Democrats agree.

Outside the courtroom, however, the legal arguments are supplanted by political realities. Democrats believe a more accurate count would help them because minorities, who tend to vote for Democrats, are the most-often-missed group. Republicans recognize the same phenomenon and charge that a census with sampling would be flawed.

"Having the power to define population as the basis both for representation and for federal funding is an enormous concentration of power," Gingrich wrote in his most recent book, "Lessons Learned the Hard Way."

In addition, Gingrich pointed out, the Census Bureau is part of Daley's Commerce Department. Daley is the son of the late mayor of Chicago Richard Daley, famed for creating a Democratic machine often accused of using unorthodox methods to ensure victory.

Gingrich wrote, "The specter of putting someone so closely connected to the Chicago Democratic machine in charge of the census with a statistical adjustment was too chilling even to contemplate."

Daley is fully aware of the tumultuous history of the census, but he believes the debate has gone beyond the normal bounds.

"People's motives are being questioned; [critics ask] how are you going to politically cook the books? It's ridiculous," he said in a July 8 interview.

"This is a career operation; we have more monitoring and oversight, and the idea that somebody is going to go in some room and cook some numbers just feeds an attitude, a cynicism that is distressing," Daley added.

Republican political operatives warn that sampling could make vulnerable 24 Republican House seats, a distressing prospect for a party with a thin, 228-206 majority.

Historians and other analysts, however, believe that number exaggerates the threat. Historically, about 10 seats shift after each census, but even that is a rough estimate.

"What the census does is count people. It has no correlation to voters," said Anderson, who wrote a respected history of the census. "The census does not count only the politically active."

She and others point out that it would be difficult to tilt the numbers even if the Census Bureau wanted to do so. And that's unlikely, Democrats said, because the bureau has only two political appointees out of a work force of over 10,000.

Republicans, however, have focused most of their criticism on fears that a Democratic administration would use the census to benefit its party and candidates.

"Our Constitution calls for an actual enumeration of citizens, not just an educated guess by Washington bureaucrats," Rep. John A. Boehner, R-Ohio, said.

"The American people deserve to be properly represented. Sampling corrupts a basic sense of fairness by treating people as numbers that can be estimated, rather than individuals who have a right to be counted. . . . Sampling is very simply an attempt by a politics-obsessed White House to politicize this important individual right and constitutional obligation," he added.

Democratic Rep. Carolyn B. Maloney of New York worries, like Boehner, that a flawed census could undermine democracy. She argued that an inaccurate census could benefit the Republicans.

"The sad truth is that the Census Bureau has developed a plan that will count everyone who lives in America, including blacks and Latinos and the poor and Asians and whites, everyone," she said on the House floor June 23. "But some members of Congress do not want that to happen. Why? Because they believe not counting certain minorities and the poor is to their political advantage."

Back and forth it goes with almost no movement or compromise. Anderson predicts a more subtle result, one deeply rooted in census history.

If the Republicans prevail, she said, "We may end up with crummy data, and we, as a society, will have to live with that." ◆

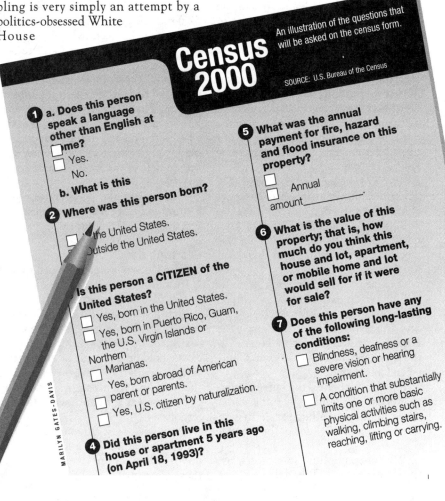

An illustration of the questions that will be asked on the census form.

SOURCE: U.S. Bureau of the Census

Politics and Public Policy

The term *public policy making* refers to action taken by the government to address issues on the public agenda; it also refers to the method by which a decision to act on policy is reached. The work of Congress, the president and the federal bureaucracy, and the judiciary is to make, implement, and rule on the policy decisions. Articles in this section discuss major policy issues that came before the federal government in the second half of 1998, most of which are likely to remain in the public eye well into 1999.

One of the most contentious issues to come before Congress in 1998 was managed health care reform. Although there was widespread agreement among Democrats and Republicans that the system needed fixing, disagreement over specific legislative proposals stymied reform efforts. The lead story in this section examines the proposals currently on the table and explains why this issue is laden with political pitfalls that could postpone a final agreement indefinitely.

Another issue that captured lawmakers' attention during the second session of the 105th Congress was Internet regulation. Much of the debate was driven by privacy concerns and the disturbing lack of protection for distributing personal information online. As Congress sought to address these concerns, it remained mindful of the costs of regulation. A pair of stories investigates the Internet policy debate, reviews Congress's legislative progress, including passage of copyright protection for digital works and a moratorium on state and local taxes of Internet commerce, and discusses the Internet issues that will occupy lawmakers in the 106th Congress.

Rounding out the section are discussions of other important public policy topics: the battle over free trade legislation that would aid businesses hit hard by the international financial crisis; the difficult question of how to spend, or not spend, the first budget surplus since 1969; the uncertain future of Social Security reform now that presidential leadership on the issue has been seriously weakened by the Monica Lewinsky scandal; and the implications of Congress's five-year reauthorization of the 1965 Higher Education Act, which reduced student loan interest rates to their lowest level in nearly two decades.

These complex public policy issues are clearly explained in the articles that follow. As many of the topics discussed here will remain at the top of Congress's agenda in the months ahead, the reports are valuable as issue studies, predictors of legislative outcomes, and primers on the policy-making process.

Lawmakers agree on the need for changes in managed care — but only in principle

Patients' Rights Bill May Die Aborning

Lawmakers are united in advocating "patients' rights," but beneath the veneer of consensus, they have deep differences over specific legislative proposals. The most likely outcome, many Congress watchers say, is either no bill at all or a narrow, scaled-back compromise designed more for politics than for patients.

Jacqueline Lee personifies the ills of managed care. During a hike in Shenandoah National Park two years ago, Lee stumbled on a rock and rolled off a 40-foot cliff, suffering multiple fractures. A second painful blow came when her insurer refused to pay the $10,000 hospital bill because Lee did not seek "pre-authorization" for treatment.

The 28-year-old woman's story has been too good for politicians to resist. She has appeared at events where Democrats and Republicans promoted their competing managed care bills.

But Lee and other consumers of health care may be excused for seeming to take both sides. For months, Democrats and Republicans have sounded the same themes in assailing managed care: Emergency care should always be covered. Insurers should not be allowed to interfere with discussions between doctors and their patients. Patients should have the right to appeal insurers' decisions. Health plans must be held accountable for their actions.

Yet underneath what seems like a ready-made consensus are deep differences that threaten to kill any potential for legislation this year that both chambers could agree on and President Clinton would sign into law. A deal on health care would require the two sides to compromise on basic and long-held beliefs about the proper role and reach of government in health care, the extent to which people should have legal recourse over the outcome of care, and the ability of free-market principles to

work in a rapidly changing industry with skyrocketing costs.

For Republicans, any legislation that would bring about substantial new regulations would entail the risk of angering their traditional political allies in the business community. It

would also involve an admission that some government intervention is necessary to resolve inequities in the current system, a partial reversal of the course the GOP set in 1994 when it rejected President Clinton's mammoth proposal that would have vastly broadened the federal government's role in the nation's health care system. (*1994 Almanac, p. 319*)

For Democrats, getting some of the patient protections they have pushed for may require abandoning others and letting the GOP take some credit for resolving an issue Democrats seized months ago.

Many experts are betting on no compromise at all.

"The smart money would probably say no," said Robert D. Reischauer, senior fellow at the Brookings Institution, when asked if he thought the two sides were likely to produce a bill that Clinton would sign into law.

Reischauer, former director of the Congressional Budget Office, said that because the issue is complex and has so many political pitfalls, it is unlikely that Congress could find the time necessary to resolve it in an already filled election year legislative agenda.

David Hebert, chairman of the Patient Access to Responsible Care Alliance, a coalition of health care providers such as chiropractors, nurse anesthetists and podiatrists, agreed that Congress is unlikely to produce a bill.

"I'm not convinced that anything will pass. There's no unanimity of opinion over what should be in the package," he said.

Even Senate Minority Leader Tom Daschle, D-S.D., pegged potential passage at "50-50."

Confusion Abounds

The Lee story reflects the confusion involved in sorting through the managed care proposals. Just understanding how the current system works is hard enough, making the development of legislation to solve perceived problems extremely difficult.

Underlying the complexities are enormous stakes. About 85 percent of Americans currently in employer-sponsored plans are in managed care, meaning any mistakes are guaranteed to come back to haunt legislators.

As managed care has taken a broader role, its ability to deliver health care has been challenged, drawing attention from both state and federal lawmakers. Horror stories such as Lee's resonate within the hearing rooms and into the media — her account has appeared on three television networks and in several newspaper and magazine articles — about how health maintenance organizations deny care and create bureaucratic snafus that, at best, are irritating to patients and, at worst, contribute to serious illness or death.

Industry officials defend managed care as a successful system that has not only helped reduce costs but has also improved the quality of care for millions of Americans. They say patient horror stories are rare and that Congress should not use such anecdotes as the basis for legislation that would drive up premiums and cause some employers to drop coverage for workers.

"Currently, the managed care reform debate is heavily politicized, and it is virtually impossible to expect any realistic, objective consideration about how any of the major legislative proposals will raise consumers' costs and vastly increase the number of uninsured Americans," said Chip Kahn, Chief Operating Officer of the Health Insurance Association of America (HIAA), a major industry group.

An article in the July/August issue of the journal Health Affairs captures the paradox that lawmakers face. Titled "Understanding the Managed Care Backlash," its authors note "two seemingly contradictory pieces of information. One suggests that Americans are satisfied with their health insurance plans, regardless of whether the plans are traditional fee-for-service or managed care. The other indicates that the public favors regulation of managed care plans, even if it raises costs. How can this seeming inconsistency be resolved?"

The question puts legislators in the position of reacting to fear of the unknown. Stories such as Lee's may generate fear even among voters who are happy with their managed care plans. And they are looking to Washington for assurances.

Points of Disagreement

One of the most significant political flashpoints in the managed care debate is the issue of whether patients should have the right to sue their health plans for damages.

Currently, patients whose health plans are governed by the federal Employee Retirement Income Security Act (ERISA) cannot sue insurers' plans in state courts over coverage disputes, because ERISA pre-empts state laws. Under the 1974 law (PL 93-406), patients can sue in federal court, but can recover only the cost of denied treatment.

Democrats have pushed for lifting the ERISA pre-emption, arguing that consumers should be able to seek legal redress and collect damages when health plans make decisions that cause serious harm or death.

But many Republicans, as well as business and industry groups, argue that removing the ERISA shield would expose employers to

CQ PHOTO / SCOTT J. FERRELL

lawsuits. They also say ERISA gives them flexibility to coordinate health plans for employees who work in different states.

Some business groups, such as the U.S. Chamber of Commerce, have even said that if the ERISA pre-emption is taken away, they would urge member companies to stop offering health insurance and instead give employees a cash equivalent, which they could use to purchase coverage. On their own, however, workers probably would not be able to buy the same type of health plan at the same price as

For months, President Clinton has been urging Congress to pass a Democratic "patients' bill of rights." His administration has threatened to veto the current House GOP version.

Side-by-Side Comparisons

Issue	Senate GOP (S 2330)	House-passed GOP (HR 4250)	Democrats (S 1890; HR 3605)
Malpractice lawsuits	No provision.	Modifies 1974 Employee Retirement Income Security Act (PL 93-406) to give patients broader legal recourse to collect damages from insurers. Health plans could be fined up to $250,000 for withholding coverage.	Amends ERISA to give patients ability to sue health plans under applicable state laws.
Malpractice damages cap	No cap.	Sets a $250,000 ceiling on non-economic (so-called pain and suffering) damages that a patient can be awarded in a lawsuit. Limit would not apply if a state already has a higher cap in place or enacts a new one.	No cap.
Primary care for women	Allows direct access to gynecologists without referral.	Similar provision.	Similar provision. Women may also choose gynecologists as their primary care physicians.
Mastectomies	Stipulates decisions regarding postoperative hospital stays be made by doctors and patients. Health plans that cover mastectomies must cover reconstructive breast surgery.	No provision.	Requires health plans to pay for a minimum 48-hour hospital stay. Requires coverage of post-mastectomy reconstructive breast surgery.
Internal appeals	Mandates an internal appeals process, giving patients more leverage to challenge a plan's coverage decision. Complaints must be addressed within 30 days, and in 72 hours for medical emergencies.	Establishes internal appeals process with same deadlines for decisions as the Senate plan.	Internal appeals must be decided within 15 business days, or 72 hours for emergencies.
External appeals	Mandates a binding external review process but limits those reviews to medical expenses exceeding $1,000 and procedures that are experimental, such as cancer treatments.	Does not limit appeals, but allows health plans to charge patients seeking an appeal between $25 and $100, or 10% of cost of medical procedure, whichever is less. Plans not complying with results of appeal could pay up to $250,000. Additional fines may be added by a judge.	Allows external appeals if care is denied because it is deemed medically unnecessary and the amount exceeds a "significant threshold," or if patient's life or health is in jeopardy. Decisions must be made within 60 days, or 72 hours for emergencies.

Side-by-Side Comparisons

Issue	Senate GOP (S 2330)	House-passed GOP (HR 4250)	Democrats (S 1890; HR 3605)
Medical savings accounts	Lifts many current restrictions on medical savings accounts (MSAs), tax-exempt savings accounts to pay medical expenses. Lifts cap on number of MSAs that can be sold nationwide.	Expands access to MSAs, with many similarities to the Senate plan.	No provision.
Gag rules	Prohibits health plans from dictating to health care providers what treatment options may or may not be discussed in conferences with patients.	Goes a step further than Senate bill, saying doctor-patient conversations could not be restricted by health plan.	Similar provision to House Republican bill.
HealthMarts	No provision.	Allows small businesses, insurers and health care providers to join forces and create purchasing pools to develop and administer health plans for workers. Effective date: Jan. 1, 2000.	No provision.
Association health plans	No provision.	Amends ERISA to allow church, trade and business organizations to form alliances and purchase insurance at rates lower than if they bought coverage individually.	No provision.
Point of service	Requires employers with more than 50 workers to offer the "point of service" option, which would permit employees to choose a health care provider from outside a pre-approved list. Employee would have to pay the difference.	Requires employers to offer the point of service option. Exceptions include companies that make health insurance available through a HealthMart or if insurance costs rise more than 1 percent.	Requires employers to offer point of service unless the employer offers at least one other health plan administered by a different company, or two or more health plans that have provider networks which "differ significantly."
Emergency care	Does not require pre-authorization for initial screenings if a "prudent layperson" would deem emergency care necessary or if patient is suffering "severe pain." For additional tests, approval of a "prudent emergency medical professional" would be required.	Uses prudent layperson definition for authorization of initial coverage. For additional tests, would require approval of a "prudent emergency medical professional."	Uses prudent layperson standard, but also includes requirement that emergency care be covered for "severe pain." Plans must cover post-stabilization and maintenance care when necessary.

employers, who can negotiate discounts based on purchasing volume.

While the White House has insisted that patients have a right to sue their health plans in state courts, there may be room for negotiation. In recent weeks, administration officials have said that giving consumers a legally enforceable right to take action against their health plans would be acceptable.

The administration's broadening of the language it will accept on the issue opens the door to compromise on one of the most problematic parts of the bill. If the two sides can reach agreement on liability, it may bode well for agreement in other areas.

Another point of dissent is over a Republican proposal to broaden the current rules governing medical savings accounts (MSAs), tax-exempt accounts that can be used for medical expenses. An experiment with such savings accounts was part of a 1996 health law (PL 104-191) designed to help make it easier for millions of Americans to keep their health insurance when they change jobs, start their own businesses or get sick. *(1996 Almanac, p. 6-28)*

The MSAs, which are included in both Senate and House Republican bills, have generated spirited partisan debate. Democrats, when pressed, may accept some broadening of the 1996 law but are unlikely to agree to completely lifting the current restrictions.

Republicans, saying the accounts are critical to giving people more choices for their health care, want to lift the limit on the number of such accounts. The accounts would be teamed with high-deductible insurance policies to cover catastrophic illnesses.

With such accounts, Republicans argue, people would be able to compare prices for medical treatment and circumvent managed care altogether.

"They simply call their doctor and say, 'Do you take Visa, Master Charge or a check?' " Sen. Phil Gramm, R-Texas, said recently.

Democrats argue that broadening the use of medical savings accounts will weaken the current health insurance system.

"Expanding the availability of medical savings accounts would give tax breaks to the healthy and wealthy while increasing costs of health insurance for the sicker and poorer," Jose E. Serrano, D-N.Y., said during House debate on the Republican bill July 24.

The parties also diverge on the issue of patient appeals. House Republicans want consumers to pay up to $100 before they seek an external appeal, because some up-front payment from patients will help ward off frivolous challenges. Senate Republicans would limit such appeals to medical expenses that exceed $1,000 or to procedures that are experimental, such as certain cancer treatments. Democrats would leave it up to the Department of Health and Human

At a Capitol Hill news conference July 16, American Medical Association Chairman Dr. Randolph D. Smoak urged passage of the Democrats' managed care bill.

Services to set a "significant threshold" before an external appeal can occur.

Disagreements exist not only between the two parties — Republicans hail a market-based solution while Democrats urge more federal involvement — but within the GOP. *(Bill comparison, p. 2076)*

House GOP members back purchasing cooperatives that would allow small businesses and groups to combine resources and buy health coverage at more affordable rates that would be exempt from many — possibly all — state

regulations. Backers of the alliances say they would help reduce the number of uninsured individuals. Democrats and consumer groups have said establishing those purchasing cooperatives would destroy the delicate balance that spreads risk in the current insurance market. Senate Republicans are unwilling to take such regulatory power away from states.

Republicans are battling not only among themselves but also with their traditional bases of support, business and insurance groups, which GOP leaders hesitate to regulate. Those interests have waged an all-out campaign to block both the Democrats' and Republicans' plans.

The American Medical Association, a longtime ally of Republicans and a hefty party contributor, has sided with Democrats in part because doctors have grown tired of the constant tussle with managed care companies and believe that the Democrats' bill gives them and their patients more power to fight back. The group has praised many of the provisions in the Democratic bill, including the lifting of the ERISA protection for insurers.

"The Patients' Bill of Rights will ensure that physicians can continue to be patient advocates," said Dr. Randolph D. Smoak, AMA chairman. "It will assure that patients get the care they need when they need it."

The two parties' differences over specific provisions in the bills speak to a broader disagreement over how much power managed care plans should have in decisions involving Americans' medical care. Democrats argue that doctors should always make the decision about whether a procedure is medically necessary. But Republicans are reluctant to remove that power from insurers, fearing that such an action would permanently dismantle managed care. If an insurer cannot maintain control over what procedures it will pay for, health care costs will skyrocket by double digits, GOP lawmakers say.

"This would, in essence, eliminate the concept of insurance coverage," Gingrich said July 24 when Democrats tried to block the House GOP bill over the medical necessity issue.

Lawmakers also are divided over how broadly legislation should apply. While the House Republican and House and Senate Democratic plans would extend a set of core patient protections to members of a broad array of health plans, the Senate Republican plan would give them only to the 48 million Americans in self-insured health plans. Sponsors argue that many states already have patient protection laws in place and that the federal government should not interfere. Self-insured plans are not subject to such state

health plan, 1994 CQ Almanac, p. 319)

Daschle has said the key reason he and other Democrats are insisting on floor time for amendments is that it may be the party's only chance to make changes to the GOP measure.

"There are more of them than there are of us," Daschle said. "It's too easy for them to pass nothing more than a shell" that would provide few true pro-

cording to both Democratic and Republican pollsters.

"We see it as a top-level concern in every state and congressional district," said Democratic pollster Mark Mellman. "This issue will be everywhere during this campaign year."

The topic is a key issue in state governor races, including Florida and Arizona, in Senate races in Kentucky and North Carolina, and in dozens of House races.

Despite such evidence that managed care is hot politically, Rep. John Linder, R-Ga., chairman of the National Republican Congressional Committee, said other issues are more important to voters.

"This election is going to be fought over taxes and spending, not over managed care and tobacco," he said.

Trying to stake out a middle ground, Joseph I. Lieberman, D-Conn., John H. Chafee, R-R.I., and Bob Graham, D-Fla., on July 29 proposed a bipartisan managed care proposal.

laws.

Political Hurdles

After more than a year of hammering away at the managed care issue, Democrats and Clinton may not want to surrender ground unless they can maintain the momentum they began to build last fall when a presidential advisory commission proposed a health care "bill of rights." It called for covering emergency care; allowing patients to appeal plans' decision on coverage, payment or treatment to an outside panel and broader access to specialty care. *(1997 CQ Weekly, p. 2909)*

Democrats introduced their own managed care bill in March, soon after Republican task forces in both chambers began meeting to form their approaches to the issue. The GOP health panels emerged after Republicans initially criticized Clinton's moves on managed care as a blatant second attempt at passing his failed Health Security Act, a massive undertaking that would have altered every facet of the nation's health care system. *(Democrats' plan, 1998 CQ Weekly, p. 893; Clinton's*

tections for patients in managed care plans, he said.

Republicans are hurling similar charges at Democrats. Senate Majority Leader Trent Lott, R-Miss., said Democrats should think twice before putting their energies into making the managed care debate an issue for the fall elections instead of focusing on passing a bill this year.

"If they want an issue, they can try to do that, but I don't think it's going to sell [to the public]," Lott said.

Rep. Dave Weldon, R-Fla., who worked with the House GOP task force to develop its bill, the echoed Lott's assessment.

"It's pretty clear to everyone that Democrats want to make it a campaign issue" rather than work with Republicans to pass a bill, he said.

National Appeal

Lawmakers are under intense pressure to act because the managed care issue has resonated far beyond Washington. It has become a rallying point for candidates across the country, ac-

With comprehensive tobacco legislation dead this year on Capitol Hill, however, voters now face an advertising campaign on managed care.

The American Association of Health Plans, a managed care industry trade group, has spent $2 million so far this year on ads that charge Washington involvement will drive up costs and may cause people to lose their insurance. The group's recent spots conclude with the chilling prediction: "When politicians play doctor, real people can get hurt." *(1998 CQ Weekly, p. 1835)*

The AFL-CIO launched its own nationwide campaign July 16 to push lawmakers to enact the Democrats' measure. *(1998 CQ Weekly, p. 1933)*

Perhaps the most unusual approach taken on the issue was from the Health Benefits Coalition, a collection of business groups including the Chamber of Commerce, the National Association of Manufacturers and the National Federation of Independent Business. The group, which has spent more than $2 million so far on advertising to block pending managed care bills, and recently sent a Frankenstein look-alike to Capitol Hill to proclaim how "frightening" and "monstrous" the Democrats' bill would be for consumers.

Bill Frist, R-Tenn., a doctor who helped develop the Senate GOP managed care proposal, said he feared such advertising campaigns could intensify over the August recess, transforming the debate from one over policy to one of 30-second television spots that oversimplify and distort the issues, derailing any legislation this year.

Patients' Advocates and Cost Cutters: Congress Forced Into Contradictions

Trying to score points on the campaign trail, lawmakers rail against managed care, reciting horror stories of individuals mistreated or misdiagnosed, and promising swift action.

Back in Washington, Congress as an institution is trying to tempt, prod and even force millions of Americans in the mammoth Medicare and Medicaid programs into managed care.

A classic case of Washington double speak? Not exactly. The conflicting messages reflect the contradictory roles Congress has been forced to assume on health care.

On one hand, the public expects lawmakers to act as their advocate against what polls show many view as heavy-handed regulation in the private market. At the same time, the federal government, as the nation's largest health care purchaser, is under intense pressure to hold down costs.

The sheer size of federal programs makes it imperative to ratchet down spending. Led by states, which jointly fund Medicaid, lawmakers are turning to cheaper managed care.

Congress' tightening embrace of managed care is fraught with many of the same benefits and difficulties facing private purchasers. In government programs, as in the marketplace, managed care reduces costs and can improve services but also breeds bureaucracy and consumer confusion. Further, the well-off, who have greater political influence, have wider choices and more personal control over their care than do the poor.

"In both the private sector and the government, you've got to strike a balance between cost containment and access to good quality," said Sen. Ron Wyden, D-Ore.

Medicare, which provides health care to those 65 and older, and Medicaid, which insures the poor and provides long-term care for the elderly and disabled, together made up 19 percent of the fiscal 1997 federal budget. The administration projects fiscal 1999 Medicare spending at $224.7 billion and federal Medicaid spending at nearly $108 billion.

Consumer Protection

Both Democrats and Republicans stress that part of the consumer protections Congress is debating for private insurers were approved for Medicare and Medicaid in the 1997 balanced-budget law (PL 105-33). (*1997 Almanac, p. 2-47*)

Among the beneficiary protections were greater access to emergency room care, an appeals process and an assurance that doctors could inform patients of all their medical options.

Further, in February, President Clinton directed that federal programs come into compliance with recommendations from a presidential commission on patients' rights, guaranteeing choice of providers and confidentiality of health information. (*1998 CQ Weekly, p. 441*)

Republicans point to the Medicare guarantees to counter Democratic attacks that the GOP is reluctant to champion patients' rights.

"There's a tremendous continuity here that nobody is seeing," said Rep. Nancy L. Johnson, R-Conn., a member of the Ways and Means Health Subcommittee, which has jurisdiction over Medicare.

Lawmakers also emphasize that in Medicare, the government is providing tempting incentives, but is not herding anyone into managed care.

Seniors can now pick between traditional Medicare fee-for-service or health maintenance organizations (HMOs). In coming months under the Medicare+Choice program, seniors will be allowed, but not required, to choose from an expanded menu of managed care plans as well as medical savings accounts — options not available to millions of Americans whose coverage is limited to whatever policy their employer offers.

"We're not pushing them," said Rep. E. Clay Shaw Jr., R-Fla. "The choice is there, and the choice is theirs."

That does not mean that the path to Medicare managed care is rosy. The Clinton administration has scaled back implementation of Medicare+Choice, worried that seniors are confused about the options.

Medicaid Managed Care

While Congress expanded Medicare in the 1997 budget deal, that same law gave states increased power to mandate managed care as the sole Medicaid option.

Medicaid covers about 40 million poor, disabled and elderly Americans. It also pays for about half the nation's nursing home care. More than 15 million Medicaid recipients are enrolled in managed care plans, up from 2.7 million in 1991.

Governors for a decade have been experimenting with managed care, desperate to tame soaring costs. In the late 1980s and early 1990s, Medicaid spending was increasing 20 percent a year, squeezing out other state priorities. The rate of growth has since leveled off.

"The federal government has got to be vigilant on this issue to be sure that poor, vulnerable people aren't taken advantage of," said Rep. Henry A. Waxman, D-Calif., a main architect of the modern Medicaid program.

Managed care has been seen as more than a financial tonic. It was also a means to improve quality. While middle-class consumers, losing the freedom to choose their doctors, chafe under HMOs, the situation may be far different for those who have had limited health care access.

"From a welfare client's point of view, the option is going to an emergency room, sitting six to eight hours to get care, and watching police and trauma cases go by . . . or having your own pediatrician," said William Waldman, the executive director of the American Public Human Services Association, a group of state welfare officials. "It [managed care] was a major step up."

Nearly all states now use managed care, but the ideal of better access has not always been met. Studies show that half of Medicaid patients still use emergency rooms for care, and a third do not have a regular doctor. Savings may also not be as large as expected. The Urban Institute, a nonpartisan think tank, estimates states are shaving costs by 5 percent to 10 percent, a level that is less than earlier forecasts.

Because reimbursement from Medicaid has traditionally been less than doctors and insurers said was needed to operate profitably, governors initially had trouble attracting commercial insurers. As more states moved into managed care, big firms followed. But some large insurers have recently left, complaining that payment is stingy and the paperwork overwhelming.

Analysts worry that could affect quality of care, especially if states turn to less experienced firms.

In the past, states that wanted to offer only managed care in their Medicaid programs were required to obtain a federal waiver. The 1997 budget law ended that requirement, with some exceptions. It also ended a policy that Medicaid recipients make up no more than 75 percent of patients in a managed care plan. The 75/25 split was an effort to prod firms into offering higher quality services.

Robert E. Hurley, a health care expert at Virginia Commonwealth University, said that since many states had gotten waivers both to implement Medicaid-only managed care and avoid the 75/25 rule, the change may not have a dramatic effect. But others said the move eroded choice, the best guarantor of quality.

"The Medicaid population is a very undemanding population. . . . They have very low expectations about their health care," said Barbara Smith of George Washington University's Center for Health Policy Research. "You'd like to have them treated in a plan that is competing for people with higher expectations."

After years of experience and some earlier scandals, states have

strengthened consumer protections. For example, after trouble with door-to-door marketing scams, many now use brokers — sort of state-paid benefits managers — to enroll recipients.

An open question is where governors go next. States have used managed care to cover poor women and children, who make up most of their caseload but account for only one-third of spending. They are cautiously experimenting with managed care for the more costly elderly and disabled.

Medicare Managed Care

The 1997 budget act was a mixture of the status quo and the next frontier for Medicare. Congress ensured the program's solvency through 2007, mainly though the tried and true practice of cutting payments. It went further, however, to usher in what sponsors hope will be a new era.

Medicare+Choice will let seniors pick from a bevy of health products, including provider sponsored organizations, known as PSOs, in which doctors and hospitals band together to provide services, and tax-deferred medical savings accounts. Recipients can begin using the accounts on Jan. 1, 1999, with enrollment for other options the following November.

Even without government prodding, seniors have been turning away from fee-for-service. The number of HMOs in Medicare has more than doubled since 1993, now covering about 14 percent of the caseload. The administration projects that one-quarter of beneficiaries will opt out of traditional Medicare by the year 2000.

There are many reasons for the trend, analysts said, chief among them the fact that Medicare's benefits package is relatively stingy, even with the 1997 budget act's addition of regular mammograms and screening for diabetes and prostate cancer.

Many seniors have bought "Medigap" insurance to plug the holes in Medicare coverage, including prescription drugs and eyeglasses, but Medigap costs have been rising by double digits annually in recent years.

"[Managed care] plans are marketing actively and aggressively. Employers who offer retiree health benefits are moving to offer them

through Medicare HMOs . . . and Medigap rates have been increasing," said Tricia Neuman at the Kaiser Family Foundation.

Getting Medicare+Choice launched has turned out to be more difficult than expected. In an effort to sell the concept to seniors, the Health Care Finance Administration, which administers Medicare, must mount one of the largest public relations campaigns ever undertaken by the government, educating 39 million people about the costs and benefits of the plans.

After focus groups showed that seniors did not understand the program's proposed marketing materials, the agency scaled back what was supposed to be a nationwide information campaign this fall to a five-state demonstration project.

The National Academy of Science's Institute of Medicine, advising the Health Care Finance Administration, warned in a June letter that unless it cut back its efforts, "many elderly people are likely to make ill-considered choices that will ultimately undermine Congress' efforts to restructure Medicare."

The institute cautioned that seniors did not understand their existing Medicare options, let alone the new choices, and said that an information campaign could produce a backlash.

While some lawmakers are miffed about the delay, some analysts said Congress bears part of the responsibility. The information campaign is funded through a user fee on insurers. Congress appropriated $95 million in fiscal 1998, less than half the amount authorized. The House Appropriations Committee has also scaled back the 1999 program.

Skeptics of radical change have cautioned that younger, healthier beneficiaries will leave traditional Medicare for HMOs and medical savings accounts. Because the government has paid the same amount for fee-for-service as managed care, HMOs that sign up healthier seniors realize a windfall.

The 1997 budget law will gradually adjust payments to managed care firms to more accurately reflect their costs of doing business.

"It will take people off the substance of the issues," Frist said.

Democratic pollster Bob Shrum, chairman of Shrum, Devine, Donilon Inc., said such attacks are unlikely to convince voters because consumers expect insurance companies and big business to oppose efforts to regulate the nation's health care system. "They don't have any credibility left on the issue," he said.

Prospects for Passage

Predicting the outcome on managed care legislation is tricky. Rep. John D. Dingell, D-Mich., a leading House cosponsor of the Democrats' bill (HR 3605), said prospects for enactment were uncertain.

"We may very well see we will not get a bill in this Congress, and the issue will be fought out in the next election," he said.

Dennis Hastert, R-Ill., chairman of the House GOP task force that produced the leadership proposal (HR 4250), said Republicans are sincere and are willing to work with Clinton to produce legislation this year, even though the administration has threatened to veto the House bill in its current form. "We've seen veto threats before," Hastert said.

Jim McDermott, D-Wash., maintains that many House Republicans voted for the GOP's managed care bill because they knew it would not become law.

"They know it's going to go down. . . . They can say they voted for a bill, but it will die over in the Senate," he said.

Both sides are already beginning to blame each other for the potential demise of legislation this year. In the Senate, for example, Lott said Democrats would be responsible for the delay in action because they are insisting on an unreasonable number of amendments that could tie up the chamber for weeks.

On July 29, Lott tried to begin floor consideration of the managed care bill

but Daschle objected, saying it was far too important an issue to place limits on the number of amendments Democrats could offer. The next day, Democrats wrote to Lott urging him to schedule "adequate time" for debate immediately after the August recess.

Despite such sparring, Sen. Edward M. Kennedy, D-Mass., who is sponsoring the Democrats' bill (S 1890) along with Daschle, said prospects are "still

ceptable, then passes its own version, which House Republicans dislike. A conference ensues, but no deal is cut.

"The clock runs out, members can't be blamed. The institution can be blamed. Leadership can be blamed," he said.

But members continue to try to use the issue to their advantage while the debate rages on. At the unveiling of the Senate GOP plan on July 15, Sen.

Hastert and Rep. Sue W. Kelly, R-N.Y., were among Republicans who gathered near the George Washington University Hospital on July 16 to announce introduction of the House GOP managed care bill.

promising" for enactment of a managed care measure. He points to the "very deep, ongoing and continuing concern" people have over who makes decisions about their medical care. Voters' concerns are "increasing in volume and in terms of velocity. This isn't going to go away," Kennedy said.

A bipartisan plan unveiled July 29 by a group of Senate moderates attempts to take popular elements from both parties' plans while discarding more contentious items, such as liability and medical savings accounts.

"The partisan bills are not going to pass, it's clear," said Max Baucus, D-Mont., a proponent of the measure.

But the late legislative entry is no guarantee that Congress will agree on a bill this year. One likely chain of events, Reischauer said, is that the Senate decides the House bill is unac-

Rick Santorum, R-Pa., touted a provision that would allow patients to pick their own providers rather than be limited to those in a pre-approved list from their managed care plan.

To emphasize his point, Santorum raised an HMO directory so that the packed press conference could witness him gallantly rip it in half.

"It's gone; you don't need it," he pronounced to the crowd.

Moments later, Gramm, who was also taking part in the event, picked up a piece of the torn directory. Looking knowingly at reporters, Gramm ran his finger along the edge to show its straightness. Santorum's stunt had been rehearsed, the book precut.

It was the perfect metaphor for the managed care debate: politicians are trying to make it look easier than it really is. ◆

As concern grows about on-line privacy, time for self-regulation may be short

Who's Minding Whose Business on the Internet?

Andy Tarnoff had no idea his privacy had been violated until Nations-Bank called to ask whether he had applied for a new credit card. When he answered no, the 24-year-old Web page designer from Milwaukee got some shocking news: Someone from New York City had tried to obtain credit using Tarnoff's name and Social Security number.

Tarnoff suspects the culprit gained access to his Social Security number and other personal information from the Internet.

"I'm a young, single guy who uses the Web," said Tarnoff. "I've never been to New York. . . . That's what leads me to think they got it off the Web because it's so random."

Tarnoff's story highlights the growing concern among consumers, privacy advocates and lawmakers about the lack of protection for personal information on the Internet. The Internet is a boundless, vast medium that is proving to be fertile ground for those who seek private information about others for financial or personal gain. Information can be accessed anywhere in the world, making the Internet's reach both exciting and treacherous.

Sen. Patrick J. Leahy, D-Vt., an Internet-savvy lawmaker, said he often warns his colleagues to consider, "If you're using the Internet for sending a message, is it a message you would put on a postcard?"

Leahy said he thinks this is one area where Congress may need to provide a legislative fix. So far, lawmakers have yet to focus on the issue in any depth.

Even though several bills aimed at bolstering privacy on-line have been introduced, many key lawmakers seem willing at this point to give industry the opportunity to tackle the issue first.

"I think it will make a lot of sense to take our time" on this issue, said Rep. Rick White, R-Wash., who has helped arrange a series of hearings in the House Commerce Committee on issues surrounding electronic commerce. "We've been guilty in the past of rushing to judgment and getting it wrong."

Capitol Hill has been following the Clinton administration's lead in giving industry a chance to show that self-regulation will work before resorting to government intervention.

"There are 10,000 new Web pages forming each week. It would be difficult for any agency to monitor," said Ira Magaziner, the White House Internet policy adviser. "If you have a law but no way of enforcing it, you're giving [Internet users] a false sense of security."

Despite such views, the administration, like many lawmakers, is not ruling out legislation or new regulation if industry action fails to address the problem adequately.

And patience appears to be growing thin among some regulators. At a July 21 hearing before the House Commerce Committee's Telecommunications, Trade and Consumer-Protection Subcommittee, Federal Trade Commission (FTC) Chairman Robert Pitofsky said that if the industry's efforts are not working by the end of the year, Congress should intervene to ensure that consumers are protected when surfing the Internet.

"We have not given up on self-regulation," said Pitofsky. "If it does not work out, we believe Congress should seriously consider legislation." Administration officials and lawmakers also are worried about the confidentiality of on-line medical records. Democrats and Republicans have added provisions in their managed care proposals to increase medical record privacy.

Information Blitz

The most common invasions of privacy involve the use of personal information by marketers who gain information from Web surfers voluntarily or through technology.

Some Web sites require patrons to register before they can enter. Many of these on-line registration forms often ask for a wide array of

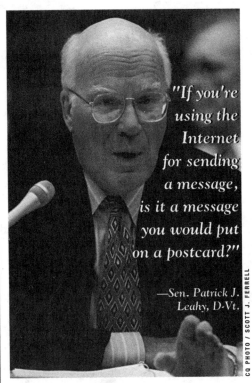

"If you're using the Internet for sending a message, is it a message you would put on a postcard?"

—Sen. Patrick J. Leahy, D-Vt.

CQ PHOTO / SCOTT J. FERRELL

personal information. Many sites also have ways of tracking what types of information Web users seek out when they visit their sites, information that could prove useful for marketing products to individuals.

But some sites are trying to make money from information available on-line. They offer to provide sensitive information such as Social Security numbers to any taker for a fee, information that is increasingly being used by thieves to gain access to credit.

Many Web users are often unaware that this information is collected or how it is used.

"A lot of people think government is the primary threat [to] privacy," said Jason Catlett, CEO of Junkbusters, an on-line company that provides resources for protecting privacy. That has "long been surpassed by private companies."

This is precisely why Catlett and others say the federal government needs to establish a basic level of protection for personal privacy on the Internet.

"There needs to be a clear national standard," said Jeff Chester, executive director of the Center for Media Education, a Washington think tank which studies media policies.

Critics and supporters of the administration's hands-off approach say that industry has an interest in ensuring that Americans are comfortable conducting on-line commerce. If not, they fear, electronic commerce

may not grow to its full potential even as use of the Internet increases.

In 1998, there are 100 million customers on-line worldwide, up from 3 million, mostly in the United States, in 1994, according to an April Commerce Department report.

"People will not put their faith, their trust or their cash into electronic commerce if they feel that in order to buy a product, they must first sell their privacy," Vice President Al Gore warned in a June 24 speech to a technology conference in Fairfax, Va.

While he says he is unlikely to stop surfing the Web, Tarnoff, who has made a few purchases on-line, said he is unlikely to shop on the Internet any time soon because of his privacy worries. "I'm gun-shy," Tarnoff said.

The Ease of Data Collection

The Internet has increased the ease and speed with which companies can collect vast amounts of information about consumers and even children.

The FTC, in a June 4 report on Internet privacy, found that 92 percent of 1,189 sites it sampled collected personal information from its visitors, such as their name, e-mail address, postal address or telephone number. A separate sample of 212 children's sites found that 89 percent collect personal information from their underage visitors.

Few sites post privacy policies that would tell visitors what information is being collected and how it is used, the report said.

Transactions on the Internet can be protected from hackers by using encryption technology, which scrambles data or electronic communications to prevent unauthorized access.

But even if a commercial transaction is encrypted, there is no guarantee that a business receiving the information will keep it private.

In addition, many Web sites track a visitor's habits and preferences through the use of "cookies," bits of data placed on the user's computer hard disk that record which Web pages are visited.

Many users do not realize cookies are be-

Some of the Internet privacy bills introduced in the 105th Congress and their chief sponsors:

● **HR 98:** Rep. Bruce F. Vento, D-Minn. — Would require Internet service providers to get a subscriber's permission before releasing personal information about the person.

● **HR 1287:** Rep. Bob Franks, R-N.J. — Would ban computer services from disclosing a Social Security number without the person's permission.

● **HR 1330:** Rep. Paul E. Kanjorski, D-Pa. — Would ban federal agencies from releasing personal information about citizens on the Internet without consent.

● **HR 2368:** Rep. W.J. "Billy" Tauzin, R-La. — Would prohibit the commercial marketing of government information about an individual obtained via the Internet and displaying an individual's Social Security number on the internet. Also would ban the commercial marketing of personal medical information obtained from the Internet without consent.

● **S 600:** Sen. Dianne Feinstein, D-Calif. — Would prohibit credit card bureaus from releasing personal information such as Social Security numbers.

ing placed on their computer hard disk by the Web site they are visiting.

There are ways to prevent sites from placing cookies on a computer. However, some sites, such as the discount travel site Lowestfare (www.lowestfare.com), require users to accept cookies to access their site.

Some of the information collected by Web sites is sold to third parties for advertising or other reasons. Others might use the information to send junk e-mail messages, also known as "spamming," a growing annoyance for many Internet users.

By using data collected from cookies

tity, as Tarnoff discovered. He said he thinks his personal information was simply grabbed off the Internet.

While many identity-theft cases are perpetrated by those who access information off-line, the Internet is easy pickings for thieves seeking to obtain personal identifying information, according to a May 1998 report by the General Accounting Office.

"The advent of the Internet has made this information much more accessible," said Rep. Gerald D. Kleczka, D-Wis., sponsor of legislation (HR 1813) that would prohibit credit bureaus from releasing Social Security

Consumer Trepidation

Polls have found that many Americans are worried that their privacy will be compromised on the Internet.

While only 6 percent of Internet users reported being the victim of privacy invasion, 86 percent said they were concerned about potential threats to their privacy, according to a poll released in June by Louis Harris and Associates Inc. and Alan F. Westin, a public law professor at Columbia University. (*1998 CQ Weekly, p. 1918*)

"It's a little like how many people have had an experience with their [car] brakes failing. You don't need to have that experience to want to have brakes" that work, said Marc Rotenberg, director of the Electronic Privacy Information Center, a public interest research group in Washington, D.C., focusing on electronic privacy, security and civil liberties issues.

Of those surveyed who do not regularly use the Internet, 44 percent said they would be more likely to do so if they could be assured that their personal information would be kept private.

"It's holding back the [full] development of commerce on the Internet," said the FTC's Pitofksy.

Industry officials say such information collection on the Internet is necessary to provide customers with better service, and not for sinister motives.

"Very few [Web sites] are exchanging information with other marketers," said Chet Dalzell, a spokesman for the Direct Marketing Association, an industry association of companies that sell and market products and services by phone, mail or via the Internet. "What we're trying to do is be better communicators" by making Web sites easier to navigate and targeting ads to meet consumers' interests.

The Clinton administration in 1997 challenged industry representatives to develop and implement policies aimed at protecting privacy on-line.

"Self-regulation can have one important feature: It builds a marketplace for privacy and makes consumers demand privacy protections," said Becky Burr, acting associate administrator of international affairs in the Commerce Department's National Telecommunications and Information Administration.

After some initial attempts, industry leaders unveiled a proposal that

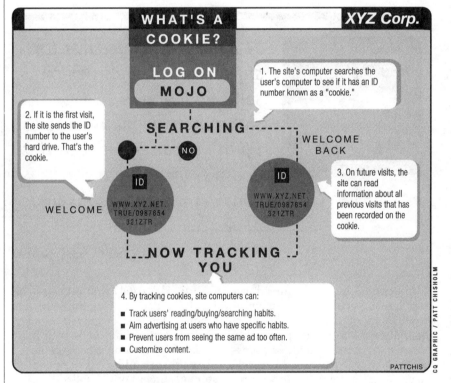

WHAT'S A COOKIE?   **XYZ Corp.**

LOG ON
MOJO

1. The site's computer searches the user's computer to see if it has an ID number known as a "cookie."

SEARCHING - - - - - -
NO

WELCOME BACK

2. If it is the first visit, the site sends the ID number to the user's hard drive. That's the cookie.

ID
WWW.XYZ.NET.
TRUE/0987654
321ZTR

ID
WWW.XYZ.NET.
TRUE/0987654
321ZTR

WELCOME

3. On future visits, the site can read information about all previous visits that has been recorded on the cookie.

NOW TRACKING YOU

4. By tracking cookies, site computers can:
- Track users' reading/buying/searching habits.
- Aim advertising at users who have specific habits.
- Prevent users from seeing the same ad too often.
- Customize content.

PATTCHIS

CQ GRAPHIC / PATT CHISHOLM

or other means, an "unprecedented dossier can be assembled of what a person has seen, revealing their interests and embarrassing facts," said Ohio State University law professor Peter P. Swire, an expert on Internet privacy and security issues.

Many companies have sprung up on the Internet, offering to sell much more sensitive information. One Web site called "Lou's Clues," (www.lousclues.com) which promotes itself as an "information service for women," advertises that it can deliver Social Security numbers to those who pay $22, as well as furnish the name and address of the subject.

This kind of information in the wrong hands can be used to commit fraud or to steal another person's iden-

numbers and other personal information, and ban commercial use of a Social Security number without written consent.

Kleczka's bill and a similar measure, (S 600) introduced in the Senate by Dianne Feinstein, D-Calif., are aimed at tackling identity fraud.

The Senate Judiciary Committee approved a separate bill (S 512) July 9 that would make it a crime to steal personal identifying information such as a Social Security number. (*1998 CQ Weekly, p. 1884*)

Current federal law bans the fraudulent possession, transfer and production of identity documents. But law enforcement officials must catch a culprit in possession of such documents in order to prosecute.

many see as the most serious attempt at self-regulation.

A coalition called the Online Privacy Alliance, which includes about 50 of the biggest companies and organizations doing business on the Internet or providing products and services for Internet commerce, announced in June a series of privacy guidelines. Among the group's members are IBM, America Online, Yahoo! and the Direct Marketing Association.

The guidelines call for members to adopt, implement and post on their Web sites privacy policies that state what information is being collected and how it is used. The group also requires members to allow consumers to decide whether the information can be used for other purposes. Members also agree not to collect information from children under 13 without the consent of their parents.

Many of the companies involved with the alliance also have signed on to other initiatives, such as the Better Business Bureau's BBBonline and TRUSTe. These groups offer privacy seals that can be placed on Web sites to assure consumers that the privacy policies of those sites have been reviewed and are being monitored by the organizations providing the seals.

Industry officials say such approaches empower consumers and provide them with the necessary information to be on the lookout for privacy violators.

"The Internet is a global place," said Harriet Pearson, IBM's director of public affairs. "When you go on the Internet, you should be as self-aware as when" you are conducting business elsewhere.

Industry officials said legislation to force companies to comply with privacy guidelines is unworkable and would quickly be outdated as technology changes.

"Laws are two-by-fours," said former FTC Commissioner Christine Varney, who is advising the Online Privacy Alliance. "They are very broad. . . . They retard innovation."

Varney and others say consumers have some recourse under current FTC regulations that bar deceptive practices. For example, the FTC can take action against companies that post privacy policies on their Web sites but do not adhere to them.

While praised for its initiative, the alliance was criticized for not includ-

ing a plan for enforcing the guidelines and instead setting a deadline of Sept. 15 for completing work on this issue.

Following the alliance's announcement, Commerce Secretary William M. Daley expressed disappointment June 23 during a two-day departmental summit on privacy, saying, "I have taken some hits for supporting the industry on self-regulation. . . . I sincerely hope industry steps up to the plate first. But if it doesn't, we will have to consider all the options we have for protecting the American consumer."

"I have taken some hits for supporting the industry on self-regulation. . . . I sincerely hope industry steps up to the plate first. But if it doesn't, we will have to consider all the options we have. . . ."

— **William M. Daley, Commerce Secretary**

Jill Lesser, America Online's director of law and public policy, defended the alliance's efforts, saying the Internet industry "moved more quickly than many others" to address the issue. America Online faced an onslaught of negative publicity and recently agreed to a monetary settlement after an employee revealed to a Navy investigator in a telephone call the name of a sailor who had identified himself as gay in an electronic message posted on the company's service.

In response to pressure from the administration and others, the alliance released its enforcement provisions July 20. The group called for members to sign on to a privacy seal program that has standards similar to the alliance's and a mechanism for punishing those that violate their privacy policies.

Magaziner hailed the alliance's effort as a "very good step forward" and said he believed it should be given a chance to work.

Bad Apples

But privacy advocates complained that the alliance's effort does not go far enough. Industry self-regulation and technological innovations to protect privacy need to be backed up with regulation, they argue.

They say self-regulation does not address the bad apples — those who are unwilling to sign on to privacy policies.

"The industry doesn't have a way of legally policing the renegades within the industry who will seek to capitalize upon gathering this information," said Rep. Edward J. Markey, D-Mass.

Markey has sponsored a broad priva-

cy bill (HR 1964) that requires the FTC and Federal Communications Commission to issue guidelines mandating that consumers be told what personal information is being collected about them and have the option of stopping unauthorized collection, use or sale of this information.

Some privacy advocates also say the federal government needs to establish a full-time federal commission or office to address privacy concerns.

Establishing some ground rules for protecting privacy on the Internet is "the responsible thing to do if we care about privacy in this country," said Rep. Bruce F. Vento, D-Minn., who has proposed legislation (HR 98) to prohibit Internet service providers from revealing a subscriber's sensitive personal information to a third party without that subscriber's consent.

While numerous bills similar to Vento's have been introduced, none has seen any action, and they appear unlikely to go anywhere in the 105th Congress. Nonetheless, some lawmakers have been seeking other ways to tackle the problem.

Markey has been trying to attach privacy amendments to other pieces of legislation. During a June markup before a House Commerce subcommittee, Markey gained adoption of an amendment to ensure that legislation (HR 2281) aimed at updating the nation's copyright laws for the digital age would not prohibit consumers from taking steps to block cookies from being placed on their computers. *(1998 CQ Weekly, p. 1704)*

But Magaziner and industry leaders say that if the industry guidelines catch on and consumers become accustomed to looking for privacy seals, they will put pressure on the rogues by refusing to visit their sites.

"The power of the marketplace on the Internet is incredible," said Harris N. Miller, president of the Information Technology Association of America, an Arlington, Va.-based computer and communications industry association.

If the marketplace fails, however, many expect Congress will step in.

Rep. W.J. "Billy" Tauzin, R-La., chairman of the House Commerce Committee's telecommunications subcommittee, praised the administration for giving industry a chance to address the issue first.

While he favors enacting legislation only as a last resort, he said, "It might be useful to have some legislation [moving through Congress] to incentivize the industry to do it right."

He has introduced a bill (HR 2368) to prohibit commercial marketing of personal health or medical information over the Internet without consent and to ban the display on the Internet of individuals' Social Security numbers.

Magaziner said the administration backs legislation to protect privacy in a few specific areas, such as measures to protect medical records and to prohibit the collection of information from children without parental consent.

In its report, the FTC called for legislation barring Web site operators from collecting personal information from children 12 and under unless their parents know about it.

Sen. Richard H. Bryan, D-Nev., introduced a bill (S 2326) on July 17 that would implement the FTC's recommendations to protect children's

How Private Is Private?

A survey of 1,011 adults conducted April 22-27 by Louis Harris and Associates and Alan F. Westin of Columbia University found Americans are concerned about privacy and the Internet.

How concerned are you about threats to your personal privacy in America today?

- 86 percent of Internet users say they are concerned.
- 81 percent of Internet users who buy products and services over the Internet are concerned about threats to their personal privacy while on-line.
- 6 percent of Internet users say they have been victims of on-line privacy invasion.
- 53 percent of Internet users are confident that most companies offering products and services over the Internet use the information properly.
- 72 percent are concerned about someone tracking what Web sites people visit and using this information improperly.
- 70 percent are concerned about Web sites collecting the e-mail addresses of site visitors without their knowledge or consent to compile e-mail marketing lists.
- 53 percent of Internet users are confident that most companies offering products and services on the Internet use the personal and confidential information that customers provide in a proper way.

What should be done to protect privacy on-line?

- 80 percent of Internet users agree with the Clinton administration's policy of allowing industry and public interest groups to develop privacy rules for the Internet and of considering legislation only if the private sector fails to implement sufficient policies.
- 79 percent of women vs. 71 percent of men are in total agreement with the administration.
- 34 percent of men vs. 19 percent of women are in total agreement that a business incentive will be enough to take care of the problem.

privacy on the Internet.

Senate Commerce Committee chairman John McCain, R-Ariz., a co-sponsor of S 2326, said his panel may act on the bill before the end of the year.

If industry does not move soon to protect the privacy of every user, the FTC has proposed that Congress require Web sites to take several actions. These include notifying consumers about information being collected about them and how it is used.

International Pressure

Overshadowing the debate in the United States is a 1995 European Union directive set to go into effect Oct. 25 that would require companies that process information in 15 European countries to give consumers the right to access and correct data about themselves. It would require the companies to gain consumers' permission to use information for any purposes other than those for which it was collected.

European officials were skeptical about whether U.S. proposals for self-regulation would comply with the di-

rective. Some privacy advocates were hopeful the Europeans would put pressure on the administration to push for comprehensive privacy legislation because privacy protections are important in a global economy.

"Fortunately for us, the Europeans are pushing [the U.S.] government to do something about privacy," said Shari Steele, staff counsel for the Electronic Frontier Foundation, a San Francisco-based think tank specializing in high-technology issues.

Magaziner, who has been negotiating with the Europeans on the issue, said he is confident that if the administration is satisfied that the U.S. Internet industry has come up with effective privacy policies, the Europeans will accept them.

Gerard de Graaf, the first secretary for trade for the European Commission's U.S. delegation, said that in theory, "self-regulation can meet the guidelines."

But he added that "We have some questions about what is appropriate self-regulation. . . . We want to be sure there is substance" to these proposals. ◆

Congress Haltingly Begins Writing The Book on Internet Regulation

In measures on taxation, copyright, gambling and pornography, lawmakers seem divided between letting commerce flourish and reining in abuses

Congress spent more time debating Internet policy issues in the last session than it ever has in the relatively short history of the medium.

With legislation addressing everything from taxation to copyright infringement, lawmakers are beginning to forge the rules of the road for the Information Age.

But Congress still seems divided over when to let the Internet grow and flourish, and when to put the brakes on potential abuses.

Consider this: Concerned that Internet growth could be hampered by the imposition of a barrage of state and local taxes, lawmakers agreed Oct. 15 to add legislation to the massive omnibus spending bill (HR 4328) that would impose a moratorium on new state and local levies on Internet access and commerce. *(1998 CQ Weekly, p. 2797)*

On Oct. 12, lawmakers cleared a bill aimed at improving copyright protections for digital works such as computer software and compact discs, legislation that supporters say is essential to increase the availability of such materials on the Internet.

At the same time, Congress added legislation to HR 4328, expected to be cleared the week of Oct. 19, that would require commercial Web site operators to take steps to keep children from accessing on their sites pornography or any other material deemed "harmful to minors."

"Congress still hasn't come to terms with the politics and morality of the Internet," said James Boyle, a law professor at American University who focuses on legal issues relating to the Internet.

He said that although many other policy areas have distinct sides, issues concerning the Internet do not break down along easily defined lines.

David McClure, executive director of the Association of Online Professionals, a trade group for the Internet industry, points to the Internet pornography legislation as one example of this. He said while most Internet industry representatives favor the goal of keeping pornography away from children, they argue that the solution mandated by Congress will not stop the problem and instead will impose new burdens on Web site operators and users.

McClure and others say part of the problem is that some lawmakers remain unfamiliar with the technology. "We still have members of Congress who don't understand how the Internet works," McClure said.

Yet even though the Clinton administration agrees with those who opposed the Internet pornography bill, White House Internet policy adviser Ira Magaziner said the administration got much of what it sought on Internet policy issues this Congress. He noted in particular the passage of the Internet tax moratorium, legislation to protect children's privacy, the digital copyright bill and a measure to require federal agencies to make on-line versions of their forms available and allow the use of digital signatures on those forms.

"I think it's a good bipartisan record," Magaziner said in an interview on Oct. 15.

The policy issues that the 106th Congress may address include ways to protect all Americans' privacy when surfing the Internet and legislation to ban gambling.

Following are highlights of the major issues taken up during this session of the 105th Congress:

Tax Moratorium

The tax moratorium was among the most hotly contested technology issues Congress tackled this year. *(1998 CQ Weekly, pp. 2112, 1774)*

Supporters of a moratorium say the decentralized nature of the Internet makes it vulnerable to taxation from the 30,000 U.S. taxing jurisdictions. They say a timeout period is necessary to develop rational tax policies before state and local governments rush to profit from new Internet taxes. But state and local officials said that few states had imposed new Internet levies and that a moratorium was an unfair preemption of their taxing authority.

The legislation added to the omnibus spending bill mirrors a measure (S 442) passed by the Senate Oct. 8. It would impose a three-year moratorium on new state and local taxes targeted at Internet access and commerce. During the timeout period, a 19-member commission would be charged with studying what type of tax treatment should be applied to the Internet.

The measure also calls for the commission to examine whether states should be allowed to force companies to collect sales taxes from customers in states where the companies do not have a physical presence. Under current law, the companies are not required to do so. The provision was sought by state and local officials who say the current loophole in the law has cost them billions of dollars in lost sales tax revenues.

They also won another key concession from the measure's supporters: inclusion of a grandfather clause allowing at least a dozen states and those local jurisdictions that have been imposing Internet access taxes before Oct. 1, 1998, to continue doing so after the measure's enactment. In exchange, they agreed to back the three-year moratorium.

The legislation also includes a provision that would exempt from the moratorium Internet service providers who fail to offer customers filtering software that can be used to block out objectionable material when surfing the Internet.

Digital Copyright

Among the other major high-tech issues completed this Congress was a measure aimed at updating the nation's copyright laws for the digital age.

The legislation (HR 2281) would implement two international treaties aimed at improving worldwide protection for digital works. HR 2281's conference report was cleared Oct. 12 by the House on a voice vote. President Clinton said he would sign it.

Supporters say the bill would increase the amount of copyrighted works available on the Internet by providing creators of such materials with new protections against theft. *(1998 CQ Weekly, p. 2182)*

Pirates steal an estimated $20 billion worth of copyrighted materials a year, industry officials say. An average of 40 percent of computer software alone is pirated every year worldwide.

"Passage of the legislation brings us a step closer to being able to utilize the Internet as a means of providing information and entertainment to consumers," said Rich Taylor, spokesman for the Motion Picture Association of America.

HR 2281 was a top priority for movie and record creators, software makers and publishers.

Hollywood alone contributed more than $2.5 million in individual and political action committee donations to members of Congress in the 1997-98 election cycle, according to the nonpartisan Center for Responsive Politics. Among the top recipients were key players on HR 2281: Rep. Howard Coble, R-N.C., the bill's sponsor; and Sens. Orrin G. Hatch, R-Utah, and Patrick J. Leahy, D-Vt., the top leaders on the Senate Judiciary Committee.

Even though various interest groups and lawmakers reached a compromise the week of Oct. 5, the legislation was held up briefly by House Majority Whip Tom DeLay, R-Texas, over an unrelated dispute concerning who should head an electronics industry group.

Angered by the appointment of a Democrat, former Rep. David McCurdy of Oklahoma (1981-1995), to head the Electronic Industries Alliance, DeLay yanked the bill from the House floor schedule Oct. 9 in protest.

When asked about it, DeLay said, "We think it's an insult to the majority to hire a partisan Democrat" to head the organization.

However, pulling the bill was not much of a punishment for the alliance. One of its member groups, the Consumer Electronics Manufacturing Association, fought to modify the legislation to make it more acceptable.

"It was a piece of legislation that consumer [electronics] folks could live with. They were not championing this legislation," said alliance spokesman Mark Rosenker.

The consumer electronics association was among several groups critical of a key provision in the bill that would ban the use, manufacture or sale of devices primarily designed to circumvent technology aimed at protecting copyrighted material. They expressed concern that the provision would require them to design their products around anti-copying technology used by copyright holders.

In response to the association's concerns, the legislation includes language that says electronic, telecommunications or computer products do not have to be designed or built to work with anti-copying technology.

The legislation includes exceptions to the ban on circumvention technology for a few specific activities, including encryption research, computer security testing and reverse engineering, which would allow software creators to make sure their products work on certain types of computers.

HR 2281 also includes language aimed at ensuring that Americans will have "fair use" of copyrighted digital works. Librarians, educators and others feared the circumvention ban would jeopardize fair use of the material by punishing Americans even if they bypassed a technological protection only for the purpose of using a product in a non-infringing way.

The legislation requires the Librarian of Congress to waive the ban in cases where non-infringing use of a particular work would be adversely affected by the circumvention ban.

"We hope [the ban] will not prove in practice as potentially threatening as it does on its face," said Adam Eisgrau, legislative counsel for the American Library Association. But he added that "having a safety valve built into the bill is encouraging."

Pornography

On-line pornography was among the first issues Congress tried to tackle relating to the Internet, and is possibly the hardest to resolve.

With no hearings and little debate, Congress included legislation known as the Communications Decency Act in the 1996 telecommunications overhaul (PL 104-104) that banned on-line distribution to minors of indecent or "patently offensive" material. *(1996 Almanac, p. 3-46)*

The Supreme Court struck down part of the legislation in 1997, saying it was too broad and limited adults' free speech rights. *(1997 Almanac, p. 5-25)*

Sen. Daniel R. Coats, R-Ind., and Rep. Michael G. Oxley, R-Ohio, introduced new versions of the legislation (S 1482 and HR 3783) in this Congress, tailored to address many of the problems raised by the high court with the Communications Decency Act.

"We bent over backwards . . . to make it constitutional," Oxley said.

Despite objections from the administration, congressional leaders added Oxley's version of the legislation, which passed the House by voice vote Oct. 7, to the omnibus spending bill.

Oxley's measure would require commercial sites on the World Wide Web to ensure that only adults can access material deemed "harmful to minors." Web sites would have to require users to provide a credit card, password or other technologically feasible means of verifying that they are adults.

Violators could face a $50,000 fine and six months in prison. Web sites that fail to take the steps to keep children from accessing smut on their sites also would not benefit from the tax moratorium as stipulated by a provision added to that legislation.

Supporters pointed to several reasons why they believe the legislation is constitutional.

They noted that Oxley's bill is limited to commercial sites on the World Wide Web and does not apply to all speech on the entire Internet, addressing problems the high court raised in its decision on the Communications Decency Act. They also said the "harmful to minors" standard has been upheld by the Supreme Court for the state level.

Nonetheless, Magaziner, the White House adviser, said the administration opposed the legislation because the administration would prefer to promote the use of software filtering and other voluntary initiatives to limit children's exposure to on-line smut.

In addition, he said the Justice Department raised concerns about the bill's constitutionality, saying the court might not uphold the statute if it was too difficult and costly for Web site operators to comply with it without infringing on the protected speech of adults and minors.

The American Civil Liberties Union, the Electronic Privacy Information Center and Electronic Frontier Foundation have vowed to challenge the legislation in court. The groups were among those that filed suit against the Communications Decency Act.

"It is the height of irony that the same Congress that plastered the salacious Starr report all over the Internet now passes a plainly unconstitutional law to suppress a vaguely defined category of 'harmful' material," said Barry Steinhardt, president of the Electronic Frontier Foundation, a San Francisco-based think tank specializing in high-tech issues.

But some argue that there is less certainty this time around as to whether they will win such a fight.

The Supreme Court has "not spoken on whether a [federal] standard such as 'harmful to minors' is constitutional as a limitation on free expression," said David Cole, a law professor at Georgetown University.

Even David Sobel, general counsel for the Electronic Privacy Information Center, a Washington, D.C., public interest research institute focusing on electronic civil liberties issues, acknowledges that "it's a closer call" than the first legislation.

But Sobel said he believes there are at least two reasons the Oxley legislation will be struck down. First, he said, it is too difficult to determine the age of a Web surfer. Second, he does not believe the Supreme Court will endorse a national "harmful to minors" standard because states' views of what is harmful to minors often differ greatly, he added.

"The kind of material prosecuted in . . . Mississippi would not be prosecuted in New York City or San Francisco," Sobel said.

Meanwhile, the House on Oct. 12 cleared legislation (HR 3494) that would increase penalties for sex offenders who use the Internet to distribute child pornography.

While legislative efforts to crack

Gambling

down on pornography on the Web may have succeeded for now, a push to curb Internet gambling fell short.

The legislation was inserted into the Senate's Commerce, Justice, State

spending bill (S 2260), by Jon Kyl, R-Ariz., during Senate floor consideration July 23. *(1998 CQ Weekly, p. 2010)*

But after the commerce spending measure was added to the omnibus bill, House and Senate negotiators chose not to keep the Internet gambling ban.

The legislation would have made Internet gambling a crime punishable by up to four years in prison and $20,000 in fines or the total amount of gambling proceeds.

It also would have required Internet service providers to cut service to gambling sites identified by law enforcement officials.

Kyl's ban was backed by a coalition that included the National Association of Attorneys General and conservative groups. But casinos and other groups supporting legalized gambling opposed any restrictions on the Internet.

Critics argued that the legislation would be impossible to enforce and would place unfair burdens on Internet service providers. Most Internet gambling operations are located outside the United States.

The House Judiciary Committee's Crime panel approved its own Internet gambling bill (HR 4427) Sept. 14. But Kyl said the bill was "unacceptable" because it contained too many loopholes. *(1998 CQ Weekly, p. 2498)*

As a result, Kyl did not make a push to add the anti-gambling provision to the omnibus spending bill because of concerns that negotiators would try to compromise between the House and Senate measures and leave in parts of HR 4427 he opposes, according to a Senate aide.

Kyl plans to pursue an Internet gambling ban in the 106th Congress.

Meanwhile, another provision added to the Senate's commerce spending bill also was apparently deleted from the omnibus measure.

It would have required schools and libraries to add technology to their computers to block out pornography and other objectionable material as a condition for receiving federal subsidies for hooking up to the Internet.

However, privacy advocates succeeded in gaining inclusion in the omnibus bill of a measure that would require Web site operators to gain parental consent before collecting personal information from children, such as an electronic mail address. ◆

Despite appeals from businesses worried by global downturn, support ebbs in both parties

Free Trade Doesn't Sell In Congress Anymore

SEATTLE — Just one year ago, K. Michael McDowell was laying the groundwork for major business contracts in Indonesia to safeguard endangered coral reefs. The founder and president of a small environmental consulting and engineering company, McDowell planned to map the reefs with his patented "Sea-All" video and satellite mapping system, thereby boosting efforts to steer development away from fragile ecosystems.

But now it is McDowell's 25-employee firm, Pentec Environmental Inc., that is endangered. When Asian currencies began their catastrophic collapse last year, the company lost nearly every potential overseas contract.

"We're kind of holding on by the fingernails trying to keep from cutting back," said McDowell, sitting in his offices just a few blocks from Puget Sound.

Pentec is not alone. The freefall of East Asian markets, along with the failure of the U.S. government to reach new trade agreements in Latin America, is roiling companies across the trade-dependent Pacific Northwest and throughout the country.

Businesses in Washington state from tiny, family-owned apple orchards to giant manufacturers such as Boeing Corp. are scrambling to cut costs in the wake of the Asian financial crisis. And with Russia on the brink of economic chaos and worldwide markets in turmoil, the situation is likely to get worse before it gets better.

Small wonder that Seattle business leaders are concerned with matters other than presidential scandals. The Capitol may be in an uproar over President Clinton's alleged misdeeds, but executives across the country want Congress this month to appropriate money for the International Monetary Fund (IMF) to help stabilize the Asian economies. Another top business priority is for Congress to give the administration "fast track" trade negotiating authority that could open markets in South America and elsewhere to U.S. companies.

"We need access to the global marketplace," said Patricia Davis, president of the Washington Council on International Trade, based in Seattle. "The kind of things that are happening in Asia and the lack of fast track . . . directly affect our companies."

With the nation's powerful business community virtually united behind free trade, its lobbyists insist that lawmakers will find time for trade in the final weeks of the 105th Congress. They contend that the recent market plunges on Wall Street and declines in U.S. exports bolster their case. "It is the eleventh hour, but so much of what is done in Congress is done in the eleventh hour," said Calman J. Cohen, president of the Emergency Committee for American Trade, a business lobbying group in the capital.

But in the post-Cold War era, House Republicans are signaling that they feel less and less urgency about international commerce. And Democrats, relying more and more on labor unions for financial support, are lining up against trade agreements that they say may hurt American working men and women.

As a result, even though House leaders have pledged a floor vote on fast-track legis-

The business community is virtually united behind free trade, but in the post-Cold War era, Republicans are signaling less urgency about international commerce, and Democrats are lining up against trade agreements that may hurt American workers.

McDowell, founder of Pentec Environmental Inc., was seeking contracts to map Asia's endangered coral reefs — until the economic collapse put his own company at risk.

lation (HR 2621), the odds of passage appear virtually nil. Legislation to promote trade with sub-Saharan Africa (HR 1432, S 2400) also faces an uphill battle. However, lawmakers are likely to clear at least some funding for the IMF as part of the fiscal 1999 spending bill (HR 4569, S 2334) for foreign operations. *(1998 CQ Weekly, p. 2507)*

Trade and Prosperity

At one time the United States led a worldwide movement toward free trade. After World War II, U.S. policymakers played a leading role in founding the IMF and negotiating to reduce tariffs — partly to keep American businesses profitable and partly to isolate the Soviet Union and its communist allies.

Spurred by trade agreements, combined imports and exports of goods and services rose from $48.1 billion in 1960 to nearly $2 trillion in 1997. Whole sectors of the economy, such as agriculture, electronics and forestry, now rely heavily on overseas markets, and free-trade advocates credit trade with everything from boosting overseas living conditions to ending the Cold War.

"The trade system has created jobs," U.S. Trade Representative Charlene Barshefsky said in a June speech. She added that it "raised living standards here and everywhere around the world, encouraged peaceful settlement of economic disputes, and moved us toward a world based more on law, transparency and free markets than on force and compulsion."

Despite such glowing praise, trade is losing its luster in the political arena.

To be sure, part of the reason the trade agenda, like so many other legislative initiatives, is stalled on Capitol Hill is because of the crisis engulfing the White House. Clinton, an ardent free-trader who steered major trade agreements through a reluctant Congress in 1993 and 1994, now is using most of his energy to stave off possible impeachment proceedings. Congressional leaders, facing serious constitutional questions within weeks of election day, are not in a position to forge sweeping trade initiatives. *(1998 CQ Weekly, p. 2467)*

But the storm over Clinton's relationship with a White House intern is only the latest cause of trade's troubles. Long before Monica Lewinsky started working at the White House, members of both parties tried unsuccessfully to resist passage of the North American Free Trade Agreement (NAFTA) and the General Agreement on Tariffs and Trade (GATT). *(GATT, 1994 Almanac, p. 123; NAFTA, 1993 Almanac, p. 171)*

Last year, opposition to trade ran so strong that the House failed to take up fast-track legislation, leaving Clinton as the first president in modern times without that key negotiating tool.

Washington's apple and wheat growers had counted on foreign demand to drive up commodity sales.

House Speaker Newt Gingrich, R-Ga., has pledged to bring it to the floor, although he has stepped back from an earlier insistence on a vote the week of Sept. 21.

A coalition of Democrats and pro-labor Republicans is confident of sinking the proposal, with some questioning whether it will even come up for a vote. "I just don't think the votes are going to be there" for passage, said Republican fast-track opponent Rep. Jack Quinn of New York.

Fast track stipulates that when the president submits a trade agreement to Congress for ratification, Congress must take an up-or-down vote within 90 days. Amendments are not allowed.

The fast-track standoff is clouding the country's trade outlook. Chile and other South American nations have declined to negotiate new agreements with the United States because Congress may insist on changing key provisions, but they are making trade deals with Canada and other nations.

"Our country has been harmed, contracts have been lost, workers have been laid off because of this inaction," said Willard A. Workman, vice president international of the U.S. Chamber of Commerce. "The rest of the world is not going to wait for us."

Also troubling to the business community, the House this year has balked for months at Clinton's request to appropriate $17.9 billion for the IMF. Although influential economists, including Federal Reserve Board Chairman Alan Greenspan, say the money would help contain Asia's financial crisis, free-market conservatives such as House Majority Leader Dick Armey, R-Texas, fault the IMF for interfering with the marketplace and aggravating already stressed economies.

Free-traders, however, are not losing every battle. The House renewed normal trading relations with China this year and turned back an effort to restrict trade with Vietnam. *(Vietnam, 1998 CQ Weekly, p. 2127; China, p. 2032)*

Furthermore, the Senate, unlike the House, remains a free-trade stronghold. Senators, more internationalist in their outlook, passed a fiscal 1999 foreign operations spending bill that fully funded the administration's $17.9 billion IMF request, and appear to favor fast track overwhelmingly.

But the shrinking number of free-trade advocates in the House feel almost hopelessly outflanked. On one side, pro-labor Democrats are lining up against trade agreements to protect American jobs; on the other side, protectionist Republicans are urging that the United States use trade barriers to retaliate for unfair trade practices overseas.

"Labor's hitting us from the left, and the [Pat] Buchanan wing, the isolationist, nationalistic wing of the Republican Party, from the right," said Rep. Robert T. Matsui of California, senior Democrat on the Ways and Means Subcommittee on Trade.

CQ PHOTO / DOUGLAS GRAHAM

Against the skyline in trade-dependent Seattle, the freighter Cho Yang Line is loaded with containers Aug. 26 near Colman Ferry Terminal.

Post-Cold War Chill

The bipartisan consensus for free trade that had existed since World War II has been fraying ever since the end of the Cold War. For the past decade, some Republicans, who had viewed worldwide trade as a tool to contain communism, have gradually returned to the isolationism that was fashionable earlier this century.

Giving voice to the growing isolationist sentiment, two 1992 presidential candidates — the Republican Buchanan and independent Ross Perot — energized large blocs of voters by denouncing trade agreements as harmful to the economy.

With the threat of Soviet expansion gone, some conservatives are no longer interested in doing business with anti-Communist dictatorships. Instead, many social conservatives, backed by such influential organizations as the Christian Coalition, want to apply the brakes to free trade and cut off commerce with countries run by repressive regimes.

"The Cold War really skewed this whole debate," said Rep. Dana Rohrabacher, R-Calif., one of the House's most conservative members. "I think the people who talk about blanket free trade are ignoring the corruption and repression going on . . . .

"We should be helping all the people who are struggling for honest government and freedom."

This concern about human rights is uniting many members of the left and the right, breeding unexpected alliances. Alongside Rohrabacher and his fellow conservatives, for example, are such liberals as Georgia Democrat Cynthia A. McKinney and Vermont independent Bernard Sanders.

The result has been a proliferation of bills to impose economic sanctions on overseas dictatorships. One of this year's most discussed proposals (HR 2431) would impose sanctions on governments that restrict religious expression. *(1998 CQ Weekly, p. 2027)*

Business lobbyists fiercely oppose the plan, contending that imposing unilateral sanctions would do nothing to help the oppressed, but rather would give business openings to U.S. competitors. The proposal, like so much trade legislation this year, appears to have little chance of clearing Congress.

While post-Cold War politics are affecting Republicans, the Democrats are moving away from trade for their own reasons. They are increasingly influenced by labor unions, which are generous campaign donors. One of the top issues on the labor agenda is stopping

trade proposals such as fast track and a potential Free Trade Area of the Americas, which could extend NAFTA to most of the Western Hemisphere.

Workers fear that sweeping free-trade agreements would encourage companies to shut domestic plants and take advantage of lower wages in other countries.

"It just opens the door even wider to exploit even more South American workers," said John C. Folk, president of the United Steel Workers local in Celina, Ohio.

Folk, 38, a father of two, is one of tens or hundreds of thousands of workers who are losing their jobs because of trade agreements. His employer, Huffy Bicycle Company, is relocating the local plant to Mexico, and Folk will be left to rely on a federal program that retrains workers whose jobs have been affected by NAFTA.

"I'm still overwhelmed by the whole thing, trying to figure out how I'm going to take care of my family," he said.

Also affecting trade issues are influential environmental groups such as the Sierra Club. Although not opposed to free trade, they insist that international agreements should include provisions to encourage countries to safeguard natural resources and improve

Rescuer of Embattled Economies
Is Now Under Siege Too

When Russia was sliding toward economic catastrophe in July, the International Monetary Fund (IMF) arranged an $11.2 billion loan package designed to shore up the country's markets and spark needed financial reforms.

The result? Russia's market and currency crumbled, its government teetered on the verge of collapse and global markets took another nosedive.

No wonder the IMF is having trouble making a case in Congress these days for $17.9 billion in increased U.S. funding.

Russian President Boris Yeltsin met in February with IMF Managing Director Michel Camdessus, setting the stage for a landmark deal.

"The Russian experience of the last several weeks is the strongest evidence yet that the IMF is a destabilizing force in international financial affairs," said House Majority Leader Dick Armey, R-Texas.

The IMF has attracted criticism over the past year for many reasons. Labor organizations say its policies undercut workers' rights overseas, environmentalists fault it for encouraging the exploitation of natural resources, and conservatives such as Armey say it intrudes in the free marketplace.

Since the Russian experience, however, lawmakers are focusing on a more basic issue: Are IMF policies making bad economies worse?

Such doubts are causing House members, despite the recent stomach-churning dips in the stock market, to balk over President Clinton's $17.9 billion appropriations request for the IMF. Instead, the House on Sept. 17 included just $3.4 billion for a special IMF credit line in the 1999 foreign operations spending bill (HR 4569).

Although many House Democrats would like to do more, powerful Republicans, including Armey and Majority Whip Tom DeLay of Texas, insist on drawing the line.

To be sure, IMF backers remain optimistic that they will get the full funding amount this year. After all, the Senate has overwhelmingly approved the money, and the powerful business community is waging an all-out battle to win over the House.

Moreover, the organization's reserves are almost depleted, and the global economy could be at risk if Congress fails to act. Treasury Secretary Robert E. Rubin warned top GOP leaders in letters this month: "We simply cannot afford any further delay."

But the administration is failing to win over crucial lawmakers, some of whom were sympathetic before the Russian loans.

"The fact is that if the IMF [funds] were well-spent, and well-handled and well-managed, I don't think anybody would quarrel with the proposal to use taxpayers' dollars to help improve the economic climate of the world," said House Appropriations Chairman Robert L. Livingston, R-La. "I'm very concerned that taxpayers' dollars are simply being mindlessly wasted by the IMF, and we need to make sure that doesn't happen anymore."

A Changed Mission

All sides agree that the IMF has drifted far from its initial mission in the 1940s.

The international cooperative organization, founded by the United States and other countries to help stabilize world commerce, started out by encouraging unrestricted currency exchanges and clear values for each currency. But with the onset of floating exchange rates in the 1970s, the organization began focusing on loans to poorer nations.

environmental cleanups.

This focus by unions and environmentalists on trade issues is relatively new. Before the 1990s, trade agreements dealt mostly with tariffs and generated little interest outside of a few affected industries.

But that has all changed with NAFTA and other sweeping agreements that encompassed such issues as health and safety standards. Environmentalists, who blame NAFTA for causing increased pollution in U.S.-Mexico border areas and importation of contaminated fruit from Mexico, say trade has become one of their most important issues.

"Since our economies are globalizing, we have to think on a global level," said John Audley, trade and environment program manager for the National Wildlife Federation.

Northwest Jobs

To many business officials in the Seattle area, all the talk about trade costing jobs and degrading the environment is just empty rhetoric. On the

The loans have grown ever larger, spawning controversy. In its latest annual report, the IMF said it lent a record $25.6 billion in the fiscal year that ended April 30, a fourfold increase over the previous year.

"This year has been truly momentous for the IMF, and it has confronted us and the whole global system with major challenges," said Stanley Fischer, the organization's first deputy managing director.

Despite the massive 1997 bailouts — including a record-breaking $21 billion loan to South Korea — the world economy remains in a precarious position. Japan is mired in a recession, Russia has failed to meet loan payments, and Latin American markets are increasingly turbulent.

Critics say IMF policies are making matters even worse.

As a condition for lending money to a struggling country, the organization typically insists that the government cut expenses and start paying off debts. The countries that receive loans are pressured into cutting social programs, increasing taxes and raising interest rates.

Such an approach aims to reassure foreign investors and creditors. But critics say the austerity measures also spell terrible hardships for the working class and the poor, and handcuff governments that could otherwise try to stimulate growth through spending.

The organization is also under fire from free-market conservatives, such as Armey, who contend that the idea of lending money to countries with crashing economies is counterproductive. That is because the loans may cause a "moral hazard" that encourages other nations to take financial risks, believing they too will be bailed out for their mistakes.

On the other hand, IMF officials

and their supporters in the Clinton administration say the global economy would be even shakier now if the organization did not act quickly to stabilize the East Asian crisis. As for Russia, they say the IMF did what it could, but that the nation failed to follow through on needed economic changes.

"You cannot do for people what they won't do for themselves, and

IMF Loans

The International Monetary Fund, hoping to prevent default, committed billions of dollars in loans to countries whose economies were hit hardest by the 1997 Asian financial crisis: Thailand, Indonesia and South Korea. When Russia's ruble plunged in value, the IMF committed loans to prevent what had happened in Asia: a domino effect of failing economies. Listed below are the loan amounts, in U.S. dollars. The amounts refer only to crisis aid and do not include previous outstanding loans.

Thailand – $4 billion over 34 months committed on Aug. 20, 1997. The Asian financial crisis started with Thailand's weakened economy. The Thai baht was devalued in July 1997 in response to sell-offs by foreign currency speculators.

Indonesia – $10 billion over three years committed on Nov. 5, 1997. The Indonesian rupiah fell in value in August 1997 after the Indonesian central bank allowed its value to float. The rupiah, like the baht, was the focus of speculative attacks.

South Korea – $21 billion over three years committed on Dec. 4, 1997. The Asian currency crisis spread to South Korea, the world's 11th largest economy, as investors lost confidence in the won.

Russia – $11.2 billion over two years committed on July 20, 1998. After the ruble's value plunged in May 1998, the Russia Central Bank calmed the crisis by raising interest rates. But the IMF, fearing a currency collapse, soon began bailout negotiations.

Russia simply did not put in place an effective economic program," Rubin told CNN.

Still, even IMF supporters say the organization needs to change. Lawmakers generally say it needs to move toward greater openness and accountability; some Democrats also want it to put a greater emphasis on human rights and the environment.

Some IMF supporters, such as Rep. Doug Bereuter, R-Neb., chairman of the International Relations Subcommittee on Asia and the Pacific, say the organization needs to better predict such economic crises as the Asian currency devaluations. But IMF officials say accurate monitoring, or "surveillance," requires that its 182 member nations work closely with the organization — which often fails to happen.

"Effective surveillance depends fundamentally on the willingness of members to take the IMF's advice," the organization's annual report states.

Since IMF policies are voted on by the 182 members, Congress cannot dictate changes. The organization's officials have pledged to try to move toward opening up more of their records, but that may take time.

In the meantime, they say, it is imperative for the United States and other nations to boost financial support. The organization has just $5 billion to $9 billion available to lend, which might not cover an economic crisis in Latin America or elsewhere.

"The situation in the global economy unfortunately, very regrettably, is becoming extremely difficult, and the resources now available are limited in ways that are unhelpful to increasing confidence in the international system," IMF's Fischer said at a Sept. 13 news conference. "There are countries out there who need assistance."

contrary, their goals and their livelihoods depend on healthy commerce across the Pacific.

In Washington, for example, foreign exports reached $28.2 billion in 1995, making it the most trade-dependent state on a per capita basis in the country, according to state officials.

The collapse of Asian markets has hit

Washington hard, with exports to Asia through the Port of Seattle dropping by nearly 25 percent in the first six months of 1998. Many companies are shipping empty containers to Asian ports to handle a growing flood of imports.

Overall, the state's economy remains strong, thanks in part to the availability of inexpensive raw materi-

als from Asia. But the economic crisis has severely set back companies that rely on Asian exports.

Two years ago, for example, suburban Seattle-based Pacific Housing Materials and Design enjoyed a thriving business exporting pre-designed houses to Japan and South Korea. The sturdy houses, constructed with two-by-fours,

International Trade in Goods and Services

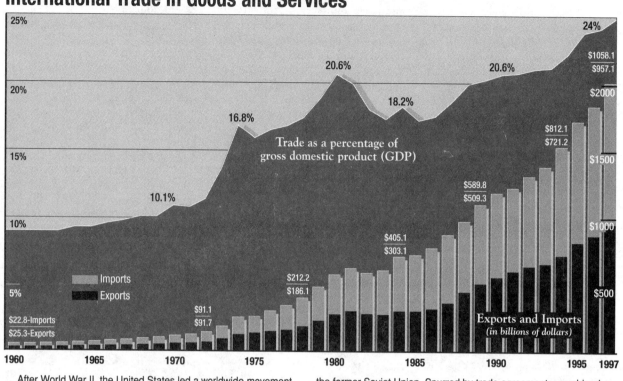

After World War II, the United States led a worldwide movement toward free trade. U.S. policy-makers played a key role in founding the International Monetary Fund and negotiating to reduce tariffs — partly to keep American businesses profitable and partly to isolate the former Soviet Union. Spurred by trade agreements, combined imports and exports rose from $48.1 billion in goods and services in 1960 (9.1 percent of GDP) to nearly $2 trillion in 1997 (24.9 percent of GDP).

SOURCE: Department of Commerce

were more resistant to earthquakes and other natural disasters than traditional Asian houses built with corner posts.

But when Asian currencies plunged last year, the company's Japanese exports skidded from 400 houses a year to about 175, and its exports to Korea hit zero. It has laid off more than half its employees and is pinning its hopes on opening retail building stores overseas.

Small wonder that company officials take issue with lawmakers who oppose expanding trade agreements.

"It's just stupid," said A. Greg Danielson, the company's chief financial officer. "Trade is the most important thing we have. Without trade, we have no jobs."

Seafood processors voice similar sentiments. The steep currency declines have led to drastic reductions in the price of seafood in Asia, leaving many companies on the brink of bankruptcy.

"The market value is too low to sustain the fisherman and the processor," said Terry Gardiner, president of NorQuest Seafoods in Seattle. "If this trend continues . . . our company will be forced to reassess whether we can economically pursue all the fisheries

we have historically pursued."

Gardiner and other Washingtonians say overseas sales are critical because the U.S. market is virtually stable. Much of the world's population growth and potential emerging middle class is overseas, and tapping those markets is vital for the expansion of American companies.

The nation's farmers, for example, including Washington apple and wheat growers, have been counting on foreign demand to drive up commodity sales. Indeed, part of the reason Congress was able to limit farm subsidies in the 1996 farm bill (PL 104-127) was that farmers believed booming export markets would drive their business for years to come. (*1996 Almanac, p. 3-15*)

Now, with Asian markets in turmoil and U.S. trade negotiations with South American nations stalled, small growers in Washington and throughout the country are facing catastrophe.

"It's killing these growers," said Tony Buak, who oversees export sales for Columbia Marketing International in Wenatchee. "We're entering such a bad time in Washington as we've never seen before."

For McDowell at Pentec Environ-

mental, the concerns are a little different. By stitching together domestic cleanup projects with a few small Asian contracts in Guam and Palau, McDowell has been able to avoid laying off any employees, although the company's growth has stalled.

But he is in the painful position of watching continued environmental degradation in Asia. Nations such as the Philippines that planned to work with Pentec to help clean up polluted rivers are now putting off any major cleanups. The coral reefs that were to have been mapped and protected instead are facing increased damage.

"In my opinion, you have to have a healthy economy to have a healthy, thriving environment," McDowell said. "If people are just interested in survival, they're a whole lot less interested in what the environment is like."

But he remains confident that Asian economies will recover within a few years, and the nations will still be able to tend to their damaged natural resources.

"Another couple of years, it's not desirable," he said. "But it's not the end of the world either." ◆

Promises of frugality give way to tax cut effort, spending initiatives

Can the Surplus Be Saved? Clinton, Congress Waver

Whatever happened to "save Social Security first"? President Clinton's January vow to leave the budget surplus alone until the sacrosanct retirement system is fixed put the freeze on Republican tax cut plans for months. At first, top Republicans such as House Speaker Newt Gingrich of Georgia agreed: Any tax cut would be paid for by cuts in other programs, or perhaps a tobacco tax increase.

At the same time, Clinton promised not to dip into the first budget surplus since Woodstock to finance additional federal spending. But that commitment weakened during the week of Sept. 21 as he sent Congress two new surplus-financed requests for supplemental spending for embassy security and farm relief — and signaled a willingness to support more defense spending.

In short, both the Clinton administration and congressional Republicans — who have spent all year seeking credit for the unexpected surplus and posing as its true guardians — are now falling over themselves to spend it.

Budget hawks are climbing the walls.

"Two wrongs don't make a right," said former Sen. Warren B. Rudman, R-N.H. (1980-93), co-chairman of the Concord Coalition, a bipartisan budget watchdog group. "Pre-election horse-trading could result in long-term fiscal damage. . . . This is far too high a price to pay for short-term political appeal."

The budget debate this year has featured initiatives from all sides crafted with an eye toward political rather than legislative gain. But as lawmakers near the end of the session, they are succumbing to the temptation to use the surplus as the magic answer to the difficult budget and tax questions that have been hanging over them all year: whether to cut taxes and how to finance those cuts, and whether to violate the tight spending caps that are supposed to strictly limit discretionary spending in the annual appropriations bills.

As it turns out, many lawmakers are willing to do both. Most of the major appropriations bills are stuck in conference. Senior GOP leaders and the White House agree that perhaps $17 billion in additional spending above the caps should be added to an unstoppable catchall bill that everyone expects will contain the half-dozen spending bills that cannot advance on their own.

On the other hand, House Republicans are pushing an $80.1 billion election-year tax cut (HR 4579) that would be financed almost exclusively by the surplus, using about 15 percent of it over five years. That has prompted Democrats to howl that Republicans are cutting taxes at the expense of Social Security. They point out that the budget surplus consists exclusively of Social Security surpluses.

"Democrats are saying that 'if we've got

Quick Contents

The Clinton administration and congressional Republicans posed all year as guardians of the budget surplus, but now they are falling all over themselves to spend it.

Fiscal 1999 Spending at a Glance

Appropriations
- Of 13 regular appropriations bills, President Clinton has signed one, the military construction bill (HR 4059—PL105-237).
- Five or six spending bills are expected to become part of a catchall bill, which will be attached to a regular spending bill making its way through a House-Senate conference.

Supplemental
The supplemental, or emergency, spending bill could cost up to $17 billion, including the following:

$1.9 billion	Bosnia peacekeeping
$3.25 billion	Year 2000 computer problems
$1.8 billion	Security at embassies
$254 million	U.S. facilities in Korea
About $2 billion	Defense readiness
$7 billion	Agriculture disasters
$500 million	Strategic Petroleum Reserve
Unspecified	Medical research and education

The supplemental spending bill may be attached to the catchall spending bill.

Taxes
- The tax bill (HR 4579) would cut taxes by $80.1 billion over five years, including $6.6 billion in cuts in fiscal 1999.
- The House was poised to vote on HR 4579 on Sept. 26.
- The tax bill stands alone, although some GOP leaders want to attach it to the catchall bill.

SOURCE: Senate Budget Committee

this surplus, you can't spend a penny of it until we save Social Security first,' " said Vice President Al Gore at a Sept. 24 campaign-style rally on the Capitol steps. Republicans, Gore said, "have another think coming, because we will fight them every step of the way — and they will lose."

Republicans counterpunched by saying Clinton cannot have it both ways; he cannot lambaste Republicans on taxes while proposing to use the surplus for extra spending.

"The Democrats shouldn't oppose using the surplus for tax cuts if they support using it for more spending," said House Ways and Means Committee Chairman Bill Archer, R-Texas. "If the president supports using the surplus to help the people of Bosnia, he shouldn't oppose using a portion of it to help the taxpayers of America."

It is clear, however, that Republicans view the tax issue as fodder for election campaigns. The bill, for one thing, does not contain GOP priorities such as a cut in capital gains taxes. It contains so many Democratic-tilting provisions that it appears aimed as much at making Democrats squirm as at providing tax cuts to married couples, raising the Social Security earnings limit or easing inheritance taxes.

But an overwhelming proportion of Democrats were poised to oppose the measure. It appeared unlikely to get the big House vote that supporters hoped for to put pressure on the Senate. Senate Minority Leader Tom Daschle, D-S.D., worked hard behind the scenes to minimize defections, and there are also a handful of Republicans opposed to surplus-financed tax cuts. Daschle is confident he can block the measure — though he suggested he might avoid a filibuster and let it advance for a high-profile Clinton veto. "Filibusters are murky for a lot of Americans," Daschle said. "Vetoes are not." Critical to uniting Democrats was obtaining an ironclad assurance from the White House that Clinton would kill any measure that tapped the surplus for tax cuts.

What is so galling to Republicans is that Clinton appears poised not only to stop their tax cut plans but also to prevail on many of his emergency spending initiatives, such as the Bosnia peacekeeping mission, aid to farmers, additional embassy security and a fix for Year 2000 computer glitches.

Despite his weakened political condition, Clinton may be able to have his cake and eat it too. Republicans support most of his extra spending, and they want to add some of their own, particularly money for military readiness.

Some top Republicans say they are shocked that Clinton wants to dip into the surplus to skirt budget caps imposed by the 1997 balanced-budget law (PL 105-33). (1997 Almanac, p. 2-3)

"By calling your new spending proposals 'emergency spending,' you are taking advantage of budget rules that say emergency spending does not require offsetting spending cuts," wrote Gingrich and House Majority Leader Dick Armey, R-Texas, in a Sept. 22 letter to Clinton. They wrote that the emergency spending Clinton requested "will in fact spend the surplus — though not on Social Security as you promised."

But Gingrich is among the chief proponents of emergency spending for farm relief and increasing the defense budget. Conspicuously absent from the letter — despite a request from Gingrich's office — was the signature of House Appropriations Committee Chairman Robert L. Livingston, R-La., who supports emergency spending and also views it as the only way to obtain Clinton's signature on the bills.

Administration officials point out that budget rules provide for unanticipated emergencies. But it is also clear that the definition of "emergency" is beginning to include annual items such as the Bosnia peacekeeping mission and may be stretched to provide for greater military readiness and even funding for medical research.

Budget hawks recoil at the prospect of busting the budget caps. They fear that Congress and Clinton are setting a precedent that will be repeated every year, eating up a big chunk of future surpluses. If lawmakers cannot meet the caps this year, they say, they surely cannot make the much more painful cuts envisioned for future years.

"A large part of these future surpluses is predicated on living with those very tight budget caps," said Martha Phillips, executive director of the Concord Coalition. "If they have twelve, fifteen, eighteen billion in emergency spending this year, how can you possibly say you're going to get a 10 percent real reduction by 2002?"

Political Year

Congress typically takes a breather after passing big deficit-reduction bills like last year's. But the emergence of the budget surplus — and later, its growth to an estimated $1.6 trillion over the next 10 years — turned the budget debate upside down.

White House officials such as former Office of Management and Budget Director Franklin D. Raines acknowledged that the administration's move on Social Security was aimed chiefly at curbing Republicans' desire for tax cuts.

Next, the Clinton budget arrived, studded with "investments" and tax breaks to boost federal aid for child care, education and health care. But his financing for these poll-tested initiatives relied on creative accounting and tobacco-related revenues that never appeared. Little of his ambitious budget will be enacted. (*Tobacco, 1998 CQ Weekly*, p. 2346)

At least Clinton has been consistent. Republicans have been all over the map. First, Gingrich surrendered to the Social Security argument. Later, House Republicans sought to rewrite the budget agreement with a $101 billion tax and spending cut plan (H Con Res 284) that fizzled after it passed in June. After floating a 10-year, $700 billion tax cut trial balloon that was quickly popped by the Senate, Republicans agreed to push the current plan: $80.1 billion in tax cuts over five years. At no time over the past nine months have Republicans and the Clinton team had anything approaching a search for common ground.

Some Republicans have suggested attaching a tax cut to the catchall spending bill — a move reminiscent of their failed 1995 attempt to use a debt limit increase to carry their balanced-budget bill. (*1995 Almanac*, p. 2-44)

"We haven't made a final decision on it, but we probably won't do that," said Senate Majority Leader Trent Lott, R-Miss. Attaching tax cuts to the must-pass spending bill would give Daschle enormous parliamentary leverage.

The budget endgame is a mess, making predictions difficult. First Republicans have to sort out what issues they want to confront the president with. Then they must begin negotiations with the White House, which is preoccupied with the Clinton sex scandal. "There's no direction downtown, either," said a high-ranking Senate GOP aide. "Don't just point your finger at us." ◆

With Social Security Ripe for Action, Can Clinton Seize the Moment?

Lawmakers work behind the scenes for an overhaul that will appeal to the majority, but they need the president to force tough choices

Quick Contents

With the first federal budget surplus in decades, the notion that a Social Security fix could be sidelined by scandal is a distressing thought for many lawmakers. Even some who have called for the president's resignation are working behind the scenes to develop a solution. Clinton's ability to lead the way on this issue will be an important test of his clout on Capitol Hill.

Sen. Judd Gregg, R-N.H., was one of the first members of Congress to publicly demand the president's resignation over the White House sex scandal.

That has not stopped him from working with the administration to ensure that the Monica Lewinsky affair does not swamp prospects for an overhaul of Social Security in 1999 that is supposed to ensure the retirement program's long-term solvency.

"The Senate has a working coalition [on Social Security] that is very broad-based, where there is a fair amount of agreement. If we had some presidential leadership we could fix the Social Security system for the next 100 years," Gregg said in an interview.

With the House poised to begin impeachment hearings, the trillion-dollar question now is whether Clinton has enough political clout to move from his current role as great facilitator, guiding a general discussion about Social Security, to that of tough leader able to force hard choices on an issue that has defined modern political demagoguery.

There is a sense of alarm among lawmakers and interest groups that they may lose a golden opportunity to deal with the issue, and lawmakers are determined to keep the process alive.

The joint desire to move forward does not mean there is a consensus on a solution. There are deep and possibly insoluble splits over whether to raise the retirement age, increase payroll taxes or reduce annual cost of living increases. Lawmakers who want to divert a portion of the program's 12.4 percent payroll tax to private savings accounts have been undercut by a stock market that has taken a series of stomach-turning lurches downward in recent weeks.

In his Jan. 27 State of the Union address, Clinton called on Congress to "save Social Security first" by dedicating any budget surplus to the program. Because of the aging of the Baby Boom generation, the program is expected to begin running a deficit in 2032. (*1998 CQ Weekly Report*, p. 215)

At an April 7 "town hall" meeting in Kansas City, Mo., the president kicked off a yearlong debate on the future of Social Security, which provides retirement, disability and survivors' aid to more than 44 million Americans. The process was to culminate in a White House summit with congressional leaders after the elections, followed by a comprehensive bill next year — a bill that could cement both the program's future and Clinton's political legacy. (*1998 CQ Weekly*, p. 1038)

While they wonder whether he will have the political ability to lead on the issue, some lawmakers believe the impeachment threat has increased Clinton's determination to take action on Social Security.

A related question is how the politics of the debate will affect policy choices. Liberals hope their unflinching support of Clinton during the Lewinsky saga will make him less willing to embrace changes they oppose, such as private investment accounts. Other analysts believe Clinton now needs more than ever to reach out to moderates in both parties to secure reform, and save his presidency.

"This issue is bigger than the politics of [impeachment]. The president is going to have to be supportive of something that fixes the system," said Sen. John B. Breaux, D-La., who wants Clinton to move to the middle.

Breaux was one of a bipartisan coalition of eight senators, including Gregg, Daniel Patrick Moynihan, D-N.Y., and Craig Thomas, R-Wyo., who signed a "dear colleague" letter on Sept. 24 laying out principles for a Social Security overhaul, including a payroll tax cut, personal accounts, a change in annual cost of living adjustments and a further increase in the program's retirement age, already scheduled to gradually rise from 65 to 67.

Business as Usual, Sort of

While the scandal has diverted the public's attention from Social Security, below the surface business has proceeded apace.

Social Security Commissioner Kenneth S. Apfel and White House aides have been quietly sounding out lawmakers about overhaul.

Breaux and others who met with administration officials said no decisions had been made about the shape of any reform proposal. They worry that a preoccupation with impeachment has left the White House behind schedule in planning the December summit with congressional leaders.

"The very early discussions for the White House conference are still going forward. The serious planning probably won't take place for a couple of weeks," Apfel said in an interview. He added the administration planned to participate in a final forum in coming days to refocus public attention on Social Security. There had been talk it would be canceled.

"I actually haven't seen a flagging of desire to move forward on this issue," Apfel said.

In an indication lawmakers think this is an issue with a future, senators scrambled to join a recently announced Democratic task force on Social Security, headed by Jeff Bingaman, D-N.M. The task force is to forge a caucus-wide position on overhaul.

House Ways and Means Committee Chairman Bill Archer, R-Texas, said he had not talked to the White House recently but added, "We're prepared to join with them." He said Clinton would have to endorse a set plan. "It's essential that they send up a specific, concrete proposal, not a series of options."

But the call for bipartisan compromise to save the program has not stopped bare-knuckle politicking on Social Security in current campaigns. Indeed, the political attacks are being justified as a necessary evil to keep the overhaul process on track.

"Is all hope lost? Not necessarily," said Rep. Earl Pomeroy, D-N.D., who has been coordinating House Democratic efforts on the issue. "He [Clinton] still has a veto pen, he can still create a circumstance where Republican members of Congress will want to get down to business on Social Security."

Pomeroy said Clinton's ability to successfully paint the House-passed $80.1 billion Republican tax bill (HR 4579) as a raid on Social Security was evidence of the issue's public resonance. (*1998 CQ Weekly, p. 2655*)

Clinton opposed the tax bill because it would be funded by tapping a budget surplus that consists mainly of Social Security trust funds, even though the White House has proposed using the surplus for spending priorities.

To inoculate themselves against political charges, Republicans passed a bill (HR 4578) on Sept. 25 that would hold 90 percent of the surplus in reserve until Social Security was solvent. (*CQ Weekly, p. 2579*)

In the Kentucky Senate race, for example, Republican Rep. Jim Bunning, who voted for the tax bill, and Democratic Rep. Scotty

Clinton, shown at a Social Security conference Feb. 9, may lack the political clout to force a solution on an issue he had hoped would help form his legacy.

Baesler, who voted no, are trading charges about who is the better friend of seniors.

The AFL-CIO, which opposes private accounts, hopes to rev up the rhetoric even more. It has begun running advertisements against the tax bill in selected districts and plans to pump millions of dollars more into the fight next year. Angry about the tactics, Republicans may attempt to hang a tax cut on any Social Security overhaul, aides said.

Outside the Capitol, other interest groups are betting that the issue will be joined next year. The National Association of Manufacturers is creating a coalition, including the U.S. Chamber of Commerce and other groups, called the Alliance for Worker Retirement Security, to lobby for private accounts and against payroll tax increases.

Leanne Abdnor, the coalition's executive director, said the group will probably run ads.

The liberal Center on Budget and Policy Priorities on Oct. 5 will release a study attacking findings by the conservative Heritage Foundation that Social Security was a bad deal for blacks and Hispanics. Civil rights leaders are expected to ask minorities to get involved in the debate.

Opinion polls show strong support for tackling Social Security — though division on how — and opposition to impeaching the president, findings that are driving lawmakers' work on the issue.

"As long as he's the president, you've got to work with him," Gregg said. ◆

Student Loan Interest Rate Cut Heads for Clinton's Signature

Higher Education Act reauthorization will also increase grants for low-income students

Without a single dissenting vote, Congress on Sept. 29 cleared a five-year reauthorization of the 1965 Higher Education Act that reduces student loan interest rates to their lowest level in nearly two decades, increases grants for needy students and sets up a new teacher training program.

In sharp contrast to the bitter sparring among lawmakers over possible impeachment hearings, a Republican-proposed tax cut, and appropriations bills, the conference report won overwhelming bipartisan support.

"I am sure that some are surprised that this Congress, in this political environment, would be able to produce a conference report of this magnitude," said Howard P. "Buck" McKeon, R-Calif., chairman of the House Education and the Workforce Subcommittee on Postsecondary Education, Training and Life-Long Learning.

The House passed the bill (HR 6) by voice vote Sept 28; the Senate followed with a 96-0 vote Sept. 29. (*1998 CQ Weekly, p. 2686*)

President Clinton, in a statement, praised the measure and urged lawmakers to appropriate the money needed to fund its new initiatives. Eager to claim credit on an issue that is highly popular with Americans, Clinton is expected to sign the bill the week of Oct. 5. [The president signed the bill Oct. 7. — Ed.]

"This bill will make it easier for millions of Americans to get the higher education they need to succeed in the global economy," Clinton said.

The U.S. Student Association, an organization that represents college students, said it was taking a "vocally silent" position on the bill. The group, college associations and the Education Department are unhappy that Congress decided to apply the lower interest rate only through Feb. 1, 1999, to students who consolidate outstanding loans for easier repayment. Students and colleges were also unhappy about a provision making it more difficult for students to discharge student loan debt if they declared bankruptcy.

Some Democrats were upset that conferees dropped a provision by Sen. Paul Wellstone, D-Minn., that would have made it easier for welfare recipients to attend college or vocational schools without losing their benefits.

"If you are able to go on and complete two years or four years of higher education, you are going to be in a better position to find a good job and give your children the care you know they need and deserve," Wellstone said.

The Wellstone amendment would have allowed states to count education toward work requirements imposed by Congress in the 1996 welfare law (PL 104-193). The final bill calls for a General Accounting Office study on the role of education in helping welfare recipients become employed. (*Welfare law, 1996 Almanac, p. 6-3*)

The bill reduces interest rates to students, at least initially, by nearly a full percentage point. Interest rates in academic year 1999-2000 will be 7.46 percent for students during the standard 10-year repayment period, down from 8.23 percent earlier this year. To help lenders' profitability, the government would provide a subsidy to ensure that banks make 7.96 percent on student loans. The rates are set by a formula based on short-term Treasury notes and vary annually.

Lending Controversy

Earlier this year, some commercial banks threatened to drop out of the college lending program unless Congress rolled back a long-planned July 1 change in the federal formula for setting interest rates, which would have sharply reduced their expected returns.

That rate cut was included in the 1993 budget-reconciliation law (PL 103-66) that also created the Education Department's direct student lending program. The Clinton administration had hoped the lending program would have captured a majority of the student aid market by now. Furthermore, the plan would have pegged student loans to long-term, as opposed to short-term, interest rates. But in the meantime, long-term rates have fallen, making the formula unacceptable to banks. (*1998 CQ Weekly Report, p. 323*)

To avoid a disruption, Congress on May 22 included a provision in the surface transportation reauthorization bill (PL 105-178) that put in place a temporary compromise rate, based on 91-day Treasury bill yields, from July 1 to Oct. 1. Until HR 6 is signed, the Education Department has the power to maintain the status quo.

Under the reauthorization, the temporary fix will be extended until 2003.

While the rates vary from year to year, lawmakers estimated that a student who borrowed $12,000 would save $650 in interest over the 10-year repayment period. The White House complained that the two-tiered rate was too generous to bankers, but lenders asserted that they were still taking a financial hit.

"While this legislation requires significant sacrifices on the part of student loan providers, it ensures that students will continue to have access [to loans]," said Mark R. Cannon, executive director of the Coalition for Student Loan Reform, a group of guarantee agencies.

The bill lets the Education Department apply the lower rate only until Feb. 1, 1999, for students who consolidate outstanding loans. After Congress approved the temporary fix this summer, the department announced it would extend the reduced rate to consolidation loans. That prompted howls from bankers who said it would give the department, which runs a direct lending program in competition with the commercial market, an unfair advantage.

The measure gradually increases the maximum allowable Pell grant for low-income students to $5,800 in academic year 2003-04, up from the current appropriated level of $3,000. Need criteria are relaxed to make it easier for students to work without exceeding income limits for financial aid and help non-traditional students, many with children, to qualify.

The authorization for college work-study programs increases to $1 billion in fiscal 1999, up from the appropriated level of $830 million.

The bill sets up a performance-based organization in the Department of Education to run student aid programs and requires the education secretary to provide information to the public about college tuition increases.

To pay for the interest rate changes, the legislation alters provisions of bankruptcy law to make it more difficult for students to discharge student loan debt. Students will still be able to discharge their payments if they prove severe economic hardship. The bill also increased the Government National Mortgage Association's (Ginnie Mae) guarantee fee to nine basis points, from six basis points, in fiscal 2005-07.

It calls for a study of using market-based mechanisms, such as auctions, to set college loan interest rates.

Training Programs

Responding to reports that more than one-third of teachers of core sub-jects such as math and science were not trained in their subject area, the bill consolidates more than a dozen programs into block grants to states to improve teacher preparation. It authorizes $300 million for the initiative in fiscal 1999.

States can use the funds to improve certification programs, provide merit pay for excellent teachers and create alternative certification programs, where individuals with expertise in an outside field can quickly be prepared to teach. Further, states are required to identify teacher-training programs that performed poorly.

"This bill will take giant steps in improving teacher preparation," said Senate Labor Committee Chairman James M. Jeffords, R-Vt.

In a second effort to address a shortage of qualified teachers, especially in poor areas, the bill provides up to $5,000 in loan forgiveness for new teachers who work in underserved school areas for five years. Teachers must have a degree in the subject matter they teach.

The bill takes steps to reach out to non-traditional students, such as older individuals or those who take longer than the standard four years to earn an undergraduate degree.

The act provides child care grants to help low-income students attend school. It allows experiments with "distance learning" so that students who live far away from a regular campus can attend via computers and other technology.

"Distance learning can open the doors of higher education to many students who cannot attend classes on college campuses because they live in remote areas or because of their job and family responsibilities," said Sen. Edward M. Kennedy, D-Mass.

The legislation blends House, Senate and White House suggestions to create a new "GEAR UP" program of outreach to low-income middle school students. The initiative, authorized at $200 million in fiscal 1999, is designed to help low-income students attend college.

The bill eases some federal regulations on vocational schools or career colleges, which in the past have been plagued by high student loan default rates and other problems. Lawmakers said they were satisfied that the schools had improved their performance.

The bill bars federal aid to students convicted on a drug charge. Students lose eligibility for one year after a first conviction, two years after a second and indefinitely after a third. ◆

Appendix

The Legislative Process in Brief

Note: Parliamentary terms used below are defined in the glossary.

Introduction of Bills

A House member (including the resident commissioner of Puerto Rico and non-voting delegates of the District of Columbia, Guam, the Virgin Islands and American Samoa) may introduce any one of several types of bills and resolutions by handing it to the clerk of the House or placing it in a box called the hopper. A senator first gains recognition of the presiding officer to announce the introduction of a bill. If objection is offered by any senator, the introduction of the bill is postponed until the following day.

As the next step in either the House or Senate, the bill is numbered, referred to the appropriate committee, labeled with the sponsor's name and sent to the Government Printing Office so that copies can be made for subsequent study and action. Senate bills may be jointly sponsored and carry several senators' names. Until 1978, the House limited the number of members who could cosponsor any one bill; the ceiling was eliminated at the beginning of the 96th Congress. A bill written in the executive branch and proposed as an administration measure usually is introduced by the chairman of the congressional committee that has jurisdiction.

Bills — Prefixed with HR in the House, S in the Senate, followed by a number. Used as the form for most legislation, whether general or special, public or private.

Joint Resolutions — Designated H J Res or S J Res. Subject to the same procedure as bills, with the exception of a joint resolution proposing an amendment to the Constitution. The latter must be approved by two-thirds of both houses and is thereupon sent directly to the administrator of general services for submission to the states for ratification instead of being presented to the president for his approval.

Concurrent Resolutions — Designated H Con Res or S Con Res. Used for matters affecting the operations of both houses. These resolutions do not become law.

Resolutions — Designated H Res or S Res. Used for a matter concerning the operation of either house alone and adopted only by the chamber in which it originates.

Committee Action

With few exceptions, bills are referred to the appropriate standing committees. The job of referral formally is the responsibility of the Speaker of the House and the presiding officer of the Senate, but this task usually is carried out on their behalf by the parliamentarians of the House and Senate. Precedent, statute and the jurisdictional mandates of the committees as set forth in the rules of the House and Senate determine which committees receive what kinds of bills. An exception is the referral of private bills, which are sent to whatever committee is designated by their sponsors. Bills are technically considered "read for the first time" when referred to House committees.

When a bill reaches a committee it is placed on the committee's calendar. At that time the bill comes under the sharpest congressional focus. Its chances for passage are quickly determined — and the great majority of bills falls by the legislative roadside. Failure of a committee to act on a bill is equivalent to killing it; the measure can be withdrawn from the committee's purview only by a discharge petition signed by a majority of the House membership on House bills, or by adoption of a special resolution in the Senate. Discharge attempts rarely succeed.

The first committee action taken on a bill usually is a request for comment on it by interested agencies of the government. The committee chairman may assign the bill to a subcommittee for study and hearings, or it may be considered by the full committee. Hearings may be public, closed (executive session) or both. A subcommittee, after considering a bill, reports to the full committee its recommendations for action and any proposed amendments.

The full committee then votes on its recommendation to the House or Senate. This procedure is called "ordering a bill reported." Occasionally a committee may order a bill reported unfavorably; most of the time a report, submitted by the chairman of the committee to the House or Senate, calls for favorable action on the measure since the committee can effectively "kill" a bill by simply failing to take any action.

After the bill is reported, the committee chairman instructs the staff to prepare a written report. The report describes the purposes and scope of the bill, explains the committee revisions, notes proposed changes in existing law and, usually, includes the views of the executive branch agencies consulted. Often committee members opposing a measure issue dissenting minority statements that are included in the report.

Usually, the committee "marks up" or proposes amendments to the bill. If they are substantial and the measure is complicated, the committee may order a "clean bill" introduced, which will embody the proposed amendments. The original bill then is put aside and the clean bill, with a new number, is reported to the floor.

The chamber must approve, alter or reject the committee amendments before the bill itself can be put to a vote.

Floor Action

After a bill is reported back to the house where it originated, it is placed on the calendar.

There are five legislative calendars in the House, issued in one cumulative calendar titled *Calendars of the United States House of Representatives and History of Legislation.* The House

How a Bill Becomes Law

This graphic shows the most typical way in which proposed legislation is enacted into law. There are more complicated, as well as simpler, routes, and most bills never become law. The process is illustrated with two hypothetical bills, House bill No. 1 (HR 1) and Senate bill No. 2 (S 2). Bills must be passed by both houses in identical form before they can be sent to the president. The path of HR 1 is traced by a black line, that of S 2 by a gray line. In practice, most bills begin as similar proposals in both houses.

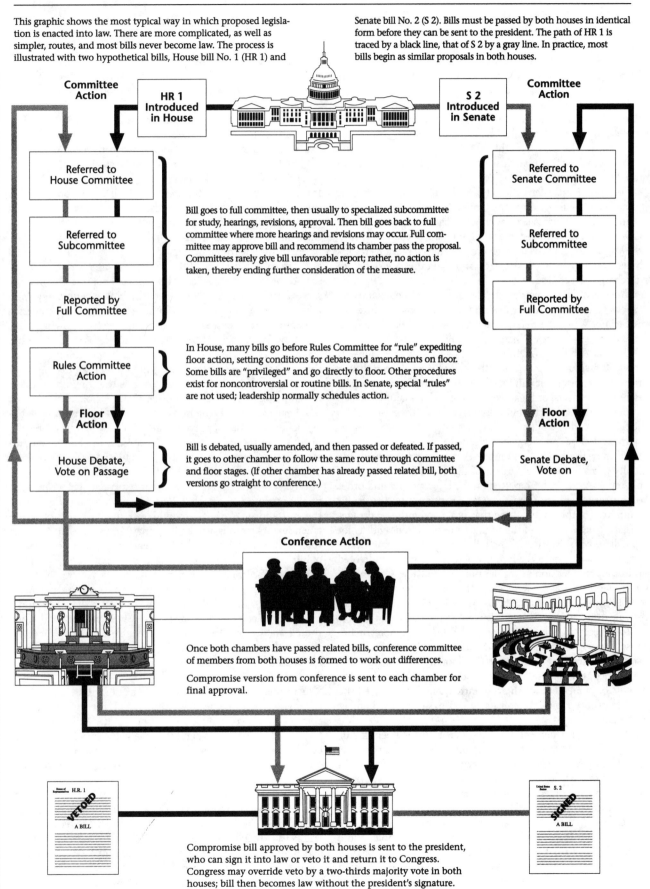

Committee Action

HR 1 Introduced in House

S 2 Introduced in Senate

Committee Action

Referred to House Committee

Referred to Senate Committee

Referred to Subcommittee

Referred to Subcommittee

Reported by Full Committee

Reported by Full Committee

Bill goes to full committee, then usually to specialized subcommittee for study, hearings, revisions, approval. Then bill goes back to full committee where more hearings and revisions may occur. Full committee may approve bill and recommend its chamber pass the proposal. Committees rarely give bill unfavorable report; rather, no action is taken, thereby ending further consideration of the measure.

Rules Committee Action

In House, many bills go before Rules Committee for "rule" expediting floor action, setting conditions for debate and amendments on floor. Some bills are "privileged" and go directly to floor. Other procedures exist for noncontroversial or routine bills. In Senate, special "rules" are not used; leadership normally schedules action.

Floor Action

Floor Action

House Debate, Vote on Passage

Bill is debated, usually amended, and then passed or defeated. If passed, it goes to other chamber to follow the same route through committee and floor stages. (If other chamber has already passed related bill, both versions go straight to conference.)

Senate Debate, Vote on

Conference Action

Once both chambers have passed related bills, conference committee of members from both houses is formed to work out differences.

Compromise version from conference is sent to each chamber for final approval.

H.R. 1 VETOED A BILL

S. 2 SIGNED A BILL

Compromise bill approved by both houses is sent to the president, who can sign it into law or veto it and return it to Congress. Congress may override veto by a two-thirds majority vote in both houses; bill then becomes law without the president's signature.

calendars are:

The Union Calendar to which are referred bills raising revenues, general appropriations bills and any measures directly or indirectly appropriating money or property. It is the Calendar of the Committee of the Whole House on the State of the Union.

The House Calendar to which are referred bills of public character not raising revenue or appropriating money.

The Corrections Calendar to which are referred bills to repeal rules and regulations deemed excessive or unnecessary when the Corrections Calendar is called the second and fourth Tuesday of each month. (Instituted in the 104th Congress to replace the seldom-used Consent Calendar.) A three-fifths majority is required for passage.

The Private Calendar to which are referred bills for relief in the nature of claims against the United States or private immigration bills that are passed without debate when the Private Calendar is called the first and third Tuesdays of each month.

The Discharge Calendar to which are referred motions to discharge committees when the necessary signatures are signed to a discharge petition.

There is only one legislative calendar in the Senate and one "executive calendar" for treaties and nominations submitted to the Senate. When the Senate Calendar is called, each senator is limited to five minutes' debate on each bill.

Debate. A bill is brought to debate by varying procedures. If a routine measure, it may await the call of the calendar. If it is urgent or important, it can be taken up in the Senate either by unanimous consent or by a majority vote. The majority leader, in consultation with the minority leader and others, schedules the bills that will be taken up for debate.

In the House, precedence is granted if a special rule is obtained from the Rules Committee. A request for a special rule usually is made by the chairman of the committee that favorably reported the bill, supported by the bill's sponsor and other committee members. The request, considered by the Rules Committee in the same fashion that other committees consider legislative measures, is in the form of a resolution providing for immediate consideration of the bill. The Rules Committee reports the resolution to the House where it is debated and voted on in the same fashion as regular bills. If the Rules Committee fails to report a rule requested by a committee, there are several ways to bring the bill to the House floor — under suspension of the rules, on Calendar Wednesday or by a discharge motion.

The resolutions providing special rules are important because they specify how long the bill may be debated and whether it may be amended from the floor. If floor amendments are banned, the bill is considered under a "closed rule," which permits only members of the committee that first reported the measure to the House to alter its language, subject to chamber acceptance.

When a bill is debated under an "open rule," amendments may be offered from the floor. Committee amendments always are taken up first but may be changed, as may all amendments up to the second degree; that is, an amendment to an amendment to an amendment is not in order.

Duration of debate in the House depends on whether the bill is under discussion by the House proper or before the House when it is sitting as the Committee of the Whole House on the State of the Union. In the former, the amount of time for debate either is determined by special rule or is allocated with an hour for each member if the measure is under consideration without a rule. In the Committee of the Whole the amount of time agreed on for general debate is equally divided between proponents and opponents. At the end of general discussion, the bill is read section by section for amendment. Debate on an amendment is limited to five minutes for each side; this is called the "five-minute rule." In practice, amendments regularly are debated more than ten minutes, with members gaining the floor by offering pro forma amendments or obtaining unanimous consent to speak longer than five minutes.

Senate debate usually is unlimited. It can be halted only by unanimous consent by "cloture," which requires a three-fifths majority of the entire Senate except for proposed changes in the Senate rules. The latter requires a two-thirds vote.

The House considers almost all important bills within a parliamentary framework known as the Committee of the Whole. It is not a committee as the word usually is understood; it is the full House meeting under another name for the purpose of speeding action on legislation. Technically, the House sits as the Committee of the Whole when it considers any tax measure or bill dealing with public appropriations. It also can resolve itself into the Committee of the Whole if a member moves to do so and the motion is carried. The Speaker appoints a member to serve as the chairman. The rules of the House permit the Committee of the Whole to meet when a quorum of 100 members is present on the floor and to amend and act on bills, within certain time limitations. When the Committee of the Whole has acted, it "rises," the Speaker returns as the presiding officer of the House and the member appointed chairman of the Committee of the Whole reports the action of the committee and its recommendations. The Committee of the Whole cannot pass a bill; instead it reports the measure to the full House with whatever changes it has approved. The full House then may pass or reject the bill — or, on occasion, recommit the bill to committee. Amendments adopted in the Committee of the Whole may be put to a second vote in the full House.

Votes. Voting on bills may occur repeatedly before they are finally approved or rejected. The House votes on the rule for the bill and on various amendments to the bill. Voting on amendments often is a more illuminating test of a bill's support than is the final tally. Sometimes members approve final passage of bills after vigorously supporting amendments that, if adopted, would have scuttled the legislation.

The Senate has three different methods of voting: an untabulated voice vote, a standing vote (called a division) and a recorded roll call to which members answer "yea" or "nay" when their names are called. The House also employs voice and standing votes, but since January 1973 yeas and nays have been recorded by an electronic voting device, eliminating the need for time-consuming roll calls.

Another method of voting, used in the House only, is the teller vote. Traditionally, members filed up the center aisle past counters; only vote totals were announced. Since 1971, one-fifth of a quorum can demand that the votes of individual members be recorded, thereby forcing them to take a public position on amendments to key bills. Electronic voting now is commonly used for this purpose.

After amendments to a bill have been voted upon, a vote may be taken on a motion to recommit the bill to committee. If carried, this vote removes the bill from the chamber's calendar and is usually a death blow to the bill. If the motion is unsuccessful, the bill then is "read for the third time." An actual reading usually is dispensed with. Until 1965, an opponent of a bill could delay this move by objecting and asking for a full reading of an engrossed (certified in final form) copy of the bill. After the "third reading," the vote on final passage is taken.

Examples of Legislative Documents

The final vote may be followed by a motion to reconsider, and this motion may be followed by a move to lay the motion on the table. Usually, those voting for the bill's passage vote for the tabling motion, thus safeguarding the final passage action. With that, the bill has been formally passed by the chamber. While a motion to reconsider a Senate vote is pending on a bill, the measure cannot be sent to the House.

Action in Second House

After a bill is passed it is sent to the other chamber. This body may then take one of several steps. It may pass the bill as is — accepting the other chamber's language. It may send the bill to committee for scrutiny or alteration, or reject the entire bill, advising the other house of its actions. Or it simply may ignore the bill submitted while it continues work on its own version of the proposed legislation. Frequently, one chamber may approve a version of a bill that is greatly at variance with the version already passed by the other house, and then substitute its contents for the language of the other, retaining only the latter's bill number.

A provision of the Legislative Reorganization Act of 1970 permits a separate House vote on any non-germane amendment added by the Senate to a House-passed bill and requires a majority vote to retain the amendment. Previously the House was forced to act on the bill as a whole; the only way to defeat the non-germane amendment was to reject the entire bill.

Often the second chamber makes only minor changes. If these are readily agreed to by the other house, the bill then is routed to the president. However, if the opposite chamber significantly alters the bill submitted to it, the measure usually is "sent to conference." The chamber that has possession of the "papers" (engrossed bill, engrossed amendments, messages of transmittal) requests a conference and the other chamber must agree to it. If the second house does not agree, the bill dies.

Conference, Final Action

Conference. A conference works out conflicting House and Senate versions of a legislative bill. The conferees usually are senior members appointed by the presiding officers of the two houses, from the committees that managed the bills. Under this arrangement the conferees of one house have the duty of trying to maintain their chamber's position in the face of amending actions by the conferees (also referred to as "managers") of the other house.

The number of conferees from each chamber may vary, the range usually being from three to nine members in each group, depending upon the length or complexity of the bill involved. There may be five representatives and three senators on the conference committee, or the reverse. But a majority vote controls the action of each group so that a large representation does not give one chamber a voting advantage over the other chamber's conferees.

Theoretically, conferees are not allowed to write new legislation in reconciling the two versions before them, but this curb sometimes is bypassed. Many bills have been put into acceptable compromise form only after new language was provided by the conferees. The 1970 Reorganization Act attempted to tighten restrictions on conferees by forbidding them to introduce any language on a topic that neither chamber sent to conference or to modify any topic beyond the scope of the different House and Senate versions.

Frequently the ironing out of difficulties takes days or even weeks. Conferences on involved appropriations bills sometimes are particularly drawn out.

As a conference proceeds, conferees reconcile differences between the versions, but generally they grant concessions only insofar as they remain sure that the chamber they represent will accept the compromises. Occasionally, uncertainty over how either house will react, or the positive refusal of a chamber to back down on a disputed amendment, results in an impasse, and the bills die in conference even though each was approved by its sponsoring chamber.

Conferees sometimes go back to their respective chambers for further instructions, when they report certain portions in disagreement. Then the chamber concerned can either "recede and concur" in the amendment of the other house or "insist on its amendment."

When the conferees have reached agreement, they prepare a conference report embodying their recommendations (compromises). The report, in document form, must be submitted to each house.

The conference report must be approved by each house. Consequently, approval of the report is approval of the compromise bill. In the order of voting on conference reports, the chamber which asked for a conference yields to the other chamber the opportunity to vote first.

Final Steps. After a bill has been passed by both the House and Senate in identical form, all of the original papers are sent to the enrolling clerk of the chamber in which the bill originated. He then prepares an enrolled bill, which is printed on parchment paper. When this bill has been certified as correct by the secretary of the Senate or the clerk of the House, depending on which chamber originated the bill, it is signed first (no matter whether it originated in the Senate or House) by the Speaker of the House and then by the president of the Senate. It is next sent to the White House to await action.

If the president approves the bill, he signs it, dates it and usually writes the word "approved" on the document. If he does not sign it within 10 days (Sundays excepted) and Congress is in session, the bill becomes law without his signature.

However, should Congress adjourn before the 10 days expire, and the president has failed to sign the measure, it does not become law. This procedure is called the pocket veto.

A president vetoes a bill by refusing to sign it and, before the 10-day period expires, returning it to Congress with a message stating his reasons. The message is sent to the chamber that originated the bill. If no action is taken on the message, the bill dies. Congress, however, can attempt to override the president's veto and enact the bill, "the objections of the president to the contrary notwithstanding." Overriding a veto requires a two-thirds vote of those present, who must number a quorum and vote by roll call.

Debate can precede this vote, with motions permitted to lay the message on the table, postpone action on it or refer it to committee. If the president's veto is overridden by a two-thirds vote in both houses, the bill becomes law. Otherwise it is dead.

When bills are passed finally and signed, or passed over a veto, they are given law numbers in numerical order as they become law. There are two series of numbers, one for public and one for private laws, starting at the number "1" for each two-year term of Congress. They are then identified by law number and by Congress — for example, Private Law 21, 97th Congress; Public Law 250, 97th Congress (or PL 97–250).

The Budget Process in Brief

Through the budget process, the president and Congress decide how much to spend and tax during the upcoming fiscal year. More specifically, they decide how much to spend on each activity, ensure that the government spends no more and spends it only for that activity, and report on that spending at the end of each budget cycle.

The President's Budget

The law requires that, by the first Monday in February, the president submit to Congress his proposed federal budget for the next fiscal year, which begins on October 1. In order to accomplish this, the president establishes general budget and fiscal policy guidelines. Based on these guidelines, executive branch agencies make requests for funds and submit them to the White House's Office of Management and Budget (OMB) nearly a year prior to the start of a new fiscal year. The OMB, receiving direction from the president and administration official, reviews the agencies' requests and develops a detailed budget by December. From December to January the OMB prepares the budget documents, so that the president can deliver it to Congress in February.

The president's budget is the executive branch's plan for the next year — but it is just a proposal. After receiving it, Congress has its own budget process to follow from February to October. Only after Congress passes the required spending bills — and the president signs them — has the government created its actual budget.

Action in Congress

Congress first must pass a "budget resolution" — a framework within which the members of Congress will make their decisions about spending and taxes. It includes targets for total spending, total revenues, and the deficit, and allocations within the spending target for the two types of spending — discretionary and mandatory.

Discretionary spending, which currently accounts for about 33 percent of all federal spending, is what the president and Congress must decide to spend for the next year through the thirteen annual appropriations bills. It includes money for such activities as the FBI and the Coast Guard, for housing and education, for NASA and highway and bridge construction, and for defense and foreign aid.

Mandatory spending, which currently accounts for 67 percent of all spending, is authorized by laws that have already been passed. It includes entitlement spending — such as for Social Security, Medicare, veterans' benefits, and food stamps — through which individuals receive benefits because they are eligible based on their age, income, or other criteria. It also includes interest on the national debt, which the government pays to individuals and institutions that hold Treasury bonds and other government securities. The only way the president

and Congress can change the spending on entitlement and other mandatory programs is if they change the laws that authorized the programs.

Currently, the law imposes a limit or "cap" through 1998 on total annual discretionary spending. Within the cap, however, the president and Congress can, and often do, change the spending levels from year to year for the thousands of individual federal programs.

In addition, the law requires that legislation that would raise mandatory spending or lower revenues — compared to existing law — be offset by spending cuts or revenue increases. This requirement, called "pay-as-you-go" is designed to prevent new legislation from increasing the deficit.

Once Congress passes the budget resolution, it turns its attention to passing the thirteen annual appropriations bills and, if it chooses, "authorizing" bills to change the laws governing mandatory spending and revenues.

Congress begins by examining the president's budget in detail. Scores of committees and subcommittees hold hearings on proposals under their jurisdiction. The House and Senate Armed Services Authorizing Committees, and the Defense and Military Construction Subcommittees of the Appropriations Committees, for instance, hold hearings on the president's defense budget. The White House budget director, cabinet officers, and other administration officials work with Congress as it accepts some of the president's proposals, rejects others, and changes still others. Congress can change funding levels, eliminate programs, or add programs not requested by the president. It can add or eliminate taxes and other sources of revenue, or make other changes that affect the amount of revenue collected. Congressional rules require that these committees and subcommittees take actions that reflect the congressional budget resolution.

The president's budget, the budget resolution, and the appropriations or authorizing bills measure spending in two ways — "budget authority" and "outlays." Budget authority is what the law authorizes the federal government to spend for certain programs, projects, or activities. What the government actually spends in a particular year, however, is an outlay. For example, when the government decides to build a space exploration system, the president and Congress may agree to appropriate $1 billion in budget authority. But the space system may take ten years to build. Thus, the government may spend $100 million in outlays in the first year to begin construction and the remaining $900 million during the next nine years as the construction continues.

Congress must provide budget authority before the federal agencies can obligate the government to make outlays. When Congress fails to complete action on one or more of the regular annual appropriations bills before the fiscal year begins on October 1, budget authority may be made on a temporary basis through continuing resolutions. Continuing resolutions make budget authority available for limited periods of time, generally at rates related through some formula to the rate provided in the previous year's appropriation.

Monitoring the Budget

Once Congress passes and the president signs the federal appropriations bills or authorizing laws for the fiscal year, the government monitors the budget through (1) agency program managers and budget officials, including the Inspectors General, who report only to the agency head; (2) the Office of Management and Budget; (3) congressional committees; and (4) the General Accounting Office, an auditing arm of Congress.

This oversight is designed to (1) ensure that agencies comply with legal limits on spending, and that they use budget authority only for the purposes intended; (2) see that programs are operating consistently with legal requirements and existing policy; and (3) ensure that programs are well managed and achieving the intended results.

The president may withhold appropriated amounts from obligation only under certain limited circumstances — to provide for contingencies, to achieve savings made possible through changes in requirements or greater efficiency of operations, or as otherwise provided by law. The Impoundment Control Act of 1974 specifies the procedures that must be followed if funds are withheld. Congress can also cancel previous authorized budget authority by passing a rescissions bill — but it also must be signed by the president.

Glossary of Congressional Terms

Absolute Majority—A vote requiring approval by a majority of all members of a house rather than a majority of members present and voting. Also referred to as constitutional majority.

Act—(1) A bill passed in identical form by both houses of Congress and signed into law by the president or enacted over his veto. A bill also becomes an act without the president's signature if he does not return it to Congress within 10 days (Sundays excepted) and if Congress has not adjourned within that period. (2) Also, the technical term for a bill passed by at least one house and engrossed.

Adjourn for More Than Three Days—Under Article I, Section 5 of the Constitution, neither house may adjourn for more than three days without the approval of the other. The necessary approval is given in a concurrent resolution and agreed to by both houses, which may permit one or both to take such an adjournment.

Adjournment Sine Die—Final adjournment of an annual or two-year session of Congress; literally, adjournment without a day. The two houses must agree to a privileged concurrent resolution for such an adjournment. A sine die adjournment precludes Congress from meeting again until the next constitutionally fixed date of a session (January 3 of the following year) unless Congress determines otherwise by law or the president calls it into special session. Article II, Section 3 of the Constitution authorizes the president to adjourn both houses until such time as he thinks proper when the two houses cannot agree to a time of adjournment, but no president has ever exercised this authority.

Adjournment to a Day (and Time) Certain—An adjournment that fixes the next date and time of meeting for one or both houses. It does not end an annual session of Congress.

Advice and Consent—The Senate's constitutional role in consenting to or rejecting the president's nominations to executive branch and judicial offices and the treaties he submits. Confirmation of nominees requires a simple majority vote of the full Senate. Treaties must be approved by a two-thirds majority of senators present and voting.

Amendment—A formal proposal to alter the text of a bill, resolution, amendment, motion, treaty, or some other text. Technically, it is a motion. An amendment may strike out (eliminate) part of a text, insert new text, or strike out and insert—that is, replace all or part of the text with new text. The texts of amendments considered on the floor are printed in full in the *Congressional Record*.

Amendment in the Nature of a Substitute—Usually, an amendment to replace the entire text of a measure. It strikes out everything after the enacting clause and inserts a version that may be somewhat, substantially, or entirely different. When a committee adopts extensive amendments to a measure, it often incorporates them into such an amendment. Occasionally, the term is applied to an amendment that replaces a major portion of a measure's text.

Annual Authorization—Legislation that authorizes appropriations for a single fiscal year and usually for a specific amount. Under the rules of the authorization-appropriation process, an annually authorized agency or program must be reauthorized each year if it is to receive appropriations for that year. Sometimes Congress fails to enact the reauthorization but nevertheless provides appropriations to continue the program, circumventing the rules by one means or another.

Appeal—A member's formal challenge of a ruling or decision by the presiding officer. On appeal, a house or a committee may overturn the ruling by majority vote. The right of appeal ensures the body against arbitrary control by the chair. Appeals are rarely made in the House and are even more rarely successful. Rulings are more frequently appealed in the Senate and occasionally overturned, in part because its presiding officer is not the majority party's leader, as in the House.

Apportionment—The action, after each decennial census, of allocating the number of members in the House of Representatives to each state. By law, the total number of House members (not counting delegates and a resident commissioner) is fixed at 435. The number allotted to each state is based approximately on its proportion of the nation's total population. Since the Constitution guarantees each state one representative no matter how small its population, exact proportional distribution is virtually impossible. The mathematical formula currently used to determine the apportionment is called the Method of Equal Proportions. (*See Method of Equal Proportions.*)

Appropriation—(1) Legislative language that permits a federal agency to incur obligations and make payments from the Treasury for specified purposes, usually during a specified period of time. (2) The specific amount of money made available by such language. The Constitution prohibits payments from the Treasury except "in Consequence of Appropriations made by Law." With some exceptions, the rules of both houses forbid consideration of appropriations for purposes that are unauthorized in law or of appropriation amounts larger than those authorized in law. The House of Representatives claims the exclusive right to originate appropriation bills—a claim the Senate denies in theory but accepts in practice.

Appendix

Authorization—(1) A statutory provision that establishes or continues a federal agency, activity or program for a fixed or indefinite period of time. It may also establish policies and restrictions and deal with organizational and administrative matters. (2) A statutory provision that authorizes appropriations for an agency, activity, or program. The appropriations may be authorized for one year, several years, or an indefinite period of time, and the authorization may be for a specific amount of money or an indefinite amount ("such sums as may be necessary"). Authorizations of specific amounts are construed as ceilings on the amounts that subsequently may be appropriated in an appropriation bill, but not as minimums; either house may appropriate lesser amounts or nothing at all.

Backdoor Spending Authority—Authority to incur obligations that evades the normal congressional appropriations process because it is provided in legislation other than appropriation acts. The most common forms are borrowing authority, contract authority, and entitlement authority.

Baseline—A projection of the levels of federal spending, revenues, and the resulting budgetary surpluses or deficits for the upcoming and subsequent fiscal years, taking into account laws enacted to date and assuming no new policy decisions. It provides a benchmark for measuring the budgetary effects of proposed changes in federal revenues or spending, assuming certain economic conditions.

Bill—The term for the chief vehicle Congress uses for enacting laws. Bills that originate in the House of Representatives are designated as H.R., those in the Senate as S., followed by a number assigned in the order in which they are introduced during a two-year Congress. A bill becomes a law if passed in identical language by both houses and signed by the president, or passed over his veto, or if the president fails to sign it within 10 days after he has received it while Congress is in session.

Bills and Resolutions Introduced—Members formally present measures to their respective houses by delivering them to a clerk in the chamber when their house is in session. Both houses permit any number of members to join in introducing a bill or resolution. The first member listed on the measure is the sponsor; the other members listed are its cosponsors.

Bills and Resolutions Referred—After a bill or resolution is introduced, it is normally sent to one or more committees that have jurisdiction over its subject, as defined by House and Senate rules and precedents. A Senate measure is usually referred to the committee with jurisdiction over the predominant subject of its text, but it may be sent to two or more committees by unanimous consent or on a motion offered jointly by the majority and minority leaders. In the House, a rule requires the Speaker to refer a measure to the committee that has primary jurisdiction. The Speaker is also authorized to refer measures sequentially to additional committees.

Borrowing Authority—Statutory authority permitting a federal agency, such as the Export-Import Bank, to borrow money from the public or the Treasury to finance its operations. It is a form of backdoor spending. To bring such spending under the control of the congressional appropriation process, the Congressional Budget Act requires that new borrowing authori-

ty shall be effective only to the extent and in such amounts as are provided in appropriations acts.

Budget—A detailed statement of actual or anticipated revenues and expenditures during an accounting period. For the national government, the period is the federal fiscal year (October 1–September 30). The budget usually refers to the president's budget submission to Congress early each calendar year. The president's budget estimates federal government income and spending for the upcoming fiscal year and contains detailed recommendations for appropriation, revenue, and other legislation. Congress is not required to accept or even vote directly on the president's proposals, and it often revises the president's budget extensively. (*See Fiscal Year.*)

Budget Act—Common name for the Congressional Budget and Impoundment Control Act of 1974, which established the basic procedures of the current congressional budget process; created the House and Senate budget committees; and enacted procedures for reconciliation, deferrals, and rescissions. (*See Budget Process, Deferral, Impoundment, Reconciliation, Rescission. See also Gramm-Rudman-Hollings Act of 1985.*)

Budget and Accounting Act of 1921—The law that, for the first time, authorized the president to submit to Congress an annual budget for the entire federal government. Prior to the act, most federal agencies sent their budget requests to the appropriate congressional committees without review by the president.

Budget Authority—Generally, the amount of money that may be spent or obligated by a government agency or for a government program or activity. Technically, it is statutory authority to enter into obligations that normally result in outlays. The main forms of budget authority are appropriations, borrowing authority, and contract authority. It also includes authority to obligate and expend the proceeds of offsetting receipts and collections. Congress may make budget authority available for only one year, several years, or an indefinite period, and it may specify definite or indefinite amounts.

Budget Process—(1) In Congress, the procedural system it uses (a) to approve an annual concurrent resolution on the budget that sets goals for aggregate and functional categories of federal expenditures, revenues, and the surplus or deficit for an upcoming fiscal year; and (b) to implement those goals in spending, revenue, and, if necessary, reconciliation and debt-limit legislation. (2) In the executive branch, the process of formulating the president's annual budget, submitting it to Congress, defending it before congressional committees, implementing subsequent budget-related legislation, impounding or sequestering expenditures as permitted by law, auditing and evaluating programs, and compiling final budget data. The Budget and Accounting Act of 1921 and the Congressional Budget and Impoundment Control Act of 1974 established the basic elements of the current budget process. Major revisions were enacted in the Gramm-Rudman-Hollings Act of 1985 and the Budget Enforcement Act of 1990.

Budget Resolution—A concurrent resolution in which Congress establishes or revises its version of the federal budget's broad financial features for the upcoming fiscal year and several

additional fiscal years. Like other concurrent resolutions, it does not have the force of law, but it provides the framework within which Congress subsequently considers revenue, spending, and other budget-implementing legislation. The framework consists of two basic elements: (1) aggregate budget amounts (total revenues, new budget authority, outlays, loan obligations and loan guarantee commitments, deficit or surplus, and debt limit); and (2) subdivisions of the relevant aggregate amounts among the functional categories of the budget. Although it does not allocate funds to specific programs or accounts, the budget committees' reports accompanying the resolution often discuss the major program assumptions underlying its functional amounts. Unlike those amounts, however, the assumptions are not binding on Congress.

By Request—A designation indicating that a member has introduced a measure on behalf of the president, an executive agency, or a private individual or organization. Members often introduce such measures as a courtesy because neither the president nor any person other than a member of Congress can do so. The term, which appears next to the sponsor's name, implies that the member who introduced the measure does not necessarily endorse it. A House rule dealing with by-request introductions dates from 1888, but the practice goes back to the earliest history of Congress.

Calendar—A list of measures or other matters (most of them favorably reported by committees) that are eligible for floor consideration. The House has five calendars; the Senate has two. A place on a calendar does not guarantee consideration. Each house decides which measures and matters it will take up, when, and in what order, in accordance with its rules and practices.

Calendar Wednesday—A House procedure that on Wednesdays permits its committees to bring up for floor consideration nonprivileged measures they have reported The procedure is so cumbersome and susceptible to dilatory tactics, however, that committees rarely use it.

Call of the Calendar—Senate bills that are not brought up for debate by a motion, unanimous consent, or a unanimous consent agreement are brought before the Senate for action when the calendar listing them is "called." Bills must be called in the order listed. Measures considered by this method usually are noncontroversial, and debate on the bill and any proposed amendments is limited to a total of five minutes for each senator.

Caucus—(1) A common term for the official organization of each party in each house. (2) The official title of the organization of House Democrats. House and Senate Republicans and Senate Democrats call their organizations "conferences." (3) A term for an informal group of members who share legislative interests, such as the Black Caucus, Hispanic Caucus, and Children's Caucus.

Censure—The strongest formal condemnation of a member for misconduct short of expulsion. A house usually adopts a resolution of censure to express its condemnation, after which the presiding officer reads its rebuke aloud to the member in the presence of his colleagues.

Chamber—The Capitol room in which a house of Congress normally holds its sessions. The chamber of the House of Repre-

sentatives, officially called the Hall of the House, is considerably larger than that of the Senate because it must accommodate 435 representatives, four delegates, and one resident commissioner. Unlike the Senate chamber, members have no desks or assigned seats. In both chambers, the floor slopes downward to the well in front of the presiding officer's raised desk. A chamber is often referred to as "the floor," as when members are said to be on or going to the floor. Those expressions usually imply that the member's house is in session.

Christmas Tree Bill—Jargon for a bill adorned with amendments, many of them unrelated to the bill's subject, that provide benefits for interest groups, specific states, congressional districts, companies, and individuals.

Classes of Senators—A class consists of the 33 or 34 senators elected to a six-year term in the same general election. Since the terms of approximately one-third of the senators expire every two years, there are three classes.

Clean Bill—After a House committee extensively amends a bill, it often assembles its amendments and what is left of the bill into a new measure that one or more of its members introduces as a "clean bill." The revised measure is assigned a new number.

Clerk of the House—An officer of the House of Representatives responsible principally for administrative support of the legislative process in the House. The clerk is invariably the candidate of the majority party.

Cloture—A Senate procedure that limits further consideration of a pending proposal to 30 hours in order to end a filibuster. Sixteen senators must first sign and submit a cloture motion to the presiding officer. One hour after the Senate meets on the second calendar day thereafter, the chair puts the motion to a yea-and-nay vote following a live quorum call. If three-fifths of all senators (60 if there are no vacancies) vote for the motion, the Senate must take final action on the cloture proposal by the end of the 30 hours of consideration and may consider no other business until it takes that action. Cloture on a proposal to amend the Senate's standing rules requires approval by two-thirds of the senators present and voting.

Code of Official Conduct—A House rule that bans certain actions by House members, officers, and employees; requires them to conduct themselves in ways that "reflect creditably" on the House; and orders them to adhere to the spirit and the letter of House rules and those of its committees. The code's provisions govern the receipt of outside compensation, gifts, and honoraria, and the use of campaign funds; prohibit members from using their clerk-hire allowance to pay anyone who does not perform duties commensurate with that pay; forbids discrimination in members' hiring or treatment of employees on the grounds of race, color, religion, sex, handicap, age, or national origin; orders members convicted of a crime who might be punished by imprisonment of two or more years not to participate in committee business or vote on the floor until exonerated or reelected; and restricts employees' contact with federal agencies on matters in which they have a significant financial interest. The Senate's rules contain some similar prohibitions.

College of Cardinals—A popular term for the subcommittee chairmen of the appropriations committees, reflecting their influence over appropriation measures. The chairmen of the full appropriations committees are sometimes referred to as popes.

Committee—A panel of members elected or appointed to perform some service or function for its parent body. Congress has four types of committees: standing, special or select, joint, and, in the House, a Committee of the Whole.

Committees conduct investigations, make studies, issue reports and recommendations, and, in the case of standing committees, review and prepare measures on their assigned subjects for action by their respective houses. Most committees divide their work among several subcommittees. With rare exceptions, the majority party in a house holds a majority of the seats on its committees, and their chairmen are also from that party.

Committee of the Whole—Common name of the Committee of the Whole House on the State of the Union, a committee consisting of all members of the House of Representatives. Measures from the union calendar must be considered in the Committee of the Whole before the House officially completes action on them; the committee often considers other major bills as well. A quorum of the committee is 100, and it meets in the House chamber under a chairman appointed by the Speaker. Procedures in the Committee of the Whole expedite consideration of legislation because of its smaller quorum requirement, its ban on certain motions, and its five-minute rule for debate on amendments. Those procedures usually permit more members to offer amendments and participate in the debate on a measure than is normally possible. The Senate no longer uses a Committee of the Whole.

Committee Veto—A procedure that requires an executive department or agency to submit certain proposed policies, programs, or action to designated committees for review before implementing them. Before 1983, when the Supreme Court declared that a legislative veto is unconstitutional, these provisions permitted committees to veto the proposals. They no longer do so, and the term is now something of a misnomer. Nevertheless, agencies usually take the pragmatic approach of trying to reach a consensus with the committees before carrying out their proposals, especially when an appropriations committee is involved.

Concurrent Resolution—A resolution that requires approval by both houses but is not sent to the president for his signature and therefore cannot have the force of law. Concurrent resolutions deal with the prerogatives or internal affairs of Congress as a whole. Designated H. Con. Res. in the House and S. Con. Res. in the Senate, they are numbered consecutively in each house in their order of introduction during a two-year Congress.

Conference—(1) A formal meeting or series of meetings between members representing each house to reconcile House and Senate differences on a measure (occasionally several measures). Since one house cannot require the other to agree to its proposals, the conference usually reaches agreement by compromise. When a conference completes action on a measure, or as much action as appears possible, it sends its recommendations to both houses in the form of a conference report, accompanied by an explanatory statement. (2) The official title of the organi-

zation of all Democrats or Republicans in the Senate and of all Republicans in the House of Representatives. (*See Party Caucus.*)

Confirmations—(*See Nomination.*)

Congress—(1) The national legislature of the United States, consisting of the House of Representatives and the Senate. (2) The national legislature in office during a two-year period. Congresses are numbered sequentially; thus, the 1st Congress of 1789–1791 and the 102d Congress of 1991–1993. Before 1935, the two-year period began on the first Monday in December of odd-numbered years. Since then it has extended from January of an odd-numbered year through noon on January 3 of the next odd-numbered year. A Congress usually holds two annual sessions, but some have had three sessions and the 67th Congress had four. When a Congress expires, measures die if they have not yet been enacted.

Congressional Record—The daily, printed, and substantially verbatim account of proceedings in both the House and Senate chambers. Extraneous materials submitted by members appear in a section titled "Extensions of Remarks." A "Daily Digest" appendix contains highlights of the day's floor and committee action plus a list of committee meetings and floor agendas for the next day's session.

Although the official reporters of each house take down every word spoken during the proceedings, members are permitted to edit and "revise and extend" their remarks before they are printed. In the Senate section, all speeches, articles, and other material submitted by senators but not actually spoken or read on the floor are set off by large black dots, called bullets. However, bullets do not appear when a senator reads part of a speech and inserts the rest. In the House section, undelivered speeches and materials are printed in a distinctive typeface. The term "permanent *Record*" refers to the bound volumes of the daily *Records* of an entire session of Congress.

Congressional Terms of Office—A term normally begins on January 3 of the year following a general election and runs two years for representatives and six years for senators. A representative chosen in a special election to fill a vacancy is sworn in for the remainder of his predecessor's term. An individual appointed to fill a Senate vacancy usually serves until the next general election or until the end of the predecessor's term, whichever comes first. Some states, however, require their governors to call a special election to fill a Senate vacancy shortly after an appointment has been made.

Continuing Resolution (CR)—A joint resolution that provides funds to continue the operation of federal agencies and programs at the beginning of a new fiscal year if their annual appropriation bills have not yet been enacted; also called continuing appropriations.

Contract Authority—Statutory authority permitting an agency to enter into contracts or incur other obligations even though it has not received an appropriation to pay for them. Congress must eventually fund them because the government is legally liable for such payments. The Congressional Budget Act of 1974 requires that new contract authority may not be used unless provided for in advance by an appropriation act, but it permits a few exceptions.

Controllable Expenditures—Federal spending that is permitted but not mandated by existing authorization law and therefore may be adjusted by congressional action in appropriation bills. (*See Appropriation.*)

Correcting Recorded Votes—The rules of both houses prohibit members from changing their votes after a vote result has been announced. Nevertheless, the Senate permits its members to withdraw or change their votes, by unanimous consent, immediately after the announcement. In rare instances, senators have been granted unanimous consent to change their votes several days or weeks after the announcement.

Votes tallied by the electronic voting system in the House may not be changed. But when a vote actually given is not recorded during an oral call of the roll, a member may demand a correction as a matter of right. On all other alleged errors in a recorded vote, the Speaker determines whether the circumstances justify a change. Occasionally, members merely announce that they were incorrectly recorded; announcements can occur hours, days, or even months after the vote and appear in the *Congressional Record*.

Corrections Calendar—Members of the House may place on this calendar bills reported favorably from committee that repeal rules and regulations considered excessive or unnecessary. Bills on the Corrections Calendar normally are called on the second and fourth Tuesday of each month at the discretion of the Speaker in consultation with the minority leader. A bill must be on the calendar for at least three legislative days before it can be brought up for floor consideration. Once on the floor, a bill is subject to one hour of debate equally divided between the chairman and ranking member of the committee of jurisdiction. A vote may be called on whether to recommit the bill to committee with or without instructions. To pass, a three-fifths majority, or 261 votes if all House members vote, is required.

Cosponsor—A member who has joined one or more other members to sponsor a measure. (*See Bills and Resolutions Introduced.*)

Current Services Estimates—Executive branch estimates of the anticipated costs of federal programs and operations for the next and future fiscal years at existing levels of service and assuming no new initiatives or changes in existing law. The president submits these estimates to Congress with his annual budget and includes an explanation of the underlying economic and policy assumptions on which they are based, such as anticipated rates of inflation, real economic growth, and unemployment, plus program caseloads and pay increases.

Custody of the Papers—Possession of an engrossed measure and certain related basic documents that the two houses produce as they try to resolve their differences over the measure.

Dance of the Swans and the Ducks—A whimsical description of the gestures some members use in connection with a request for a recorded vote, especially in the House. When a member wants his colleagues to stand in support of the request, he moves his hands and arms in a gentle upward motion resembling the beginning flight of a graceful swan. When he wants his colleagues to remain seated in order to avoid such a vote, he moves his hands and arms in a vigorous downward motion resembling a diving duck.

Dean—Within a state's delegation in the House of Representatives, the member with the longest continuous service.

Debt Limit—The maximum amount of outstanding federal public debt permitted by law. The limit (or ceiling) covers virtually all debt incurred by the government except agency debt. Each congressional budget resolution sets forth the new debt limit that may be required under its provisions.

Deferral—An impoundment of funds for a specific period of time that may not extend beyond the fiscal year in which it is proposed. Under the Impoundment Control Act of 1974, the president must notify Congress that he is deferring the spending or obligation of funds provided by law for a project or activity. Congress can disapprove the deferral by legislation.

Deficit—The amount by which the government's outlays exceed its budget receipts for a given fiscal year. Both the president's budget and the annual congressional budget resolution provide estimates of the deficit or surplus for the upcoming and several future fiscal years.

Degrees of Amendment—Designations that indicate the relationships of amendments to the text of a measure and to each other. In general, an amendment offered directly to the text of a measure is an amendment in the first degree, and an amendment to that amendment is an amendment in the second degree. Both houses normally prohibit amendments in the third degree—that is, an amendment to an amendment to an amendment.

Dilatory Tactics—Procedural actions intended to delay or prevent action by a house or a committee. They include, among others, offering numerous motions, demanding quorum calls and recorded votes at every opportunity, making numerous points of order and parliamentary inquiries, and speaking as long as the applicable rules permit. The Senates rules permit a battery of dilatory tactics, especially lengthy speeches, except under cloture. In the House, possible dilatory tactics are more limited. Speeches are always subject to time limits and debate-ending motions. Moreover, a House rule instructs the Speaker not to entertain dilatory motions and lets the Speaker decide whether a motion is dilatory. However, the Speaker may not override the constitutional right of a member to demand the yeas and nays, and in practice usually waits for a point of order before exercising that authority. (*See Cloture.*)

Discharge a Committee—Remove a measure from a committee to which it has been referred in order to make it available for floor consideration. Noncontroversial measures are often discharged by unanimous consent. However, because congressional committees have no obligation to report measures referred to them, each house has procedures to extract controversial measures from recalcitrant committees. Six discharge procedures are available in the House of Representatives. The Senate uses a motion to discharge, which is usually converted into a discharge resolution.

Discharge Calendar—The House calendar to which motions to discharge committees are referred when they have the required number of signatures (218) and are awaiting floor action.

Appendix

Discharge Petition—(*See Discharge a Committee.*)

Discharge Resolution—In the Senate, a special motion that any senator may introduce to relieve a committee from consideration of a bill before it. The resolution can be called up for Senate approval or disapproval in the same manner as any other Senate business. (*House procedure, see Discharge a Committee.*)

Division Vote—A vote in which the chair first counts those in favor of a proposition and then those opposed to it, with no record made of how each member votes. In the Senate, the chair may count raised hands or ask senators to stand, whereas the House requires members to stand; hence, often called a standing vote. Committees in both houses ordinarily use a show of hands. A division usually occurs after a voice vote and may be demanded by any member or ordered by the chair if there is any doubt about the outcome of the voice vote. The demand for a division can also come before a voice vote. In the Senate, the demand must come before the result of a voice vote is announced. It may be made after a voice vote announcement in the House, but only if no intervening business has transpired and only if the member was standing and seeking recognition at the time of the announcement. A demand for the yeas and nays or, in the house, for a recorded vote, takes precedence over a division vote.

Enacting Clause—The opening language of each bill, beginning "Be it enacted by the Senate and House of Representatives of the United States of America in Congress assembled…" This language gives legal force to measures approved by Congress and signed by the president or enacted over his veto. A successful motion to strike it from a bill kills the entire measure.

Engrossed Bill—The official copy of a bill or joint resolution as passed by one chamber, including the text as amended by floor action, and certified by the clerk of the House or the secretary of the Senate (as appropriate). Amendments by one house to a measure or amendments of the other also are engrossed. House engrossed documents are printed on blue paper; the Senate's are printed on white paper.

Enrolled Bill—The final official copy of a bill or joint resolution passed in identical form by both houses. An enrolled bill is printed on parchment. After it is certified by the chief officer of the house in which it originated and signed by the House Speaker and the Senate president pro tempore, the measure is sent to the president for his signature.

Entitlement Program—A federal program under which individuals, businesses, or units of government that meet the requirements or qualifications established by law are entitled to receive certain payments if they seek such payments. Major examples include Social Security, Medicare, Medicaid, unemployment insurance, and military and federal civilian pensions. Congress cannot control their expenditures by refusing to appropriate the sums necessary to fund them because the government is legally obligated to pay eligible recipients the amounts to which the law entitles them.

Executive Calendar—The Senate's calendar for committee reports on its executive business, namely treaties and nominations. The calendar numbers indicate the order in which items were referred to the calendar but have no bearing on when or if the Senate will consider them. The Senate, by motion or unanimous consent, resolves itself into executive session to consider them

Executive Document—A document, usually a treaty, sent by the president to the Senate for approval. It is referred to a committee in the same manner as other measures. Executive documents are designated as Executive A, 102d Congress, 1st Session; Executive B; and so on.

Executive Order—A unilateral proclamation by the president that has a policy-making or legislative impact. Members of Congress have challenged some executive orders on the grounds that they usurped the authority of the legislative branch. Although the Supreme Court has ruled that a particular order exceeded the president's authority, it has upheld others as falling within the president's general constitutional powers.

Executive Privilege—The assertion that presidents have the right to withhold certain information from Congress. Presidents have based their claim on: (1) the constitutional separation of powers; (2) the need for secrecy in military and diplomatic affairs; (3) the need to protect individuals from unfavorable publicity; (4) the need to safeguard the confidential exchange of ideas in the executive branch; and (5) the need to protect individuals who provide confidential advice to the president.

Executive Session—A meeting of a Senate or House committee (or occasionally of either chamber) that only its members may attend. Witnesses regularly appear at committee meetings in executive session — for example, Defense Department officials during presentations of classified defense information. Other members of Congress may be invited, but the public and press are not to attend.

Expenditures—The actual spending of money as distinguished from the appropriation of funds. Expenditures are made by the disbursing officers of the administration; appropriations are made only by Congress. The two are rarely identical in any fiscal year. In addition to some current budget authority, expenditures may represent budget authority made available one, two, or more years earlier.

Expulsion—A member's removal from office by a two-thirds vote of his house; the super majority is required by the Constitution. It is the most severe and most rarely used sanction a house can invoke against a member. Although the Constitution provides no explicit grounds for expulsion, the courts have ruled that it may be applied only for misconduct during a member's term of office, not for conduct before the member's election. Generally, neither house will consider expulsion of a member convicted of a crime until the judicial processes have been exhausted. At that stage, members sometimes resign rather than face expulsion. In 1977 the House adopted a rule urging members convicted of certain crimes to voluntarily abstain from voting or participating in other legislative business.

Federal Debt—The total amount of monies borrowed and not yet repaid by the federal government. Federal debt consists of public debt and agency debt. Public debt is the portion of the federal debt borrowed by the Treasury or the Federal Financing Bank directly from the public or from another federal fund or account. For example, the Treasury regularly borrows money from the Social Security trust fund. Public debt accounts for about 99 percent of the federal debt. Agency debt refers to the debt incurred by federal agencies like the Export-Import Bank, but excluding the Treasury and the Federal Financing Bank, which are authorized by law to borrow funds from the public or from another government fund or account.

Filibuster—The use of obstructive and time-consuming parliamentary tactics by one member or a minority of members to delay, modify, or defeat proposed legislation or rules changes. Filibusters are also sometimes used to delay urgently needed measures in order to force the body to accept other legislation. The Senate's rules permitting unlimited debate and the extraordinary majority it requires to impose cloture make filibustering particularly effective in that chamber. Under the stricter rules of the House, filibusters in that body are short-lived and therefore ineffective and rarely attempted

Fiscal Year—The federal government's annual accounting period. It begins October 1 and ends on the following September 30. A fiscal year is designated by the calendar year in which it ends and is often referred to as FY. Thus, fiscal year 1992 began October 1, 1991, ended September 30, 1992, and is called FY92. In theory, Congress is supposed to complete action on all budgetary measures applying to a fiscal year before that year begins. It rarely does so.

Five-Minute Rule—In its most common usage, a House rule that limits debate on an amendment offered in Committee of the Whole to five minutes for its sponsor and five minutes for an opponent. In practice, the committee routinely permits longer debate by two devices: the offering of pro forma amendments, each debatable for five minutes, and unanimous consent for a member to speak longer than five minutes. Also a House rule that limits a committee member to five minutes when questioning a witness at a hearing until each member has had an opportunity to question that witness.

Floor Manager—A majority party member responsible for guiding a measure through its floor consideration in a house and for devising the political and procedural strategies that might be required to get the measure passed. The presiding officer gives the floor manager priority recognition to debate, offer amendments, oppose amendments, and make crucial procedural motions.

Frank—Informally, a member's legal right to send official mail postage free under his or her signature; often called the franking privilege. Technically, it is the autographic or facsimile signature used on envelopes instead of stamps that permits members and certain congressional officers to send their official mail free of charge. The franking privilege has been authorized by law since the first Congress, except for a few months in 1873. Congress reimburses the U.S. Postal Service for the franked mail it handles.

Function or Functional Category—A broad category of national need and spending of budgetary significance. A category provides an accounting method for allocating and keeping track of budgetary resources and expenditures for that function because it includes all budget accounts related to the functions subject or purpose such as agriculture, administration of justice, commerce and housing and energy. Functions do not necessarily correspond with appropriations acts or with the budgets of individual agencies.

Germane—Basically, on the same subject as the matter under consideration. A House rule requires that all amendments be germane. In the Senate, only amendments proposed to general appropriation bills and budget resolutions or under cloture must be germane. Germaneness rules can be evaded by suspension of the rules in both houses, by unanimous consent agreements in the Senate, and by special rules from the Rules Committee in the House.

Gerrymandering—The manipulation of legislative district boundaries to benefit a particular party, politician, or minority group. The term originated in 1812 when the Massachusetts legislature redrew the lines of state legislative districts to favor the party of Gov. Elbridge Gerry, and some critics said one district looked like a salamander.

Gramm-Rudman-Hollings Act of 1985—Common name for the Balanced Budget and Emergency Deficit Control Act of 1985, which established new budget procedures intended to balance the federal budget by fiscal year 1991—a goal subsequently extended to 1993. The act's chief sponsors were senators Phil Gramm (R-Texas), Warren Rudman (R-N.H.), and Ernest Hollings (D-S.C.).

Grandfather Clause—A provision in a measure, law, or rule that exempts an individual, entity, or a defined category of individuals or entities from complying with a new policy or restriction. For example, a bill that would raise taxes on persons who reach the age of 65 after a certain date inherently grandfathers out those who are 65 before that date. Similarly, a Senate rule limiting senators to two major committee assignments also grandfathers some senators who were sitting on a third major committee prior to a specified date.

Grants-in-Aid—Payments by the federal government to state and local governments to help provide for assistance programs or public services.

Hearing—(1) Committee or subcommittee meetings to receive testimony from witnesses on proposed legislation during investigations or for oversight purposes. Relatively few bills are important enough to justify formal hearings. Witnesses often include experts, government officials, spokespersons for interested groups, officials of the General Accounting Office, and members of Congress. Also, the printed transcripts of hearings.

Hold—A senator's request that his or her party leaders delay floor consideration of certain legislation or presidential nominations. The majority leader usually honors a hold for a reasonable period of time, especially if its purpose is to assure the senator that the matter will not be called up during his or her absence or to give the senator time to gather necessary information.

Hold-Harmless Clause—In legislation providing a new formula for allocating federal funds, a clause to ensure that recipients of those funds do not receive less in a future year than they did in the current year if the new formula would result in a reduction for them. Similar to a grandfather clause, it has been used most frequently to soften the impact of sudden reductions in federal grants. (*See Grandfather Clause.*)

Hopper—A box on the clerk's desk in the House chamber into which members deposit bills and resolutions to introduce them. In House jargon, to drop a bill in the hopper is to introduce it.

Hour Rule—(1) A House rule that permits members, when recognized, to hold the floor in debate for no more than one hour each. The majority party member customarily yields one-half the time to a minority member. Although the hour rule applies to general debate in Committee of the Whole as well as in the House, special rules routinely vary the length of time for such debate and its control to fit the circumstances of particular measures.

House—The House of Representatives, as distinct from the Senate, although each body is a "house" of Congress.

House as in Committee of the Whole—A hybrid combination of procedures from the general rules of the House and from the rules of the Committee of the Whole, sometimes used to expedite consideration of a measure on the floor.

House Calendar—The calendar reserved for all public bills and resolutions that do not raise revenue or directly or indirectly appropriate money or property when they are favorably reported by House committees.

House Manual—A commonly used title for the handbook of the rules of the House of Representatives, published in each Congress. Its official title is *Constitution, Jefferson's Manual, and Rules of the House of Representatives*.

House of Representatives—The house of Congress in which states are represented roughly in proportion to their populations, but every state is guaranteed at least one representative. By law, the number of voting representatives is fixed at 435. Four delegates and one resident commissioner also serve in the House; they may vote in their committees and in Committee of the Whole but not in the House sitting as the House. Although the House and Senate have equal legislative power, the Constitution gives the House sole authority to originate revenue measures. The House also claims the right to originate appropriation measures, a claim the Senate disputes in theory but concedes in practice. The House has the sole power to impeach, and it elects the president when no candidate has received a majority of the electoral votes. It is sometimes referred to as the lower body.

Immunity—(1) Members' constitutional protection from lawsuits and arrest in connection with their legislative duties. They may not be tried for libel or slander for anything they say on the floor of a house or in committee. Nor may they be arrested while attending sessions of their houses or when traveling to or from sessions of Congress, except when charged with treason, a felony, or a breach of the peace. (2) In the case of a witness before a committee, a grant of protection from prosecution based on that person's testimony to the committee. It is used to compel witnesses to testify who would otherwise refuse to do so on the constitutional ground of possible self-incrimination. Under such a grant, none of a witness testimony may be used against

him or her in a court proceeding except in a prosecution for perjury or for giving a false statement to Congress.

Impeachment—The first step to remove the president, vice president, or other federal civil officers from office and to disqualify them from any future federal office "of honor, Trust or Profit." An impeachment is a formal charge of treason, bribery, or "other high Crimes and Misdemeanors." The House has the sole power of impeachment and the Senate the sole power of trying the charges and convicting. The House impeaches by a simple majority vote; conviction requires a two-thirds vote of all senators present.

Impoundment—An executive branch action or inaction that delays or withholds the expenditure or obligation of budget authority provided by law. The Impoundment Control Act of 1974 classifies impoundments as either deferrals or rescissions, requires the president to notify Congress about all such actions, and gives Congress authority to approve or reject them. The Constitution is unclear on whether a president may refuse to spend appropriated money, but Congress usually expects the president to spend at least enough to achieve the purposes for which the money was provided whether or not he agrees with those purposes.

Item Veto—A procedure (sometimes called a line-item veto), available in 1997 for the first time, permitting a president to cancel amounts of new discretionary appropriations (budget authority), as well as new items of direct spending (entitlements) and certain limited tax benefits, unless Congress disapproves by law within a limited period of time. After the president signs a bill, he may act within five calendar days to propose the cancellation of one or more such items; a cancellation becomes permanent unless, within 30 days, Congress passes a joint resolution to disapprove it. The president may veto such a joint resolution; in that case, it requires a two-thirds vote in both houses to override the president's veto of the joint resolution disapproving his action. The authority to cancel amounts of new discretionary appropriations applies only to amounts specifically identified in the law or one of the accompanying standing or conference committee reports. The authority for this procedure expires at the end of 2004 unless Congress extends it by law.

Joint Committee—A committee composed of members selected from each house. The functions of most joint committees involve investigation, research, or oversight of agencies closely related to Congress. Permanent joint committees, created by statute, are sometimes called standing joint committees. Once quite numerous, only four joint committees remained as of 1997: Joint Economic, Joint Taxation, Joint Library, and Joint Printing. No joint committee has authority to report legislation.

Joint Resolution—A legislative measure that Congress uses for purposes other than general legislation. Like a bill, it has the force of law when passed by both houses and either approved by the president or passed over the president's veto. Unlike a bill, a joint resolution enacted into law is not called an act; it retains its original title.

Most often, joint resolutions deal with such relatively limited matters as the correction of errors in existing law, continuing appropriations, a single appropriation, or the establishment of permanent joint committees. Unlike bills, however, joint resolutions also are used to propose constitutional amendments; these do not require the president's signature and become effective only when ratified by three-fourths of the states. The House designates joint resolutions as H.J. Res., the Senate as S.J. Res. Each house numbers its joint resolutions consecutively in the order of introduction during a two-year Congress.

Journal—The official record of House or Senate actions, including every motion offered, every vote cast, amendments agreed to, quorum calls, and so forth. Unlike the *Congressional Record*, it does not provide reports of speeches, debates, statements, and the like. The Constitution requires each house to maintain a *Journal* and to publish it periodically.

King of the Mountain (or Hill Rule)—*(See Queen of the Hill Rule.)*

Lame Duck—Jargon for a member who has not been reelected, or did not seek reelection, and is serving the balance of his or her term.

Lame Duck Session—A session of a Congress held after the election for the succeeding Congress, so-called after the lame duck members still serving.

Law—An act of Congress that has been signed by the president, passed over the president's veto, or allowed to become law without the president's signature.

Legislative Day—The day that begins when a house meets after an adjournment and ends when it next adjourns. Because the House of Representatives normally adjourns at the end of a daily session, its legislative and calendar days usually coincide. The Senate, however, frequently recesses at the end of a daily session, and its legislative day may extend over several calendar days, weeks, or months. Among other uses, this technicality permits the Senate to save time by circumventing its morning hour, a procedure required at the beginning of every legislative day

Legislative Veto—A procedure, declared unconstitutional in 1983, that allowed Congress or one of its houses to nullify certain actions of the president, executive branch agencies, or independent agencies. Sometimes called congressional vetoes or congressional disapprovals. Following the Supreme Court's 1983 decision, Congress amended several legislative veto statutes to require enactment of joint resolutions, which are subject to presidential veto, for nullifying executive branch actions.

Live Pair—A voluntary and informal agreement between two members on opposite sides of an issue under which the member who is present for a recorded vote withholds or withdraws his or her vote because the other member is absent.

Loan Guarantee—A statutory commitment by the federal government to pay part or all of a loans principal and interest to a lender or the holder of a security in case the borrower defaults.

Lobby—To try to persuade members of Congress to propose, pass, modify, or defeat proposed legislation or to change or repeal existing laws. A lobbyist attempts to promote his or her own preferences or those of a group, organization, or industry. Originally the term referred to persons frequenting the lobbies or corridors of legislative chambers in order to speak to lawmakers. In a general sense, lobbying includes not only direct contact with members but also indirect attempts to influence them, such as writing to them or persuading others to write or visit them, attempting to mold public opinion toward a desired legislative goal by various means, and contributing or arranging for contributions to members election campaigns. The right to lobby stems from the First Amendment to the Constitution, which bans laws that abridge the right of the people to petition the government for a redress of grievances.

Logrolling—Jargon for a legislative tactic or bargaining strategy in which members try to build support for their legislation by promising to support legislation desired by other members or by accepting amendments they hope will induce their colleagues to vote for their bill.

Mace—The symbol of the office of the House sergeant at arms. Under the direction of the Speaker, the sergeant at arms is responsible for preserving order on the House floor by holding up the mace in front of an unruly member, or by carrying the mace up and down the aisles to quell boisterous behavior. When the House is in session, the mace sits on a pedestal at the Speaker's right; when the House is in Committee of the Whole, it is moved to a lower pedestal. The mace is 46 inches high and consists of 13 ebony rods bound in silver and topped by a silver globe with a silver eagle, wings outstretched, perched on it.

Majority Leader—The majority party's chief floor spokesman, elected by that party's caucus—sometimes called floor leader. In the Senate, the majority leader also develops the party's political and procedural strategy, usually in collaboration with other party officials and committee chairmen. He negotiates the Senates agenda and committee ratios with the minority leader and usually calls up measures for floor action. The chamber traditionally concedes to the majority leader the right to determine the days on which it will meet and the hours at which it will convene and adjourn. In the House, the majority leader is the Speaker's deputy and heir apparent. He helps plan the floor agenda and the party's legislative strategy and often speaks for the party leadership in debate.

Majority Whip—In effect, the assistant majority leader, in either the House or Senate. His job is to help marshal majority forces in support of party strategy and legislation.

Manual—The official handbook in each house prescribing in detail its organization, procedures, and operations.

Marking Up a Bill—Going through the contents of a piece of legislation in committee or subcommittee to, for example, consider its provisions in large and small portions, act on amendments to provisions and proposed revisions to the language, and insert new sections and phraseology. If the bill is extensively amended, the committee's version may be introduced as a separate bill, with a new number, before being considered by the full House or Senate. *(See Clean Bill.)*

Method of Equal Proportions—The mathematical formula used since 1950 to determine how the 435 seats in the House of Representatives should be distributed among the 50 states in the apportionment following each decennial census. It minimizes as much as possible the proportional difference between the average district population in any two states. Because the Constitution guarantees each state at least one representative, 50 seats are automatically apportioned. The formula calculates priority numbers for each state, assigns the first of the 385 remaining seats to the state with the highest priority number, the second to the state with the next highest number, and so on until all seats are distributed. *(See Apportionment.)*

Midterm Election—The general election for members of Congress that occurs in November of the second year in a presidential term.

Minority Leader—The minority party's leader and chief floor spokesman, elected by the party caucus; sometimes called minority floor leader. With the assistance of other party officials and the ranking minority members of committees, the minority leader devises the party's political and procedural strategy.

Minority Whip—Performs duties of whip for the minority party. *(See also Majority Whip.)*

Minority Staff—Employees who assist the minority party members of a committee. Most committees hire separate majority and minority party staffs, but they also may hire nonpartisan staff.

Motion—A formal proposal for a procedural action, such as to consider, to amend, to lay on the table, to reconsider, to recess, or to adjourn. It has been estimated that at least 85 motions are possible under various circumstances in the House of Representatives, somewhat fewer in the Senate. Not all motions are created equal; some are privileged or preferential and enjoy priority over others. And some motions are debatable, amendable or divisible, while others are not.

Nomination—A proposed presidential appointment to a federal office submitted to the Senate for confirmation. Approval is by majority vote. The Constitution explicitly requires confirmation for ambassadors, consuls, public Ministers (department heads), and Supreme Court justices. By law, other federal judges, all military promotions of officers, and many high-level civilian officials must be confirmed.

Oath of Office—Upon taking office, members of Congress must swear or affirm that they will "support and defend the Constitution . . . against all enemies, foreign and domestic," that they will "bear true faith and allegiance" to the Constitution, that they take the obligation "freely, without any mental reservation or purpose of evasion," and that they will "well and faithfully discharge the duties" of their office. The oath is required by the Constitution; the wording is prescribed by a statute. All House members must take the oath at the beginning of each new Congress.

Obligations—Orders placed, contracts awarded, services received, and similar transactions during a given period that will require payments during the same or future period. Such amounts include outlays for which obligations had not been previously recorded and reflect adjustments for differences between obligations previously recorded and actual outlays to liquidate those obligations.

Omnibus Bill—A measure that combines the provisions of several disparate subjects into a single and often lengthy bill.

One-Minute Speeches—Addresses by House members at the beginning of a legislative day. The speeches may cover any subject but are limited to one minute's duration.

Order of Business (House)—The sequence of events during the meeting of the House on a new legislative day prescribed by a House rule; also called the general order of business. The sequence consists of (1) the chaplain's prayer; (2) approval of the *Journal*; (3) pledge of allegiance (4) correction of the reference of public bills; (5) disposal of business on the Speaker's table; (6) unfinished business; (7) the morning hour call of committees and consideration of their bills (largely obsolete); (8) motions to go into Committee of the Whole; and (9) orders of the day (also obsolete). In practice, on days specified in the rules, the items of business that follow approval of the *Journal* are supplanted in part by the special order of business (for example, the corrections, discharge, or private calendars or motions to suspend the rules) and on any day by other privileged business (for example, general appropriation bills and special rules) or measures made in order by special rules. By this combination of an order of business with privileged interruptions, the House gives precedence to certain categories of important legislation, brings to the floor other major legislation from its calendars in any order it chooses, and provides expeditious processing for minor and noncontroversial measures.

Order of Business (Senate)—The sequence of events at the beginning of a new legislative day prescribed by Senate rules. The sequence consists of (1) the chaplain's prayer; (2) *Journal* reading and correction; (3) morning business in the morning hour; (4) call of the calendar during the morning hour; and (5) unfinished business.

Outlays—Amounts of government spending. They consist of payments, usually by check or in cash, to liquidate obligations incurred in prior fiscal years as well as in the current year, including the net lending of funds under budget authority. In federal budget accounting, net outlays are calculated by subtracting the amounts of refunds and various kinds of reimbursements to the government from actual spending.

Override a Veto—Congressional enactment of a measure over the president's veto. A veto override requires a recorded two-thirds vote of those voting in each house, a quorum being present. Because the president must return the vetoed measure to its house of origin, that house votes first, but neither house is required to attempt an override, whether immediately or at all. If an override attempt fails in the house of origin, the veto stands and the measure dies.

Oversight—Congressional review of the way in which federal agencies implement laws to ensure that they are carrying out the intent of Congress and to inquire into the efficiency of the implementation and the effectiveness of the law. The Legislative Reorganization Act of 1946 defined oversight as the function of exercising continuous watchfulness over the execution of the laws by the executive branch.

Pairing—A procedure that permits two or three members to enter into voluntary arrangements that offset their votes so that one or more of the members can be absent without changing the result. The names of paired members and their positions on the vote (except on general pairs) appear in the *Congressional Record*. Members can be paired on one vote or on a series of votes.

Parliamentarian—The official advisor to the presiding officer in each house on questions of procedure. The parliamentarian and his assistants also answer procedural questions from members and congressional staff, refer measures to committees on behalf of the presiding officer, and maintain compilations of the precedents. The House parliamentarian revises the House Manual at the beginning of every Congress and usually reviews special rules before the Rules Committee reports them to the House. Either a parliamentarian or an assistant is always present and near the podium during sessions of each house.

Party Caucus—Generic term for each party's official organization in each house. Only House Democrats officially call their organization a caucus. House and Senate Republicans and Senate Democrats call their organizations conferences. The party caucuses elect their leaders, approve committee assignments and chairmanships (or ranking minority members, if the party is in the minority), establish party committees and study groups, and discuss party and legislative policies. On rare occasions, they have stripped members of committee seniority or expelled them from the caucus for party disloyalty.

Petition—A request or plea sent to one or both chambers from an organization or private citizens' group asking support of particular legislation or favorable consideration of a matter not yet receiving congressional attention. Petitions are referred to appropriate committees.

Pocket Veto—The indirect veto of a bill as a result of the president withholding approval of it until after Congress has adjourned sine die. A bill the president does not sign, but does not formally veto while Congress is in session, automatically becomes a law 10 days (excluding Sundays) after it is received. But if Congress adjourns its annual session during that 10-day period, the measure dies even if the president does not formally veto it.

Point of Order—A parliamentary term used in committee and on the floor to object to an alleged violation of a rule and to demand that the chair enforce the rule. The point of order immediately halts the proceedings until the chair decides whether the contention is valid.

Pork or Pork Barrel Legislation—Pejorative terms for federal appropriations, bills, or policies that provide funds to benefit a legislator's district or state, with the implication that the legislator presses for enactment of such benefits to ingratiate himself or herself with constituents rather than on the basis of an impartial, objective assessment of need or merit.

The terms are often applied to such benefits as new parks, post offices, dams, canals, bridges, roads, water projects, sewage treatment plants, and public works of any kind, as well as demonstration projects, research grants, and relocation of government facilities. Funds released by the president for various kinds of benefits or government contracts approved by him allegedly for political purposes are also sometimes referred to as pork.

Postcloture Filibuster—A filibuster conducted after the Senate invokes cloture. It employs an array of procedural tactics rather than lengthy speeches to delay final action. The Senate curtailed the postcloture filibusters effectiveness by closing a variety of loopholes in the cloture rule in 1979 and 1986.

President of the Senate—The vice president of the United States in his constitutional role as presiding officer of the Senate. The Constitution permits the vice president to cast a vote in the Senate only to break a tie, but he is not required to do so.

President Pro Tempore—Under the Constitution, an officer elected by the Senate to preside over it during the absence of the vice president of the United States. Often referred to as the "pro tem," he is usually the majority party senator with the longest continuous service in the chamber and also, by virtue of his seniority, a committee chairman. When attending to committee and other duties, the president pro tempore appoints other senators to preside.

Previous Question—A nondebatable motion which, when agreed to by majority vote, usually cuts off further debate, prevents the offering of additional amendments, and brings the pending matter to an immediate vote. It is a major debate-limiting device in the House; it is not permitted in Committee of the Whole or in the Senate.

Printed Amendment—A House rule guarantees five minutes of floor debate in support and five minutes in opposition, and no other debate time, on amendments printed in the Congressional Record at least one day prior to the amendment's consideration in the Committee of the Whole. In the Senate, although amendments may be submitted for printing, they have no parliamentary standing or status. An amendment submitted for printing in the Senate, however, may be called up by any senator.

Private Bill—A bill that applies to one or more specified persons, corporations, institutions, or other entities, usually to grant relief when no other legal remedy is available to them. Many private bills deal with claims against the federal government, immigration and naturalization cases, and land titles.

Private Calendar—Commonly used title for a calendar in the House reserved for private bills and resolutions favorably reported by committees. The private calendar is officially called the Calendar of the Committee of the Whole House.

Privilege—An attribute of a motion, measure, report, question, or proposition that gives it priority status for consideration. Privileged motions and motions to bring up privileged questions are not debatable.

Privileged Questions—The order in which bills, motions, and other legislative measures are considered by Congress is governed by strict priorities. A motion to table, for instance, is more privileged than a motion to recommit. Thus, a motion to recommit can be superseded by a motion to table, and a vote would be forced on the latter motion only. A motion to adjourn, however, takes precedence over a tabling motion and thus is considered of the "highest privilege." (*See also Questions of Privilege.*)

Pro Forma Amendment—In the House, an amendment that ostensibly proposes to change a measure or another amendment by moving "to strike the last word" or "to strike the requisite number of words." A member offers it not to make any actual change in the measure or amendment but only to obtain time for debate.

Proxy Voting—The practice of permitting a member to cast the vote of an absent colleague in addition to his own vote. Proxy voting is prohibited on the floors of the House and Senate, but the Senate permits their committees to authorize proxy voting, and most do. In 1995, House rules were changed to prohibit proxy voting in committee.

Public Law—A public bill or joint resolution enacted into law. It is cited by the letters P.L. followed by a hyphenated number. The digits before the hyphen indicate the number of the Congress in which it was enacted; the digits after the hyphen indicate its position in the numerical sequence of public measures that became law during that Congress. For example, the Budget Enforcement Act of 1990 became P.L. 101-508 because it was the 508th measure in that sequence for the 101st Congress. (*See also Private Bill.*)

Queen of the Hill Rule—A special rule from the House Rules Committee that permits votes on a series of amendments, especially complete substitutes for a measure, in a specified order, but directs that the amendment receiving the greatest number of votes shall be the winning one. This kind of rule permits the House to vote directly on a variety of alternatives to a measure. In doing so, it sets aside the precedent that once an amendment has been adopted, no further amendments may be offered to the text it has amended. Under an earlier practice, the Rules Committee reported "king of the hill" rules under which there also could be votes on a series of amendments, again in a specified order. If more than one of the amendments was adopted under this kind of rule, it was the last amendment to receive a majority vote that was considered as having been finally adopted, whether or not it had received the greatest number of votes.

Questions of Privilege—These are matters affecting members of Congress individually or collectively. Matters affecting the rights, safety, dignity, and integrity of proceedings of the House or Senate as a whole are questions of privilege in both chambers.

Questions involving individual members are called questions of "personal privilege." A member rising to ask a question of personal privilege is given precedence over almost all other proceedings. An annotation in the House rules points out that the privilege rests primarily on the Constitution, which gives a member a conditional immunity from arrest and an unconditional freedom to speak in the House. (*See also Privileged Questions.*)

Quorum—The minimum number of members required to be present for the transaction of business. Under the Constitution, a quorum in each house is a majority of its members: 218 in the House and 51 in the Senate when there are no vacancies. By House rule, a quorum in Committee of the Whole is 100. In practice, both houses usually assume a quorum is present even if it is not, unless a member makes a point of no quorum in the House or suggests the absence of a quorum in the Senate. Con-

sequently, each house transacts much of its business, and even passes bills, when only a few members are present.

For House and Senate committees, chamber rules allow a minimum quorum of one-third of a committee's members to conduct most types of business.

Ramseyer Rule—A House rule that requires a committee's report on a bill or joint resolution to show the changes the measure, and any committee amendments to it, would make in existing law.

Readings of Bills—Traditional parliamentary procedure required bills to be read three times before they were passed. This custom is of little modern significance. Normally a bill is considered to have its first reading when it is introduced and printed, by title, in the *Congressional Record*. In the House, its second reading comes when floor consideration begins. (This is the most likely point at which there is an actual reading of the bill, if there is any.) The second reading in the Senate is supposed to occur on the legislative day after the measure is introduced, but before it is referred to committee. The third reading (again, usually by title) takes place when floor action has been completed on amendments.

Reapportionment—(*See Apportionment.*)

Recess—(1) A temporary interruption or suspension of a meeting of a chamber or committee. Unlike an adjournment, a recess does not end a legislative day. Because the Senate often recesses from one calendar day to another, its legislative day may extend over several calendar days, weeks, or even months. (2) A period of adjournment for more than three days to a day certain, especially over a holiday or in August during odd-numbered years.

Recognition—The power of recognition of a member is lodged in the Speaker of the House and the presiding officer of the Senate. The presiding officer names the member who will speak first when two or more members simultaneously request recognition.

Recommit—To send a measure back to the committee that reported it; sometimes called a straight motion to recommit to distinguish it from a motion to recommit with instructions. A successful motion to recommit kills the measure unless it is accompanied by instructions.

Reconciliation—A procedure for changing existing revenue and spending laws to bring total federal revenues and spending within the limits established in a budget resolution. Congress has applied reconciliation chiefly to revenues and mandatory spending programs, especially entitlements. Discretionary spending is controlled through annual appropriation bills.

Reconsider a Vote—A motion to reconsider the vote by which an action was taken has, until it is disposed of, the effect of putting the action in abeyance. In the Senate, the motion can be made only by a member who voted on the prevailing side of the original question or by a member who did not vote at all. In the House, it can be made only by a member on the prevailing side.

A common practice in the Senate after close votes on an issue is a motion to reconsider, followed by a motion to table the motion to reconsider. On this motion to table, senators vote as they voted on the original question, which allows the motion to table to prevail, assuming there are no switches. The matter then is finally closed and further motions to reconsider are not entertained. In the House, as a routine precaution, a motion to reconsider usually is made every time a measure is passed. Such a motion almost always is tabled immediately, thus shutting off the possibility of future reconsideration, except by unanimous consent.

Motions to reconsider must be entered in the Senate within the next two days of actual session after the original vote has been taken. In the House they must be entered either on the same day or on the next succeeding day the House is in session.

Recorded Vote—(1) Generally, any vote in which members are recorded by name for or against a measure; also called a record vote or roll-call vote. The only recorded vote in the Senate is a vote by the yeas and nays and is commonly called a roll-call vote. (2) Technically, a recorded vote is one demanded in the House of Representatives and supported by at least one-fifth of a quorum (44 members) in the House sitting as the House or at least 25 members in Committee of the Whole.

Report—(1) As a verb, a committee is said to report when it submits a measure or other document to its parent chamber. (2) A clerk is said to report when he or she reads a measure's title, text, or the text of an amendment to the body at the direction of the chair. (3) As a noun, a committee document that accompanies a reported measure. It describes the measure, the committee's views on it, its costs, and the changes it proposes to make in existing law; it also includes certain impact statements. (4) A committee document submitted to its parent chamber that describes the results of an investigation or other study or provides information the committee is required to provide by rule or law.

Reprimand—A formal condemnation of a member for misbehavior, considered a milder reproof than censure. The House of Representatives first used it in 1976. The Senate has not used the term. (*See also Censure, Code of Official Conduct, Expulsion.*)

Rescission—A provision of law that repeals previously enacted budget authority in whole or in part. Under the Impoundment Control Act of 1974, the president can impound such funds by sending a message to Congress requesting one or more rescissions and the reasons for doing so. If Congress does not pass a rescission bill for the programs requested by the president within 45 days of continuous session after receiving the message, the president must make the funds available for obligation and expenditure. If the president does not, the comptroller general of the United States is authorized to bring suit to compel the release of those funds. A rescission bill may rescind all, part, or none of an amount proposed by the president, and may rescind funds the president has not impounded.

Resolution—(1) A simple resolution; that is, a nonlegislative measure effective only in the house in which it is proposed and not requiring concurrence by the other chamber or approval by the president. Simple resolutions are designated H. Res. in the House and S. Res. in the Senate. Simple resolutions express nonbinding opinions on policies or issues or deal with the internal affairs or prerogatives of a house. (2) Any type of resolution: simple, concurrent, or joint. (*See Concurrent Resolution, Joint Resolution.*)

Revise and Extend One's Remarks—A unanimous consent request to publish in the *Congressional Record* a statement a member did not deliver on the floor, a longer statement than the one made on the floor, or miscellaneous extraneous material.

Rider—Congressional slang for an amendment unrelated or extraneous to the subject matter of the measure to which it is attached. Riders often contain proposals that are less likely to become law on their own merits as separate bills, either because of opposition in the committee of jurisdiction, resistance in the other house, or the probability of a presidential veto. Riders are more common in the Senate.

Rule—(1) A permanent regulation that a house adopts to govern its conduct of business, its procedures, its internal organization, behavior of its members, regulation of its facilities, duties of an officer, or some other subject it chooses to govern in that form. (2) In the House, a privileged simple resolution reported by the Rules Committee that provides methods and conditions for floor consideration of a measure or, rarely, several measures.

Secretary of the Senate—The chief administrative and budgetary officer of the Senate. The secretary manages a wide range of functions that support the operation of the Senate as an organization as well as those functions necessary to its legislative process, including recordkeeping, document management, certifications, housekeeping services, administration of oaths, and lobbyist registrations.

Select or Special Committee—A committee established by a resolution in either house for a special purpose and, usually, for a limited time. Most select and special committees are assigned specific investigations or studies, but are not authorized to report measures to their chambers.

Senate—The house of Congress in which each state is represented by two senators; each senator has one vote. Article V of the Constitution declares that "No State, without its Consent, shall be deprived of its equal Suffrage in the Senate." The Constitution also gives the Senate equal legislative power with the House of Representatives. Although the Senate is prohibited from originating revenue measures, and as a matter of practice it does not originate appropriation measures, it can amend both. Only the Senate can give or withhold consent to treaties and nominations from the president. It also acts as a court to try impeachments by the House and elects the vice president when no candidate receives a majority of the electoral votes. It is often referred to as "the upper body," but not by members of the House.

Senate Manual—The handbook of the Senate's standing rules and orders and the laws and other regulations that apply to the Senate, usually published once each Congress.

Senatorial Courtesy—The Senate's practice of declining to confirm a presidential nominee for an office in the state of a senator of the president's party unless that senator approves.

Sequestration—A procedure for canceling budgetary resources that is, money available for obligation or spending to enforce budget limitations established in law. Sequestered funds are no longer available for obligation or expenditure.

Sine Die—(*See Adjournment Sine Die.*)

Slip Law—The first official publication of a measure that has become law. It is published separately in unbound, single-sheet form or pamphlet form. A slip law usually is available two or three days after the date of the law's enactment.

Speaker—The presiding officer of the House of Representatives and the leader of its majority party. The Speaker is selected by the majority party and formally elected by the House at the beginning of each Congress. Although the Constitution does not require the Speaker to be a member of the House, in fact, all Speakers have been members.

Special Session—A session of Congress convened by the president, under his constitutional authority, after Congress has adjourned sine die at the end of a regular session. (*See Adjournment Sine Die.*)

Spending Authority—The technical term for backdoor spending. The Congressional Budget Act of 1974 defines it as borrowing authority, contract authority, and entitlement authority for which appropriation acts do not provide budget authority in advance. Under the Budget Act, legislation that provides new spending authority may not be considered unless it provides that the authority shall be effective only to the extent or in such amounts as provided in an appropriation act.

Sponsor—The principal proponent and introducer of a measure or an amendment.

Standing Committee—A permanent committee established by a House or Senate standing rule or standing order. The rule also describes the subject areas on which the committee may report bills and resolutions and conduct oversight. Most introduced measures must be referred to one or more standing committees according to their jurisdictions.

Standing Vote—An alternative and informal term for a division vote, during which members in favor of a proposal and then members opposed stand and are counted by the chair. (*See Division Vote.*)

Star Print—A reprint of a bill, resolution, amendment, or committee report correcting technical or substantive errors in a previous printing; so called because of the small black star that appears on the front page or cover.

Statutes at Large—A chronological arrangement of the laws enacted in each session of Congress. Though indexed, the laws are not arranged by subject matter nor is there an indication of how they affect or change previously enacted laws. The volumes are numbered by Congress, and the laws are cited by their volume and page number. The Gramm-Rudman-Hollings Act, for example, appears as 99 Stat. 1037.

Strike from the *Record*—Expunge objectionable remarks from the *Congressional Record*, after a member's words have been taken down on a point of order.

Strike Out the Last Word—A motion whereby a House member is entitled to speak for five minutes on an amendment then being debated by the chamber. A member gains recogni-

tion from the chair by moving to "strike out the last word" of the amendment or section of the bill under consideration. The motion is proforma, requires no vote, and does not change the amendment being debated.

Substitute—A motion, amendment, or entire bill introduced in place of the pending legislative business. Passage of a substitute measure kills the original measure by supplanting it. The substitute also may be amended. (*See also Amendment in the Nature of a Substitute.*)

Sunshine Rules—Rules requiring open committee hearings and business meetings, including markup sessions, in both houses, and also open conference committee meetings. However, all may be closed under certain circumstances and using certain procedures required by the rules.

Super Majority—A term sometimes used for a vote on a matter that requires approval by more than a simple majority of those members present and voting; also referred to as extraordinary majority.

Supplemental Appropriation Bill—A measure providing appropriations for use in the current fiscal year, in addition to those already provided in annual general appropriation bills. Supplemental appropriations are often for unforeseen emergencies.

Suspension of the Rules (House)—An expeditious procedure for passing relatively noncontroversial or emergency measures by a two-thirds vote of those members voting, a quorum being present.

Suspension of the Rules (Senate)—A procedure to set aside one or more of the Senate's rules; it is used infrequently, and then most often to suspend the rule banning legislative amendments to appropriation bills.

Table a Bill—Motions to table, or to "lay on the table," are used to block or kill amendments or other parliamentary questions. When approved, a tabling motion is considered the final disposition of that issue. One of the most widely used parliamentary procedures, the motion to table is not debatable, and adoption requires a simple majority vote.

In the Senate, however, different language sometimes is used. The motion may be worded to let a bill "lie on the table," perhaps for subsequent "picking up." This motion is more flexible, keeping the bill pending for later action, if desired. Tabling motions on amendments are effective debate-ending devices in the Senate.

Teller Vote—A voting procedure, formerly used in the House, in which members cast their votes by passing through the center aisle to be counted, but not recorded by name, by a member from each party appointed by the chair. The House deleted the procedure from its rules in 1993, but during floor discussion of the deletion a leading member stated that a teller vote would still be available in the event of a breakdown of the electronic voting system.

Treaty—A formal document containing an agreement between two or more sovereign nations. The Constitution authorizes the president to make treaties, but he must submit them to the Senate for its approval by a two-thirds vote of the senators present. Under the Senate's rules, that vote actually occurs on a resolution of ratification. Although the Constitution does not give the House a direct role in approving treaties, that body has sometimes insisted that a revenue treaty is an invasion of its prerogatives. In any case, the House may significantly affect the application of a treaty by its equal role in enacting legislation to implement the treaty.

Trust Funds—Special accounts in the Treasury that receive earmarked taxes or other kinds of revenue collections, such as user fees, and from which payments are made for special purposes or to recipients who meet the requirements of the trust funds as established by law. Of the more than 150 federal government trust funds, several finance major entitlement programs, such as Social Security, Medicare, and retired federal employees' pensions. Others fund infrastructure construction and improvements, such as highways and airports.

Unanimous Consent—Without an objection by any member. A unanimous consent request asks permission, explicitly or implicitly, to set aside one or more rules. Both houses and their committees frequently use such requests to expedite their proceedings.

Unanimous Consent Agreement—A device used in the Senate to expedite legislation. Much of the Senate's legislative business, dealing with both minor and controversial issues, is conducted through unanimous consent or unanimous consent agreements. On major legislation, such agreements usually are printed and transmitted to all senators in advance of floor debate. Once agreed to, they are binding on all members unless the Senate, by unanimous consent, agrees to modify them. An agreement may list the order in which various bills are to be considered, specify the length of time bills and contested amendments are to be debated and when they are to be voted upon, and, frequently, require that all amendments introduced be germane to the bill under consideration. In this regard, unanimous consent agreements are similar to the "rules" issued by the House Rules Committee for bills pending in the House.

Unfunded Mandate—Generally, any provision in federal law or regulation that imposes a duty or obligation on a state or local government or private sector entity without providing the necessary funds to comply. The Unfunded Mandates Reform Act of 1995 amended the Congressional Budget Act of 1974 to provide a mechanism for the control of new unfunded mandates.

Union Calendar—A calendar of the House of Representatives for bills and resolutions favorably reported by committees that raise revenue or directly or indirectly appropriate money or property. In addition to appropriation bills, measures that authorize expenditures are also placed on this calendar. The calendar's full title is the Calendar of the Committee of the Whole House on the State of the Union.

U.S. Code—Popular title for the *United States Code: Containing the General and Permanent Laws of the United States in Force on. . . .* It is a consolidation and partial codification of the general and permanent laws of the United States arranged by subject under 50 titles. The first six titles deal with general or political subjects, the other 44 with subjects ranging from agriculture to war, alphabetically arranged. A supplement is published after each session of Congress, and the entire Code is revised every six years.

Veto—The president's disapproval of a legislative measure passed by Congress. He returns the measure to the house in which it originated without his signature but with a veto message stating his objections to it. When Congress is in session, the president must veto a bill within 10 days, excluding Sundays, after he has received it; otherwise it becomes law without his signature. The 10-day clock begins to run at midnight following his receipt of the bill. (*See also Committee Veto, Item Veto, Override a Veto, Pocket Veto.*)

Voice Vote—A method of voting in which members who favor a question answer aye in chorus, after which those opposed answer no in chorus, and the chair decides which position prevails.

War Powers Act of 1973—An act that requires the president "in every possible instance" to consult Congress before he commits U.S. forces to ongoing or imminent hostilities. If he commits them to a combat situation without congressional consultation, he must notify Congress within 48 hours. Unless Congress declares war or otherwise authorizes the operation to continue, the forces must be withdrawn within 60 or 90 days, depending on certain conditions.

Whip—The majority or minority party member in each house who acts as assistant leader, helps plan and marshal support for party strategies, encourages party discipline, and advises his leader on how his colleagues intend to vote on the floor. In the Senate, the Republican whip's official title is assistant leader.

Without Objection—Used in lieu of a vote on noncontroversial motions, amendments, or bills that may be passed in either the House or Senate if no member voices an objection.

Yeas and Nays—A vote in which members usually respond "aye" or "no" (despite the official title of the vote) on a question when their names are called in alphabetical order. The Constitution requires the yeas and nays when a demand for it is supported by one-fifth of the members present, and it also requires an automatic yea-and-nay vote on overriding a veto. Senate precedents require the support of at least one-fifth of a quorum, a minimum of 11 members with the present membership of 100.

Yielding—When a member has been recognized to speak, no other member may speak unless he or she obtains permission from the member recognized. This permission is called yielding and usually is requested in the form, "Will the gentleman yield to me?" While this activity occasionally is seen in the Senate, the Senate has no rule or practice to parcel out time.

Zone Whip—A member responsible for whip duties concerning his or her party colleagues from specific geographical areas.

Constitution of the United States

We the People of the United States, in Order to form a more perfect Union, establish Justice, insure domestic Tranquility, provide for the common defence, promote the general Welfare, and secure the Blessings of Liberty to ourselves and our Posterity, do ordain and establish this Constitution for the United States of America.

ARTICLE I

Section 1. All legislative Powers herein granted shall be vested in a Congress of the United States, which shall consist of a Senate and House of Representatives.

Section 2. The House of Representatives shall be composed of Members chosen every second Year by the People of the several States, and the Electors in each State shall have the Qualifications requisite for Electors of the most numerous Branch of the State Legislature.

No Person shall be a Representative who shall not have attained to the age of twenty five Years, and been seven Years a Citizen of the United States, and who shall not, when elected, be an Inhabitant of that State in which he shall be chosen.

[Representatives and direct Taxes shall be apportioned among the several States which may be included within this Union, according to their respective Numbers, which shall be determined by adding to the whole Number of free Persons, including those bound to Service for a Term of Years, and excluding Indians not taxed, three fifths of all other Persons.][1] The actual Enumeration shall be made within three Years after the first Meeting of the Congress of the United States, and within every subsequent Term of ten Years, in such Manner as they shall by Law direct. The Number of Representatives shall not exceed one for every thirty Thousand, but each State shall have at Least one Representative; and until such enumeration shall be made, the State of New Hampshire shall be entitled to chuse three, Massachusetts eight, Rhode-Island and Providence Plantations one, Connecticut five, New-York six, New Jersey four, Pennsylvania eight, Delaware one, Maryland six, Virginia ten, North Carolina five, South Carolina five, and Georgia three.

When vacancies happen in the Representation from any State, the Executive Authority thereof shall issue Writs of Election to fill such Vacancies.

The House of Representatives shall chuse their Speaker and other Officers; and shall have the sole Power of Impeachment.

Section 3. The Senate of the United States shall be composed of two Senators from each State, [chosen by the Legislature thereof,][2] for six Years; and each Senator shall have one Vote.

Immediately after they shall be assembled in Consequence of the first Election, they shall be divided as equally as may be into three Classes. The Seats of the Senators of the first Class shall be vacated at the Expiration of the second Year, of the second Class at the Expiration of the fourth Year, and of the third Class at the Expiration of the sixth Year, so that one third may be chosen every second Year; [and if Vacancies happen by Resignation, or otherwise, during the Recess of the Legislature of any State, the Executive thereof may make temporary Appointments until the next Meeting of the Legislature, which shall then fill such Vacancies.][3]

No Person shall be a Senator who shall not have attained to the Age of thirty Years, and been nine Years a Citizen of the United States, and who shall not, when elected, be an Inhabitant of that State for which he shall be chosen.

The Vice President of the United States shall be President of the Senate, but shall have no Vote, unless they be equally divided.

The Senate shall chuse their other Officers, and also a President pro tempore, in the Absence of the Vice President, or when he shall exercise the Office of President of the United States.

The Senate shall have the sole Power to try all Impeachments. When sitting for that Purpose, they shall be on Oath or Affirmation. When the President of the United States is tried, the Chief Justice shall preside: And no Person shall be convicted without the Concurrence of two thirds of the Members present.

Judgment in Cases of Impeachment shall not extend further than to removal from Office, and disqualification to hold and enjoy any Office of honor, Trust or Profit under the United States: but the Party convicted shall nevertheless be liable and subject to Indictment, Trial, Judgment and Punishment, according to Law.

Section 4. The Times, Places and Manner of holding Elections for Senators and Representatives, shall be prescribed in each State by the Legislature thereof; but the Congress may at any time by Law make or alter such Regulations, except as to the Places of chusing Senators.

The Congress shall assemble at least once in every Year, and such Meeting shall [be on the first Monday in December],[4] unless they shall by Law appoint a different Day.

Section 5. Each House shall be the Judge of the Elections, Returns and Qualifications of its own Members, and a Majority of each shall constitute a Quorum to do Business; but a smaller Number may adjourn from day to day, and may be authorized to compel the Attendance of absent Members, in such Manner, and under such Penalties as each House may provide.

Each House may determine the Rules of its Proceedings, punish its Members for disorderly Behaviour, and, with the Concurrence of two thirds, expel a Member.

Each House shall keep a Journal of its Proceedings, and from time to time publish the same, excepting such Parts as may in their Judgment require Secrecy; and the Yeas and Nays of the Members of either House on any question shall, at the Desire of one fifth of those Present, be entered on the Journal.

Neither House, during the Session of Congress, shall, without the Consent of the other, adjourn for more than three days, nor to any other Place than that in which the two Houses shall be sitting.

Section 6. The Senators and Representatives shall receive a Compensation for their Services, to be ascertained by Law, and paid out of the Treasury of the United States. They shall in all Cases, except Treason, Felony and Breach of the Peace, be privileged from Arrest during their Attendance at the Session of their respective Houses, and in going to and returning from the same; and for any Speech or Debate in either House, they shall not be questioned in any other Place.

No Senator or Representative shall, during the Time for which he was elected, be appointed to any civil Office under the Authority of the United States, which shall have been created, or the Emoluments whereof shall have been encreased during such time; and no Person holding any Office under the United States, shall be a Member of either House during his Continuance in Office.

Section 7. All Bills for raising Revenue shall originate in the House of Representatives; but the Senate may propose or concur with Amendments as on other Bills.

Every Bill which shall have passed the House of Representatives and the Senate, shall, before it become a Law, be presented to the President of the United States; If he approve he shall sign it, but if not he shall return it, with his Objections to that House in which it shall have originated, who shall enter the Objections at large on their Journal, and proceed to reconsider it. If after such Reconsideration two thirds of that House shall agree to pass the Bill, it shall be sent, together with the Objections, to the other House, by which it shall likewise be reconsidered, and if approved by two thirds of that House, it shall become a Law. But in all such Cases the Votes of both Houses shall be determined by yeas and Nays, and the Names of the Persons voting for and against the Bill shall be entered on the Journal of each House respectively. If any Bill shall not be returned by the President within ten Days (Sundays excepted) after it shall have been presented to him, the Same shall be a Law, in like Manner as if he had signed it, unless the Congress by their Adjournment prevent its Return, in which Case it shall not be a Law.

Every Order, Resolution, or Vote to which the Concurrence of the Senate and House of Representatives may be necessary (except on a question of Adjournment) shall be presented to the President of the United States; and before the Same shall take Effect, shall be approved by him, or being disapproved by him, shall be repassed by two thirds of the Senate and House of Representatives, according to the Rules and Limitations prescribed in the Case of a Bill.

Section 8. The Congress shall have Power To lay and collect Taxes, Duties, Imposts and Excises, to pay the Debts and provide for the common Defence and general Welfare of the United States; but all Duties, Imposts and Excises shall be uniform throughout the United States;

To borrow Money on the credit of the United States;

To regulate Commerce with foreign Nations, and among the several States, and with the Indian Tribes;

To establish an uniform Rule of Naturalization, and uniform Laws on the subject of Bankruptcies throughout the United States;

To coin Money, regulate the Value thereof, and of foreign Coin, and fix the Standard of Weights and Measures;

To provide for the Punishment of counterfeiting the Securi-

ties and current Coin of the United States;

To establish Post Offices and post Roads;

To promote the Progress of Science and useful Arts, by securing for limited Times to Authors and Inventors the exclusive Right to their respective Writings and Discoveries;

To constitute Tribunals inferior to the supreme Court;

To define and punish Piracies and Felonies committed on the high Seas, and Offences against the Law of Nations;

To declare War, grant Letters of Marque and Reprisal, and make Rules concerning Captures on Land and Water;

To raise and support Armies, but no Appropriation of Money to that Use shall be for a longer Term than two Years;

To provide and maintain a Navy;

To make Rules for the Government and Regulation of the land and naval Forces;

To provide for calling forth the Militia to execute the Laws of the Union, suppress Insurrections and repel Invasions;

To provide for organizing, arming, and disciplining, the Militia, and for governing such Part of them as may be employed in the Service of the United States, reserving to the States respectively, the Appointment of the Officers, and the Authority of training the Militia according to the discipline prescribed by Congress;

To exercise exclusive Legislation in all Cases whatsoever, over such District (not exceeding ten Miles square) as may, by Cession of particular States, and the Acceptance of Congress, become the Seat of the Government of the United States, and to exercise like Authority over all Places purchased by the Consent of the Legislature of the State in which the Same shall be, for the Erection of Forts, Magazines, Arsenals, dock-Yards, and other needful Buildings; — And

To make all Laws which shall be necessary and proper for carrying into Execution the foregoing Powers, and all other Powers vested by this Constitution in the Government of the United States, or in any Department or Officer thereof.

Section 9. The Migration or Importation of such Persons as any of the States now existing shall think proper to admit, shall not be prohibited by the Congress prior to the Year one thousand eight hundred and eight, but a Tax or duty may be imposed on such Importation, not exceeding ten dollars for each Person.

The Privilege of the Writ of Habeas Corpus shall not be suspended, unless when in Cases of Rebellion or Invasion the public Safety may require it.

No Bill of Attainder or ex post facto Law shall be passed.

No Capitation, or other direct, Tax shall be laid, unless in Proportion to the Census or Enumeration herein before directed to be taken.[5]

No Tax or Duty shall be laid on Articles exported from any State.

No Preference shall be given by any Regulation of Commerce or Revenue to the Ports of one State over those of another; nor shall Vessels bound to, or from, one State, be obliged to enter, clear, or pay Duties in another.

No Money shall be drawn from the Treasury, but in Consequence of Appropriations made by Law; and a regular Statement and Account of the Receipts and Expenditures of all public Money shall be published from time to time.

No Title of Nobility shall be granted by the United States: And no Person holding any Office of Profit or Trust under them, shall, without the Consent of the Congress, accept of any present, Emolument, Office, or Title, of any kind whatever, from any King, Prince, or foreign State.

Section 10. No State shall enter into any Treaty, Alliance, or Confederation; grant Letters of Marque and Reprisal; coin Money; emit Bills of Credit; make any Thing but gold and silver Coin a Tender in Payment of Debts; pass any Bill of Attainder, ex post facto Law, or Law impairing the Obligation of Contracts, or grant any Title of Nobility.

No State shall, without the Consent of the Congress, **lay** any Imposts or Duties on Imports or Exports, except what may be absolutely necessary for executing it's inspection Laws: and the net Produce of all Duties and Imposts, laid by any State on Imports or Exports, shall be for the Use of the Treasury of the United States; and all such Laws shall be subject to the Revision and Controul of the Congress.

No State shall, without the Consent of Congress, lay any Duty of Tonnage, keep Troops, or Ships of War in time of Peace, enter into any Agreement or Compact with another State, or with a foreign Power, or engage in War, unless actually invaded, or in such imminent Danger as will not admit of delay.

ARTICLE II

Section 1. The executive Power shall be vested in a President of the United States of America. He shall hold his Office during the Term of four Years, and, together with the Vice President, chosen for the same Term, be elected, as follows

Each State shall appoint, in such Manner as the Legislature thereof may direct, a Number of Electors, equal to the whole Number of Senators and Representatives to which the State may be entitled in the Congress: but no Senator or Representative, or Person holding an Office of Trust or Profit under the United States, shall be appointed an Elector.

[The Electors shall meet in their respective States, and vote by Ballot for two Persons, of whom one at least shall not be an Inhabitant of the same State with themselves. And they shall make a List of all the Persons voted for, and of the Number of Votes for each; which List they shall sign and certify, and transmit sealed to the Seat of the Government of the United States, directed to the President of the Senate. The President of the Senate shall, in the Presence of the Senate and House of Representatives, open all the Certificates, and the Votes shall then be counted. The Person having the greatest Number of Votes shall be the President, if such Number be a Majority of the whole Number of Electors appointed; and if there be more than one who have such Majority, and have an equal Number of Votes, then the House of Representatives shall immediately chuse by Ballot one of them for President; and if no Person have a Majority, then from the five highest on the list the said House shall in like Manner chuse the President. But in chusing the President, the Votes shall be taken by States, the Representation from each State having one Vote; A quorum for this Purpose shall consist of a Member or Members from two thirds of the States, and a Majority of all the States shall be necessary to a Choice. In every Case, after the Choice of the President, the Person having the greatest Number of Votes of the Electors shall be the Vice President. But if there should remain two or more who have equal Votes, the Senate shall chuse from them by Ballot the Vice President.][6]

The Congress may determine the Time of chusing the Electors, and the Day on which they shall give their Votes; which Day shall be the same throughout the United States.

No Person except a natural born Citizen, or a Citizen of the United States, at the time of the Adoption of this Constitution, shall be eligible to the Office of President; neither shall any Person be eligible to that Office who shall not have attained to the Age of thirty five Years, and been fourteen Years a Resident within the United States.

In Case of the Removal of the President from Office, or of his Death, Resignation, or Inability to discharge the Powers and Duties of the said Office,[7] the Same shall devolve on the Vice President, and the Congress may by Law provide for the Case of Removal, Death, Resignation or Inability, both of the President and Vice President, declaring what Officer shall then act as President, and such Officer shall act accordingly, until the Disability be removed, or a President shall be elected.

The President shall, at stated Times, receive for his Services, a Compensation, which shall neither be encreased nor diminished during the Period for which he shall have been elected, and he shall not receive within that Period any other Emolument from the United States, or any of them.

Before he enter on the Execution of his Office, he shall take the following Oath or Affirmation: — "I do solemnly swear (or affirm) that I will faithfully execute the Office of President of the United States, and will to the best of my Ability, preserve, protect and defend the Constitution of the United States."

Section 2. The President shall be Commander in Chief of the Army and Navy of the United States, and of the Militia of the several States, when called into the actual Service of the United States; he may require the Opinion, in writing, of the principal Officer in each of the executive Departments, upon any Subject relating to the Duties of their respective Offices, and he shall have Power to grant Reprieves and Pardons for Offences against the United States, except in Cases of Impeachment.

He shall have Power, by and with the Advice and Consent of the Senate, to make Treaties, provided two thirds of the Senators present concur; and he shall nominate, and by and with the Advice and Consent of the Senate, shall appoint Ambassadors, other public Ministers and Consuls, Judges of the supreme Court, and all other Officers of the United States, whose Appointments are not herein otherwise provided for, and which shall be established by Law: but the Congress may by Law vest the Appointment of such inferior Officers, as they think proper, in the President alone, in the Courts of Law, or in the Heads of Departments.

The President shall have Power to fill up all Vacancies that may happen during the Recess of the Senate, by granting Commissions which shall expire at the End of their next Session.

Section 3. He shall from time to time give to the Congress Information of the State of the Union, and recommend to their Consideration such Measures as he shall judge necessary and expedient; he may, on extraordinary Occasions, convene both Houses, or either of them, and in Case of Disagreement between them, with Respect to the Time of Adjournment, he may adjourn them to such Time as he shall think proper; he shall receive Ambassadors and other public Ministers; he shall take Care that the Laws be faithfully executed, and shall Commission all the Officers of the United States.

Section 4. The President, Vice President and all civil Officers of the United States, shall be removed from Office on Impeachment for, and Conviction of, Treason, Bribery, or other high Crimes and Misdemeanors.

ARTICLE III

Section 1. The judicial Power of the United States, shall be vested in one supreme Court, and in such inferior Courts as the Congress may from time to time ordain and establish. The Judges, both of the supreme and inferior Courts, shall hold their

Offices during good Behaviour, and shall, at stated Times, receive for their Services, a Compensation, which shall not be diminished during their Continuance in Office.

Section 2. The judicial Power shall extend to all Cases, in Law and Equity, arising under this Constitution, the Laws of the United States, and Treaties made, or which shall be made, under their Authority; — to all Cases affecting Ambassadors, other public Ministers and Consuls; — to all Cases of admiralty and maritime Jurisdiction; — to Controversies to which the United States shall be a Party; — to Controversies between two or more States; — between a State and Citizens of another State;[8] — between Citizens of different States; — between Citizens of the same State claiming Lands under Grants of different States, and between a State, or the Citizens thereof, and foreign States, Citizens or Subjects.

In all Cases affecting Ambassadors, other public Ministers and Consuls, and those in which a State shall be Party, the supreme Court shall have original Jurisdiction. In all the other Cases before mentioned, the supreme Court shall have appellate Jurisdiction, both as to Law and Fact, with such Exceptions, and under such Regulations as the Congress shall make.

The Trial of all Crimes, except in Cases of Impeachment, shall be by Jury; and such Trial shall be held in the State where the said Crimes shall have been committed; but when not committed within any State, the Trial shall be at such Place or Places as the Congress may by Law have directed.

Section 3. Treason against the United States, shall consist only in levying War against them, or in adhering to their Enemies, giving them Aid and Comfort. No Person shall be convicted of Treason unless on the Testimony of two Witnesses to the same overt Act, or on Confession in open Court.

The Congress shall have Power to declare the Punishment of Treason, but no Attainder of Treason shall work Corruption of Blood, or Forfeiture except during the Life of the Person attainted.

ARTICLE IV

Section 1. Full Faith and Credit shall be given in each State to the public Acts, Records, and judicial Proceedings of every other State. And the Congress may by general Laws prescribe the Manner in which such Acts, Records and Proceedings shall be proved, and the Effect thereof.

Section 2. The Citizens of each State shall be entitled to all Privileges and Immunities of Citizens in the several States.

A Person charged in any State with Treason, Felony, or other Crime, who shall flee from Justice, and be found in another State, shall on Demand of the executive Authority of the State from which he fled, be delivered up, to be removed to the State having Jurisdiction of the Crime.

[No Person held to Service or Labour in one State, under the Laws thereof, escaping into another, shall, in Consequence of any Law or Regulation therein, be discharged from such Service or Labour, but shall be delivered up on Claim of the Party to whom such Service or Labour may be due.][9]

Section 3. New States may be admitted by the Congress into this Union; but no new State shall be formed or erected within the Jurisdiction of any other State; nor any State be formed by the Junction of two or more States, or Parts of States, without the Consent of the Legislatures of the States concerned as well as of the Congress.

The Congress shall have Power to dispose of and make all needful Rules and Regulations respecting the Territory or other Property belonging to the United States; and nothing in this Constitution shall be so construed as to Prejudice any Claims of the United States, or of any particular State.

Section 4. The United States shall guarantee to every State in this Union a Republican Form of Government, and shall protect each of them against Invasion; and on Application of the Legislature, or of the Executive (when the Legislature cannot be convened) against domestic Violence.

ARTICLE V

The Congress, whenever two thirds of both Houses shall deem it necessary, shall propose Amendments to this Constitution, or, on the Application of the Legislatures of two thirds of the several States, shall call a Convention for proposing Amendments, which, in either Case, shall be valid to all Intents and Purposes, as Part of this Constitution, when ratified by the Legislatures of three fourths of the several States, or by Conventions in three fourths thereof, as the one or the other Mode of Ratification may be proposed by the Congress; Provided [that no Amendment which may be made prior to the Year One thousand eight hundred and eight shall in any Manner affect the first and fourth Clauses in the Ninth Section of the first Article; and][10] that no State, without its Consent, shall be deprived of its equal Suffrage in the Senate.

ARTICLE VI

All Debts contracted and Engagements entered into, before the Adoption of this Constitution, shall be as valid against the United States under this Constitution, as under the Confederation.

This Constitution, and the Laws of the United States which shall be made in Pursuance thereof; and all Treaties made, or which shall be made, under the Authority of the United States, shall be the supreme Law of the Land; and the Judges in every State shall be bound thereby, any Thing in the Constitution or Laws of any State to the Contrary notwithstanding.

The Senators and Representatives before mentioned, and the Members of the several State Legislatures, and all executive and judicial Officers, both of the United States and of the several States, shall be bound by Oath or Affirmation, to support this Constitution; but no religious Test shall ever be required as a Qualification to any Office or public Trust under the United States.

ARTICLE VII

The Ratification of the Conventions of nine States, shall be sufficient for the Establishment of this Constitution between the States so ratifying the Same.

Done in Convention by the Unanimous Consent of the States present the Seventeenth Day of September in the Year of our Lord one thousand seven hundred and Eighty seven and of the Independence of the United States of America the Twelfth. IN WITNESS whereof We have hereunto subscribed our Names,

George Washington,
President and
deputy from Virginia.

New Hampshire:	John Langdon
	Nicholas Gilman.
Massachusetts:	Nathaniel Gorham,
	Rufus King.
Connecticut:	William Samuel Johnson,
	Roger Sherman.

New York: Alexander Hamilton.
New Jersey: William Livingston,
                     David Brearley,
                     William Paterson,
                     Jonathan Dayton.
Pennsylvania: Benjamin Franklin,
                     Thomas Mifflin,
                     Robert Morris,
                     George Clymer,
                     Thomas FitzSimons,
                     Jared Ingersoll,
                     James Wilson,
                     Gouverneur Morris.
Delaware: George Read,
                     Gunning Bedford Jr.,
                     John Dickinson,
                     Richard Bassett,
                     Jacob Broom.
Maryland: James McHenry,
                     Daniel of St. Thomas Jenifer,
                     Daniel Carroll.
Virginia: John Blair,
                     James Madison Jr.
North Carolina: William Blount,
                     Richard Dobbs Spaight,
                     Hugh Williamson.
South Carolina: John Rutledge,
                     Charles Cotesworth Pinckney,
                     Charles Pinckney,
                     Pierce Butler.
Georgia: William Few,
                     Abraham Baldwin.

[The language of the original Constitution, not including the Amendments, was adopted by a convention of the states on September 17, 1787, and was subsequently ratified by the states on the following dates: Delaware, December 7, 1787; Pennsylvania, December 12, 1787; New Jersey, December 18, 1787; Georgia, January 2, 1788; Connecticut, January 9, 1788; Massachusetts, February 6, 1788; Maryland, April 28, 1788; South Carolina, May 23, 1788; New Hampshire, June 21, 1788.

Ratification was completed on June 21, 1788.

The Constitution subsequently was ratified by Virginia, June 25, 1788; New York, July 26, 1788; North Carolina, November 21, 1789; Rhode Island, May 29, 1790; and Vermont, January 10, 1791.]

Amendments

Amendment I

(First ten amendments ratified December 15, 1791.)

Congress shall make no law respecting an establishment of religion, or prohibiting the free exercise thereof; or abridging the freedom of speech, or of the press; or the right of the people peaceably to assemble, and to petition the Government for a redress of grievances.

Amendment II

A well regulated Militia, being necessary to the security of a free State, the right of the people to keep and bear Arms, shall not be infringed.

Amendment III

No Soldier shall, in time of peace be quartered in any house, without the consent of the Owner, nor in time of war, but in a manner to be prescribed by law.

Amendment IV

The right of the people to be secure in their persons, houses, papers, and effects, against unreasonable searches and seizures, shall not be violated, and no Warrants shall issue, but upon probable cause, supported by Oath or affirmation, and particularly describing the place to be searched, and the persons or things to be seized.

Amendment V

No person shall be held to answer for a capital, or otherwise infamous crime, unless on a presentment or indictment of a Grand Jury, except in cases arising in the land or naval forces, or in the Militia, when in actual service in time of War or public danger; nor shall any person be subject for the same offence to be twice put in jeopardy of life or limb; nor shall be compelled in any criminal case to be a witness against himself, nor be deprived of life, liberty, or property, without due process of law; nor shall private property be taken for public use, without just compensation.

Amendment VI

In all criminal prosecutions, the accused shall enjoy the right to a speedy and public trial, by an impartial jury of the State and district wherein the crime shall have been committed, which district shall have been previously ascertained by law, and to be informed of the nature and cause of the accusation; to be confronted with the witnesses against him; to have compulsory process for obtaining witnesses in his favor, and to have the Assistance of Counsel for his defence.

Amendment VII

In Suits at common law, where the value in controversy shall exceed twenty dollars, the right of trial by jury shall be preserved, and no fact tried by a jury, shall be otherwise re-examined in any Court of the United States, than according to the rules of the common law.

Amendment VIII

Excessive bail shall not be required, nor excessive fines imposed, nor cruel and unusual punishments inflicted.

Amendment IX

The enumeration in the Constitution, of certain rights, shall not be construed to deny or disparage others retained by the people.

Amendment X

The powers not delegated to the United States by the Constitution, nor prohibited by it to the States, are reserved to the States respectively, or to the people.

Amendment XI (Ratified February 7, 1795)

The Judicial power of the United States shall not be construed to extend to any suit in law or equity, commenced or prosecuted against one of the United States by Citizens of another State, or by Citizens or Subjects of any Foreign State.

Amendment XII (Ratified June 15, 1804)

The Electors shall meet in their respective states and vote by ballot for President and Vice-President, one of whom, at least, shall not be an inhabitant of the same state with themselves; they shall name in their ballots the person voted for as President, and in distinct ballots the person voted for as Vice-President, and they shall make distinct lists of all persons voted for as President, and of all persons voted for as Vice-President, and of the number of votes for each, which lists they shall sign and certify, and transmit sealed to the seat of the government of the United States, directed to the President of the Senate; — The President of the Senate shall, in the presence of the Senate and House of Representatives, open all the certificates and the votes shall then be counted; — The person having the greatest number of votes for President, shall be the President, if such number be a majority of the whole number of Electors appointed; and if no person have such majority, then from the persons having the highest numbers not exceeding three on the list of those voted for as President, the House of Representatives shall choose immediately, by ballot, the President. But in choosing the President, the votes shall be taken by states, the representation from each state having one vote; a quorum for this purpose shall consist of a member or members from two-thirds of the states, and a majority of all the states shall be necessary to a choice. [And if the House of Representatives shall not choose a President whenever the right of choice shall devolve upon them, before the fourth day of March next following, then the Vice-President shall act as President, as in the case of the death or other constitutional disability of the President. —][11] The person having the greatest number of votes as Vice-President, shall be the Vice-President, if such number be a majority of the whole number of Electors appointed, and if no person have a majority, then from the two highest numbers on the list, the Senate shall choose the Vice-President; a quorum for the purpose shall consist of two-thirds of the whole number of Senators, and a majority of the whole number shall be necessary to a choice. But no person constitutionally ineligible to the office of President shall be eligible to that of Vice-President of the United States.

Amendment XIII (Ratified December 6, 1865)

Section 1. Neither slavery nor involuntary servitude, except as a punishment for crime whereof the party shall have been duly convicted, shall exist within the United States, or any place subject to their jurisdiction.

Section 2. Congress shall have power to enforce this article by appropriate legislation.

Amendment XIV (Ratified July 9, 1868)

Section 1. All persons born or naturalized in the United States, and subject to the jurisdiction thereof, are citizens of the United States and of the State wherein they reside. No State shall make or enforce any law which shall abridge the privileges or immunities of citizens of the United States; nor shall any State deprive any person of life, liberty, or property, without due process of law; nor deny to any person within its jurisdiction the equal protection of the laws.

Section 2. Representatives shall be apportioned among the several States according to their respective numbers, counting the whole number of persons in each State, excluding Indians not taxed. But when the right to vote at any election for the choice of electors for President and Vice President of the United States, Representatives in Congress, the Executive and Judicial officers of a State, or the members of the Legislature thereof, is denied to any of the male inhabitants of such State, being

twenty-one years of age,[12] and citizens of the United States, or in any way abridged, except for participation in rebellion, or other crime, the basis of representation therein shall be reduced in the proportion which the number of such male citizens shall bear to the whole number of male citizens twenty-one years of age in such State.

Section 3. No person shall be a Senator or Representative in Congress, or elector of President and Vice President, or hold any office, civil or military, under the United States, or under any State, who, having previously taken an oath, as a member of Congress, or as an officer of the United States, or as a member of any State legislature, or as an executive or judicial officer of any State, to support the Constitution of the United States, shall have engaged in insurrection or rebellion against the same, or given aid or comfort to the enemies thereof. But Congress may by a vote of two-thirds of each House, remove such disability.

Section 4. The validity of the public debt of the United States, authorized by law, including debts incurred for payment of pensions and bounties for services in suppressing insurrection or rebellion, shall not be questioned. But neither the United States nor any State shall assume or pay any debt or obligation incurred in aid of insurrection or rebellion against the United States, or any claim for the loss or emancipation of any slave; but all such debts, obligations and claims shall be held illegal and void.

Section 5. The Congress shall have power to enforce, by appropriate legislation, the provisions of this article.

Amendment XV (Ratified February 3, 1870)

Section 1. The right of citizens of the United States to vote shall not be denied or abridged by the United States or by any State on account of race, color, or previous condition of servitude.

Section 2. The Congress shall have power to enforce this article by appropriate legislation.

Amendment XVI (Ratified February 3, 1913)

The Congress shall have power to lay and collect taxes on incomes, from whatever source derived, without apportionment among the several States, and without regard to any census or enumeration.

Amendment XVII (Ratified April 8, 1913)

The Senate of the United States shall be composed of two Senators from each State, elected by the people thereof, for six years; and each Senator shall have one vote. The electors in each State shall have the qualifications requisite for electors of the most numerous branch of the State legislatures.

When vacancies happen in the representation of any State in the Senate, the executive authority of such State shall issue writs of election to fill such vacancies: *Provided*, That the legislature of any State may empower the executive thereof to make temporary appointments until the people fill the vacancies by election as the legislature may direct.

This amendment shall not be so construed as to affect the election or term of any Senator chosen before it becomes valid as part of the Constitution.

Amendment XVIII (Ratified January 16, 1919)[13]

Section 1. After one year from the ratification of this article the manufacture, sale, or transportation of intoxicating liquors within, the importation thereof into, or the exportation thereof from the United States and all territory subject to the jurisdiction thereof for beverage purposes is hereby prohibited.

Section 2. The Congress and the several States shall have concurrent power to enforce this article by appropriate legislation.

Section 3. This article shall be inoperative unless it shall have been ratified as an amendment to the Constitution by the legislatures of the several States, as provided in the Constitution, within seven years from the date of the submission hereof to the States by the Congress.

Amendment XIX (Ratified August 18, 1920)

The right of citizens of the United States to vote shall not be denied or abridged by the United States or by any State on account of sex.

Congress shall have power to enforce this article by appropriate legislation.

Amendment XX (Ratified January 23, 1933)

Section 1. The terms of the President and Vice President shall end at noon on the 20th day of January, and the terms of Senators and Representatives at noon on the 3d day of January, of the years in which such terms would have ended if this article had not been ratified; and the terms of their successors shall then begin.

Section 2. The Congress shall assemble at least once in every year, and such meeting shall begin at noon on the 3d day of January, unless they shall by law appoint a different day.

Section 3.[14] If, at the time fixed for the beginning of the term of the President, the President elect shall have died, the Vice President elect shall become President. If a President shall not have been chosen before the time fixed for the beginning of his term, or if the President elect shall have failed to qualify, then the Vice President elect shall act as President until a President shall have qualified; and the Congress may by law provide for the case wherein neither a President elect nor a Vice President elect shall have qualified, declaring who shall then act as President, or the manner in which one who is to act shall be selected, and such person shall act accordingly until a President or Vice President shall have qualified.

Section 4. The Congress may by law provide for the case of the death of any of the persons from whom the House of Representatives may choose a President whenever the right of choice shall have devolved upon them, and for the case of the death of any of the persons from whom the Senate may choose a Vice President whenever the right of choice shall have devolved upon them.

Section 5. Sections 1 and 2 shall take effect on the 15th day of October following the ratification of this article.

Section 6. This article shall be inoperative unless it shall have been ratified as an amendment to the Constitution by the legislatures of three-fourths of the several States within seven years from the date of its submission.

Amendment XXI (Ratified December 5, 1933)

Section 1. The eighteenth article of amendment to the Constitution of the United States is hereby repealed.

Section 2. The transportation or importation into any State, Territory, or possession of the United States for delivery or use therein of intoxicating liquors, in violation of the laws thereof, is hereby prohibited.

Section 3. This article shall be inoperative unless it shall have been ratified as an amendment to the Constitution by

conventions in the several States, as provided in the Constitution, within seven years from the date of the submission hereof to the States by the Congress.

Amendment XXII (Ratified February 27, 1951)

Section 1. No person shall be elected to the office of the President more than twice, and no person who has held the office of President, or acted as President, for more than two years of a term to which some other person was elected President shall be elected to the office of the President more than once. But this Article shall not apply to any person holding the office of President when this Article was proposed by the Congress, and shall not prevent any person who may be holding the office of President, or acting as President, during the term within which this Article become operative from holding the office of President or acting as President during the remainder of such term.

Section 2. This article shall be inoperative unless it shall have been ratified as an amendment to the Constitution by the legislatures of three-fourths of the several States within seven years from the date of its submission to the States by the Congress.

Amendment XXIII (Ratified March 29, 1961)

Section 1. The District constituting the seat of Government of the United States shall appoint in such manner as the Congress may direct:

A number of electors of President and Vice President equal to the whole number of Senators and Representatives in Congress to which the District would be entitled if it were a State, but in no event more than the least populous State; they shall be in addition to those appointed by the States, but they shall be considered, for the purposes of the election of President and Vice President, to be electors appointed by a State; and they shall meet in the District and perform such duties as provided by the twelfth article of amendment.

Section 2. The Congress shall have power to enforce this article by appropriate legislation.

Amendment XXIV (Ratified January 23, 1964)

Section 1. The right of citizens of the United States to vote in any primary or other election for President or Vice President, for electors for President or Vice President, or for Senator or Representative in Congress, shall not be denied or abridged by the United States or any State by reason of failure to pay any poll tax or other tax.

Section 2. The Congress shall have power to enforce this article by appropriate legislation.

Amendment XXV (Ratified February 10, 1967)

Section 1. In case of the removal of the President from office or of his death or resignation, the Vice President shall become President.

Section 2. Whenever there is a vacancy in the office of the Vice President, the President shall nominate a Vice President who shall take office upon confirmation by a majority vote of both Houses of Congress.

Section 3. Whenever the President transmits to the President pro tempore of the Senate and the Speaker of the House of Representatives his written declaration that he is unable to discharge the powers and duties of his office, and until he transmits to them a written declaration to the contrary, such powers and duties shall be discharged by the Vice President as Acting President.

Section 4. Whenever the Vice President and a majority of either the principal officers of the executive departments or of such other body as Congress may by law provide, transmit to the President pro tempore of the Senate and the Speaker of the House of Representatives their written declaration that the President is unable to discharge the powers and duties of his office, the Vice President shall immediately assume the powers and duties of the office as Acting President.

Thereafter, when the President transmits to the President pro tempore of the Senate and the Speaker of the House of Representatives his written declaration that no inability exists, he shall resume the powers and duties of his office unless the Vice President and a majority of either the principal officers of the executive department or of such other body as Congress may by law provide, transmit within four days to the President pro tempore of the Senate and the Speaker of the House of Representatives their written declaration that the President is unable to discharge the powers and duties of his office. Thereupon Congress shall decide the issue, assembling within forty-eight hours for that purpose if not in session. If the Congress, within twenty-one days after receipt of the latter written declaration, or, if Congress is not in session, within twenty-one days after Congress is required to assemble, determines by two-thirds vote of both Houses that the President is unable to discharge the powers and duties of his office, the Vice President shall continue to discharge the same as Acting President; otherwise, the President shall resume the powers and duties of his office.

Amendment XXVI (Ratified July 1, 1971)

Section 1. The right of citizens of the United States, who are eighteen years of age or older, to vote shall not be denied or abridged by the United States or by any State on account of age.

Section 2. The Congress shall have power to enforce this article by appropriate legislation.

Amendment XXVII (Ratified May 7, 1992)

No law varying the compensation for the services of the Senators and Representatives shall take effect, until an election of Representatives shall have intervened.

Notes

1. The part in brackets was changed by section 2 of the Fourteenth Amendment.
2. The part in brackets was changed by the first paragraph of the Seventeenth Amendment.
3. The part in brackets was changed by the second paragraph of the Seventeenth Amendment.
4. The part in brackets was changed by section 2 of the Twentieth Amendment.
5. The Sixteenth Amendment gave Congress the power to tax incomes.
6. The material in brackets has been superseded by the Twelfth Amendment.
7. This provision has been affected by the Twenty-fifth Amendment.
8. These clauses were affected by the Eleventh Amendment.
9. This paragraph has been superseded by the Thirteenth Amendment.
10. Obsolete.
11. The part in brackets has been superseded by section 3 of the Twentieth Amendment.
12. See the Nineteenth and Twenty-sixth Amendments.
13. This Amendment was repealed by section 1 of the Twenty-first Amendment.
14. See the Twenty-fifth Amendment.

SOURCE: U.S. Congress, House, Committee on the Judiciary, *The Constitution of the United States of America, as Amended*, 100th Cong., 1st sess., 1987, H Doc 100-94.

Congressional Information on the Internet

A huge array of congressional information is available for free at Internet sites operated by the federal government, colleges and universities, and commercial firms. The sites offer the full text of bills introduced in the House and Senate, voting records, campaign finance information, transcripts of selected congressional hearings, investigative reports, and much more.

THOMAS

The most important site for congressional information is THOMAS (*http://thomas.loc.gov*), which is named for Thomas Jefferson and operated by the Library of Congress. THOMAS's highlight is its databases containing the full text of all bills introduced in Congress since 1989, the full text of the *Congressional Record* since 1989, and the status and summary information for all bills introduced since 1973.

THOMAS also offers special links to bills that have received or are expected to receive floor action during the current week and newsworthy bills that are pending or that have recently been approved. Finally, THOMAS has selected committee reports, answers to frequently asked questions about accessing congressional information, publications titled *How Our Laws Are Made* and *Enactment of a Law*, and links to lots of other congressional Web sites.

House of Representatives

The U.S. House of Representatives site (*http://www.house.gov*) offers the schedule of bills, resolutions, and other legislative issues the House will consider in the current week. It also has updates about current proceedings on the House floor and a list of the next day's meeting of House committees. Other highlights include a database that helps users identify their representative, a directory of House members and committees, the House ethics manual, links to Web pages maintained by House members and committees, a calendar of congressional primary dates and candidate-filing deadlines for ballot access, the full text of all amendments to the Constitution that have been ratified and those that have been proposed but not ratified, and lots of information about Washington, D.C., for visitors.

Another key House site is The Office of the Clerk On-line Information Center (*http://clerkweb.house.gov*), which has records of all roll-call votes taken since 1990. The votes are recorded by bill, so it is a lengthy process to compile a particular representative's voting record. The site also has lists of committee assignments, a telephone directory for members and committees, mailing label templates for members and committees, rules of the current Congress, election statistics from 1920 to the present, biographies of Speakers of the House, biographies of women who have served since 1917, and a virtual tour of the House Chamber.

One of the more interesting House sites is operated by the Subcommittee on Rules and Organization of the House

Committee on Rules (*http://www.house.gov/rules_org/R&O_Reference.htm*). Its highlight is dozens of Congressional Research Service reports about the legislative process. Some of the available titles include *Legislative Research in Congressional Offices: A Primer, How to Follow Current Federal Legislation and Regulations, Hearings in the House of Representatives: A Guide for Preparation and Conduct, Investigative Oversight: An Introduction to the Law, Practice, and Procedure of Congressional Inquiry, How Measures Are Brought to the House Floor: A Brief Introduction, A Brief Introduction to the Federal Budget Process,* and *Presidential Vetoes 1789-1996: A Summary Overview.*

A final House site is the Internet Law Library (*http://law.house.gov*). This site has a searchable version of the U.S. Code, which contains the text of public laws enacted by Congress, and a tutorial for searching the Code. There also is a huge collection of links to other Internet sites that provide state and territorial laws, laws of other nations, and treaties and international laws.

Senate

At least in the Internet world, the Senate is not as active as the House. Its main Web site (*http://www.senate.gov*) has records of all roll-call votes taken since 1989 (arranged by bill), brief descriptions of all bills and joint resolutions introduced in the Senate during the past week, and a calendar of upcoming committee hearings. The site also provides the standing rules of the Senate, a directory of senators and their committee assignments, lists of nominations that the president has submitted to the Senate for approval, links to Web pages operated by senators and committees, and a virtual tour of the Senate.

Information about the membership, jurisdiction, and rules of each congressional committee is available at the U.S. Government Printing Office site (*http://www.access.gpo.gov/congress/index.html*). It also has transcripts of selected congressional hearings, the full text of selected House and Senate reports, and the House and Senate rules manuals.

General Reference

An excellent place to explore voting records of individual members of Congress is Congressional Quarterly's VoteWatch (*http://pathfinder.com/CQ*), a project of Time Warner's Pathfinder and Congressional Quarterly. The site provides voting records for the previous eighteen months and can be searched by the name of the representative or senator, popular bill name, keyword, or subject. The site also has articles about the latest key votes in the House and Senate.

Another Congressional Quarterly site, American Voter (*http://voter.cq.com*), provides detailed information about individual members of Congress. For each member, it offers a biographical profile, a list of key staff contacts, results of primary and general elections, a record of recent key votes, the text of recent floor speeches, a list of bills and resolutions introduced during the current session, and records of committee votes. The member information can be searched by name, Zip Code, or state.

The U.S. General Accounting Office, the investigative arm of Congress, operates a site *(http://www.gao.gov)* that provides the full text of its reports from 1996 to the present. The reports cover a wide range of topics: aviation safety, combating terrorism, counternarcotics efforts in Mexico, defense contracting, electronic warfare, food assistance programs, Gulf War illness, health insurance, illegal aliens, information technology, long-term care, mass transit, Medicare, military readiness, money laundering, national parks, nuclear waste, organ donation, student loan defaults, and the Year 2000 computing crisis, among others.

The GAO Daybook is an excellent current awareness tool. This electronic mailing list distributes a daily list of reports and testimony released by the GAO. Subscriptions are available by sending an E-mail message to *majordomo@www.gao.gov,* and in the message area typing "subscribe daybook" (without the quotation marks).

Current budget and economic projections are provided at the Congressional Budget Office Web site *(http://www.cbo.gov).* The site also has reports about the economic and budget outlook for the next decade, the president's budget proposals, federal civilian employment, Social Security privatization, tax reform, water use conflicts in the West, marriage and the federal income tax, and the role of foreign aid in development, among other topics. Other highlights include monthly budget updates, historical budget data, cost estimates for bills reported by congressional committees, and transcripts of congressional testimony by CBO officials.

The congressional Office of Technology Assessment was eliminated in 1995, but every report it ever issued is available at The OTA Legacy *(http://www.wws-princeton.edu:80/~ota),* a site operated by the Woodrow Wilson School of Public and International Affairs at Princeton University. The site has more than 100,000 pages of detailed reports about aging, agricultural technology, arms control, biological research, cancer, computer security, defense technology, economic development, education, environmental protection, health and health technology, information technology, space, transportation, and many other subjects. The reports are organized in alphabetical, chronological, and topical lists.

Campaign Finance

Several Internet sites provide detailed campaign finance data for congressional elections. The official site is operated by the Federal Election Commission *(http://www.fec.gov),* which regulates political spending. The site's highlight is its database of campaign reports filed from May 1996 to the present by House and presidential candidates, political action committees, and political party committees. Senate reports are not included because they are filed with the Secretary of the Senate. The re-

ports in the FEC's database are scanned images of paper reports filed with the commission.

The FEC site also has summary financial data for House and Senate candidates in the current election cycle, abstracts of court decisions pertaining to federal election law from 1976 to 1997, a graph showing the number of political action committees in existence each year from 1974 to the present, and a directory of national and state agencies that are responsible for releasing information about campaign financing, candidates on the ballot, election results, lobbying, and other issues. Another useful feature is a collection of brochures about federal election law, public funding of presidential elections, the ban on contributions by foreign nationals, independent expenditures supporting or opposing a candidate for federal office, contribution limits, filing a complaint, researching public records at the FEC, and other topics. Finally, the site provides the FEC's legislative recommendations, its annual report, a report about its first twenty years in existence, the FEC's monthly newsletter, several reports about voter registration, election results for the most recent presidential and congressional elections, and campaign guides for corporations and labor organizations, congressional candidates and committees, political party committees, and nonconnected committees.

The best online source for campaign finance data is FECInfo *(http://www.tray.com/fecinfo),* which is operated by former Federal Election Commission employee Tony Raymond. FECInfo's searchable databases provide extensive itemized information about receipts and expenditures by federal candidates and political action committees from 1980 to the present. The data, which are obtained from the FEC, are quite detailed. For example, for candidates contributions can be searched by Zip Code. The site also has data on soft money contributions, lists of the top political action committees in various categories, lists of the top contributors from each state, and much more.

Another interesting site is Campaign Finance Data on the Internet *(http://www.soc.american.edu/campfin),* which is operated by the American University School of Communication. It provides electronic files from the FEC that have been reformatted in .dbf format so they can be used in database programs such as Paradox, Access, and FoxPro. The files contain data on PAC, committee, and individual contributions to individual congressional candidates.

More campaign finance data is available from the Center for Responsive Politics *(http://www.crp.org),* a public interest organization. The center provides a list of all "soft money" donations to political parties of $100,000 or more in the current election cycle and data about "leadership" political action committees associated with individual politicians. Other databases at the site provide information about travel expenses that House members received from private sources for attending meetings and other events, activities of registered federal lobbyists, and activities of foreign agents who are registered in the United States.

Index

Index